# KEYSTONE THUNDER

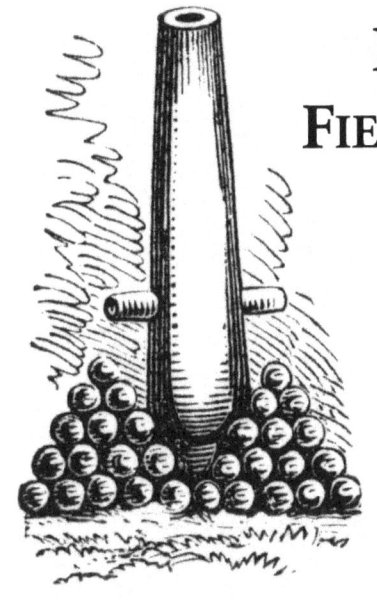

PENNSYLVANIA
FIELD ARTILLERY
IN THE
CIVIL WAR

Richard W. McCoy

HERITAGE BOOKS
2012

# HERITAGE BOOKS
*AN IMPRINT OF HERITAGE BOOKS, INC.*

Books, CDs, and more—Worldwide

For our listing of thousands of titles see our website
at
www.HeritageBooks.com

Published 2012 by
HERITAGE BOOKS, INC.
Publishing Division
100 Railroad Ave. #104
Westminster, Maryland 21157

Copyright © 2012 Richard W. McCoy

All rights reserved. No part of this book may be reproduced or transmitted in any form or by any means, electronic or mechanical, including photocopying, recording or by any information storage and retrieval system without written permission from the author, except for the inclusion of brief quotations in a review.

International Standard Book Numbers
Paperbound: 978-0-7884-5373-1
Clothbound: 978-0-7884-3424-2

# TABLE OF CONTENTS

Preface .................................. v

## I

1. The Ringgold Light Artillery Company ............ 1
2. The First Pennsylvania Artillery Regiment .......... 5
3. Pennsylvania Independent Batteries ............. 11
4. Organization of a Field Battery ................ 14

## II

1. First Shots ............................. 19
2. Armament and Re-Armament ................. 22
3. A Pennsylvania Battery at Shiloh ............... 25
4. The Peninsula Campaign .................... 26
5. The Seven Days ......................... 30
6. The Shenandoah Valley .................... 36

## III

1. Cedar Mountain and Rappahannock River ........ 41
2. Second Bull Run ........................ 44
3. Two New Batteries ....................... 52
4. South Mountain ......................... 54
5. The Bloodiest Day – Antietam ................ 57
6. The Autumn of 1862 ...................... 62
7. Fredericksburg ......................... 65
8. Murfreesboro .......................... 69
9. The Winter of 1862-63 .................... 72
10. Chancellorsville ........................ 74

## IV

1. The Invasion of Pennsylvania ................ 83
2. The Militia Batteries ..................... 86
3. Gettysburg - the First Day ................. 89
4. Gettysburg - the Second Day ................ 93
5. Gettysburg - the Third Day ................. 99
6. The Pursuit Southward .................... 106

7. Chickamauga ............................. 109

## V

1. The Autumn of 1863 ........................ 113
2. The Relief of Chattanooga .................... 118
3. Lookout Mountain and Missionary Ridge ........ 122
4. The Mine Run Campaign ..................... 125
5. The Spring of 1864 ......................... 128
6. The Overland Campaign ..................... 131
7. The Atlanta Campaign ...................... 138

## VI

1. The Siege of Petersburg ...................... 147
2. Cedar Creek ............................... 153
3. The March to the Sea ....................... 157
4. Franklin and Nashville ...................... 159
5. Triumph and Tragedy ....................... 164
6. The Guns Fall Silent ........................ 171

Epilogue ..................................... 177

Appendix A:
Officer Listings by Organization ................ 183

Appendix B:
Battery Assignments .......................... 221

Bibliography ................................. 243

Image Bibliography ........................... 247

Index ....................................... 253

# Preface

When studying the military forces of the Civil War, it is all too easy to overlook the men who served in the artillery. It is not that their stories are less interesting than those of the infantry or the cavalry, or that their martial deeds were any less impressive; rather, our fascination with the weapons themselves can lead us to overlook the men behind them. Even today, a Civil War cannon is an object of fascination. Although designed to kill, they are nonetheless works of art in their own right. Representing the pinnacle of technology in the age of their production, they waste no material in their lightweight-yet-rugged construction. The average Civil War cannon could lob a ten-pound projectile a distance of several miles, yet is light enough that one or two men can move it around by hand for short distances with relative ease. With their speed and firepower, field artillery pieces were the weapons of mass destruction of their day. As General William T. Sherman once observed, "a battery of field artillery is worth a thousand muskets."

But the men who served in the artillery were no mere mechanics passively tending the needs of their weapons. Although artillerymen may seem to lose a measure of their individuality in the collective service of their guns (an infantryman is still an infantryman even when alone, and a cavalryman needs only his horse to make him a cavalryman, but an artilleryman must be part of a gun crew to be a combatant at all), the men of the artillery shared most of the same challenges as their brethren in the other branches of service, and also faced many unique challenges exclusively their own as well.

The field artillery of the Civil War was organized into batteries, and a battery's reputation could be a source of great pride for its men. Conversely, the failure of a battery to perform well in battle could bring shame on its members, and the men of a battery would go to great lengths to protect their battery's honor. Just as infantrymen feared the disgrace of losing their colors to the enemy, artillerymen feared losing their battery's guns, and in the same way that an infantryman might die to keep the flag of his regiment out of the hands of an enemy, so too an artilleryman might fight with clubs and rammers against rifles and bayonets to protect the cannon of his battery. The men of a battery lived together, ate together, worked together, fought together, and sometimes died together. The bonds that united them were consequently very strong, and in most cases lasted long past the end of the war.

In the field, a battery of Civil War artillery needed a wide range of specialists to function properly, and the men of the artillery had far more diverse duties than the men of any other branch of service. There were carpenters and blacksmiths who maintained the six gun carriages, six caissons, over a dozen limbers, and various other pieces of heavy equipment that the battery carried with it, and often these *artificers* (as they were called) needed to make repairs in the very midst of battle. A battery also needed several dozen skilled equestrians to manage the eighty or more horses that pulled all of that heavy equipment around. A battery's cannoneers, meanwhile, needed the speed and endurance to keep up with the horse-drawn elements, and also the strength to manhandle artillery pieces that could each weigh the better part of a ton. Cannoneers also needed the coordination to work with their crewmates in an intricate ballet of rammers, sponges, primers, and lanyards in order to safely load and fire their muzzle-loading artillery pieces. The *gunners*, who led the gun crews and actually aimed the cannon, required all the skills of a good cannoneer and a good rifle marksman combined. Finally, the officers of the artillery had to coordinate the movements of all those men, horses, and machinery, which altogether could occupy several acres of ground.

The artillery, with its combination of foot-born and mounted elements, faced some unique maneuvering challenges. Even moving from a marching column "into battery" involved the most careful orchestration. Each horse-team pulling a cannon and limber combination would have to turn suddenly toward the enemy and the cannoneers would rush up and disconnect the cannon from the limber; then the horses would turn around in a wide arc and rush back through the gaps between the cannon, only inches from where the cannoneers were already busy turning their weapons to face the enemy.

Once in position, a field battery could expect to start taking fire from enemy batteries, with projectiles weighing an average of ten pounds either smashing through men, horses, and equipment, or exploding overhead to create a rain of shrapnel that fell over everything. Even more unnerving was the prospect of a charge by the enemy's infantry. Once in position, a battery of artillery was awkward to move and the only defense was to keep firing and kill or wound enough of the attackers to break the charge before it reached the muzzles of the guns.

The aim of this work is to tell the story of Pennsylvania's field batteries during the Civil War; which is, to a great extent, to tell the story of the war itself. Pennsylvania field batteries served through the entire duration and in every major theatre of the conflict. A Pennsylvania field battery was one of the first units to rush to the defense of Washington after the attack on Fort Sumter, and others fought with the Army of the Potomac in every one of its major engagements except the First Battle of Bull Run. Pennsylvania batteries were stationed in Maryland, Delaware, Virginia, Ohio, Tennessee, Kentucky, Mississippi, Alabama, Georgia, the Carolinas, and as far away as Texas. Some Pennsylvania batteries also served within their home state during the war, and during the 1863 invasion of Pennsylvania that culminated in the Battle of Gettysburg, some fought in the direct defense of their home state's soil.

But even though they were spread out across the East and the West, the North and the South, the batteries of the Keystone State were still all part of a distinct community and their stories are all interconnected. Frequently, different batteries from Pennsylvania fought alongside each other in the same battle. Many of the batteries from Pennsylvania were part of the same regiment, the 1st Pennsylvania Light Artillery, and shared a common administrative structure even though some of them never actually served together in the field. Officers and men were frequently transferred from one battery to another, and during the course of the war various batteries were merged together, split apart, disbanded, reinstated, and renamed. Such frequent reorganizations make it impossible to even definitively state the number of field batteries that were raised in Pennsylvania during the Civil War, much less write a discrete history for each. This work therefore tells the story of the entire Pennsylvania field artillery service collectively, rather than as a series of individual unit sketches. The goal is to chronicle the entire service of the Pennsylvania field artillery, and to share at each step along the way not only what each Pennsylvania battery *did*, but also what other Pennsylvania batteries *were doing at the same time*, and how their stories are all interconnected.

The men of the Pennsylvania field artillery have earned a proud place in the history of their state and their nation. They made enormous sacrifices, and in many cases the ultimate sacrifice, to preserve their country from destruction. They came together from many backgrounds and from all walks of life in order to fight that the nation might live, and it is to their memory that this work is dedicated.

●○●

*Going into Action* by William Henry Shelton (1840 – 1932).
Image from the Library of Congress.

# I

## 1. The Ringgold Light Artillery Company

On the 15th of April 1861, three days after the Confederates in Charleston opened fire on Fort Sumter, President Lincoln issued a proclamation calling for 75,000 three months' volunteer troops from the various states to help put down the rebellion. The city of Washington appeared to be in imminent danger, and the government urged the states to send whatever troops were immediately available to defend the unprotected capital.

At this early stage in the war the troops going forward to Washington were mainly from state militia organizations, and were usually no larger than small companies. One of the first units to arrive was the Ringgold Light Artillery Company of Reading, Pennsylvania.

The Ringgold Light Artillery was a militia battery that had been organized in 1850 by Captain James M. McKnight. Named for a famed artillerist of the Mexican War, the Ringgold Light Artillery was, unlike most militia organizations of the period, fully armed and equipped. At the onset of the Civil War, the company boasted four 6-pounder cannon complete with caissons, and over one hundred men to serve them.

Whereas most of the country had vainly hoped that war could be avoided, and failed to prepare for war until it was upon them, the Ringgold Light Artillery had already been holding daily drill sessions for several months and was immediately ready to answer the President's call. In fact, the organization was in the middle of a drill session when they first received the news that Fort Sumter had been attacked.

The Ringgold Light Artillery at drill. Image from the National Archives.

On the 16$^{th}$ of April, the Ringgold Light Artillery moved by rail to Harrisburg where they joined with several other Pennsylvania militia companies bound for the nation's capital. In order to hasten their departure, the unit was ordered to leave its four cannon in Harrisburg when all the militia left by train for Washington. On the 18$^{th}$, while passing through Baltimore, the militia troops were forced to march two miles through the city from one train station to another (the two rail lines used different gauge tracks and could not be linked). During this march, they found themselves surrounded by a hostile pro-secession mob that attempted to block their way while pelting them with insults, rocks, and clubs. The Pennsylvania troops were able to make their way through the mob and boarded the train to Washington without any but minor injuries. On the following day, the 6$^{th}$ Massachusetts Militia Regiment, also passing through Baltimore, was not so fortunate. The 6$^{th}$ Massachusetts was forced to exchange fire with the mob, with a number of men killed and wounded on both sides.

Upon arriving in Washington, the militia troops were billeted in the national Capitol and immediately went to work building defenses and preparing for the expected Confederate attack. On the 23$^{rd}$, the Ringgold Light Artillery was moved to the Navy Yard, where it was armed with three 12-pounder howitzers. Three days later the company returned to the Capitol, where it remained until the 15$^{th}$ of May, when it was moved to the Washington Arsenal. The following day, the 16$^{th}$, saw the company's four 6-pounder cannon returned to it, having finally been forwarded from Harrisburg.

In the months following the arrival of the first militia units, the size of the forces in and around Washington grew rapidly. By late June, a true army had formed and preparations to defend against a Confederate attack on Washington were replaced with preparations to march southward against the Confederate army encamped at Manassas Junction. As the army grew, the militia units were consolidated and reorganized. The Ringgold Light Artillery was nominally consolidated into the 25$^{th}$ Pennsylvania Infantry Regiment as Company "A,"[*] but never actually functioned in the field as a part of that regiment. The men remained in the Washington defenses for the remainder of their three-month term of service and were discharged without incident.

Although they were discharged before having an opportunity to meet the enemy in battle, the men of the Ringgold Light Artillery earned a proud place in history for being among the first to answer their country's call. Fellow artillerist John Billings would later write of such 'first defenders' that "[t]here is no doubt whatsoever but what the prompt appearance of these short-term

---

[*] Some of the men from the Ringgold Light Artillery were combined with the extra men from the National Light Infantry Company of Pottsville to create Company "C" of the 25$^{th}$ Pennsylvania Infantry Regiment. This unit, commanded by Henry Nagle, formerly a lieutenant in the Ringgold Light Artillery, was also called the "Second Ringgold Infantry."

men not only saved the Capital, but that it served also to show the Rebels that the North at short call could send a large and comparatively well equipped force into the field ...."[*]

**National Flag of the Ringgold Light Artillery Company.**
**Image from Brian Hunt and the Pennsylvania Capitol Preservation Committee.**

**The U.S. Capitol in 1860. Image from the National Archives**

---

[*] From John D. Billings, *Hardtack & Coffee: The Unwritten Story of Army Life.* (Lincoln and London: University of Nebraska Press, 1993; reprint, Boston: George M. Smith & Co., 1887), 30-33.

## 2. The First Pennsylvania Artillery Regiment

Politicians predicted a quick end to the war, and many believed that the new army would be able crush the rebellion in a single campaign. In reality, the forces gathering around Washington, composed mainly of short-term volunteers, were too inexperienced and undisciplined for the hard fighting and aggressive maneuvering that would be required to defeat the Confederates. On the 21$^{st}$ of July, the defeat at the Battle of Bull Run taught the many doubters in the North that it was going to be a long war.*

But even as the opposing armies clashed at Bull Run in what many believed was to have been the single battle that would decide the war, new regiments were already being created all over the North. In Pennsylvania, although President Lincoln had initially requested only sixteen regiments from the Commonwealth, enrollments were so high that twenty-five regiments were created to answer the call, with more on the way.

The total number of regiments from Pennsylvania quickly swelled to over forty. Governor Andrew Curtin and the General Assembly reacted by establishing the Pennsylvania Reserve Volunteer Corps. Created on the 15$^{th}$ of May 1861, the P.R.V.C. consisted of thirteen infantry regiments, one cavalry regiment, and one artillery regiment. Some confusion ensued from the practice of assigning reserve numbers to P.R.V.C. regiments that were

---

* The only volunteer artillery organizations present during the First Battle of Bull Run were Captain Charles Bookwood's New York Battery (later known as the 2$^{nd}$ New York Battery) and Captain William Reynolds' 2$^{nd}$ Rhode Island Battery (later known as Battery A, 1$^{st}$ Rhode Island Light Artillery). The artillery on the Union side that day was otherwise composed entirely of units from the regular army.

different than their line numbers. For example, the 30th Pennsylvania Regiment was also the 1st Pennsylvania Reserves; the 31st Pennsylvania Regiment was also the 2nd Pennsylvania Reserves, and so on.

Governor Andrew Curtin.
Image from the Pennsylvania Historical and Museum

The 43rd Pennsylvania Regiment, also known as the 14th Pennsylvania Reserves, was designated as the artillery regiment of the P.R.V.C. and was given yet another name and number – the 1st Pennsylvania Light Artillery Regiment. From that time onward, the new name would stick and the regiment was thereafter best known as the *1st Pennsylvania Light Artillery*.

The 1st Pennsylvania Light Artillery traced its origin to a call for volunteers issued by James Brady of Philadelphia on the 13th of April 1861, a month before the creation of the P.R.V.C. In his *History of Pennsylvania Volunteers, 1861-1865*, Samuel P. Bates relates the creation of the regiment as follows:

> On the 13th of April 1861, James Brady, a citizen of Philadelphia, issued a call for volunteers for a Light Artillery Regiment. In three days thirteen hundred men were enrolled, and their services were immediately tendered to the Secretary of War. By him the tender was referred to Governor Curtin. Governor Curtin referred it to General [Robert] Patterson, who, after considerable delay, objected to its acceptance on the ground that it was not a militia organization. In the meantime the men, eager to be in the service, enlisted in New Jersey and New York regiments. One company joined Colonel [Edward D.] Baker's California Regiment, and another joined the Twenty-seventh Regiment, commanded by Colonel [Max] Einstein. About five hundred men still remained, and were maintained at

the expense of the officers, and their friends, until the law authorizing the organization of the Reserve Corps was passed, when four companies, commanded by Captains Brady, Simpson, Flood and West, were accepted and ordered to the camp at Harrisburg. These were here joined by four other companies recruited in the counties of Franklin, Potter, York, Lawrence and Luzerne, and an organization was effected by the choice of Captain Richard H. Rush of the regular army, Colonel; Charles T. Campbell, from Captain of company A, Lieutenant Colonel; A. E. Lewis, Senior Major, and H. T. Danforth, of company B, Junior Major. Colonel Rush declined to accept the command, and soon after became Colonel of the Sixth Cavalry. The regiment, consequently, remained under the command of Lieutenant Colonel Campbell. It was clothed and equipped by the State, and received arms from the State and from the city of Philadelphia. ...[*]

The regiment's eight companies were assigned letters from "A" through "H." Companies "C," "D," "G," and "H" (under the initial command of Captains John G. Simpson, Edward H. Flood, Robert M. West, and James Brady, respectively) had been part of the original organization raised in Philadelphia. Jeremiah McCarthy soon replaced John G. Simpson as captain of Company "C," and Mark Kern succeeded Robert M. West as captain of Company "G" when West was promoted to major on the 13th of September 1861.

Company "A" was organized in Franklin County under the command of Charles T. Campbell, who was promptly promoted to lieutenant colonel, and later to colonel, leaving the command of Company "A" to Captain Hezekiah Easton.

Company "B" was first organized at Mount Jackson, in Lawrence County, on the 26th of April, under the leadership of Henry T. Danforth, who had served in Braxton Bragg's vaunted Battery C, 3rd U.S. Artillery, during the Mexican War. Captain Danforth was promptly promoted to major and command of

---

[*] From Samuel P. Bates. *History of the Pennsylvania Volunteers, 1861-1865.* (Harrisburg: B. Singerly, State Printer, 1869), vol. 1, 944.

Company "B" was given to Captain (formerly First Sergeant) James H. Cooper.

Company "E" was organized under the leadership of Captain Alfred E. Lewis primarily of men from Blair and Philadelphia counties. Captain Lewis was promoted to major upon formation of the regiment, leaving Captain Jacob M. Barr in command. Captain Barr resigned on the $12^{th}$ of December and was succeeded by Captain Theodore Miller.

Company "F" was organized under the leadership of Captain Ezra W. Matthews primarily of men from Philadelphia County.

In August of 1861, the $1^{st}$ Pennsylvania Light Artillery was moved to Washington where it was more fully trained and equipped. Individually, each company was issued the cannon, horses, and other equipment necessary for service as field artillery.

Before and during the Civil War, the United States Army classified artillery as 'foot artillery,' 'field artillery,' or 'light artillery.' 'Foot artillery' referred to units that manned large and difficult to move artillery pieces, such as those used in forts, or along the seacoast, or during sieges. The term 'field artillery' referred to units equipped with smaller cannon that could be easily drawn by horses and maneuvered with an army in the field. 'Light artillery' was a small and highly specialized subdivision of field artillery in which the cannoneers were mounted on horseback so that the entire unit, both men and equipment, was fast enough to move and operate in conjunction with cavalry. In the regular army, regiments of artillery were not individually designated as foot, field, or light artillery, but where theoretically available for service in any of these capacities.[*]

---

[*] The four regiments of regular army artillery in service before the Civil War had twelve companies each, and two companies from each regiment were designated as 'light' companies. In practice, however, the light companies were generally light artillery in name and uniform only.

**National Flag of the 1ˢᵗ Pennsylvania Light Artillery Regiment.
Image from Brian Hunt and the Pennsylvania Capitol Preservation Committee.**

A great deal of confusion has resulted because the various states gave names to their volunteer artillery units that did not use the correct terminology to identify those units' actual area of service. Volunteer foot artillery regiments (of which Pennsylvania raised four[*]) where almost invariably called "heavy" artillery and volunteer field artillery regiments where almost all named "light" artillery. The 1ˢᵗ Pennsylvania Light Artillery, despite its name, was composed entirely of field batteries and was therefore actually a regiment of field artillery.

---

[*] These were the 112ᵗʰ Pennsylvania Regiment (2ⁿᵈ Penna. Heavy Artillery), the 152ⁿᵈ Pennsylvania Regiment (3ʳᵈ Penna. Heavy Artillery), the 204ᵗʰ Pennsylvania Regiment (5ᵗʰ Penna. Heavy Artillery), and the 212ᵗʰ Pennsylvania Regiment (6ᵗʰ Penna. Heavy Artillery).

The principal maneuvering unit of the field artillery was the battery. A battery was a company of between 100 and 150 men, and either four or six cannon, and the various horses and other equipment necessary to maneuver and fire those cannon.

The men of the original eight batteries of the 1st Pennsylvania Light Artillery learned the art of field artillery service at Camp Barry, near Washington, D.C. Camp Barry was the Union army's primary camp for artillery instruction. It was named for Major William F. Barry, the Chief of Artillery for the Union army. Major Barry was also the author, along with Henry J. Hunt and William H. French, of the artillery manual then in use by the United States Army.[*]

Lt. Col. Charles T. Campbell of the 1st Pennsylvania Light Artillery. Image from the P.R.V.C. Historical Society.

After training at Camp Barry was completed, the individual batteries of the 1st Pennsylvania Light Artillery where each given assignments with various parts of the army and were never again stationed together as a regiment.

By this time, it was becoming obvious to the military leadership that it was not desirable to have the states provide complete field artillery regiments. Since field artillery batteries functioned independently of each other, the regimental system was just burdening the army with high-ranking yet inexperienced officers for which the service had no real use.

Colonel Campbell, a valuable officer, recognized how limited his service would be as the commander of an artillery regiment, and resigned to take command of the 57th Pennsylvania Infantry.

---

[*] This was the *Instruction for Field Artillery* (Philadelphia: J.B. Lippincott & Co., 1861).

Henry Danforth, meanwhile, now a lieutenant colonel, after briefly supervising the training of Batteries D and H, requested reassignment back to his own old organization, Battery B (now under Captain James Cooper, who had formerly been Danforth's first sergeant). When his request was denied, Danforth resigned his commission and enlisted in Battery B, where he was soon re-commissioned as a second lieutenant.

## 3. Pennsylvania Independent Batteries

The army decided in late 1861 that no more field artillery regiments would be accepted from the states. Thenceforward, the states were only to raise "independent" batteries of artillery. Pennsylvania would ultimately raise nine such independent batteries for service in the Union army.

The first six Pennsylvania independent batteries were raised throughout late 1861. At the time, they were given no letter designations, and were generally identified by the name of their commander, or by some other nickname, but on the 1st of May 1863 letter designations would be retroactively assigned.[*]

Pennsylvania Independent Battery "A" was recruited in August in Philadelphia and formed on September 19th 1861 under Captain Frank Schaffer, and would spend its entire tenure of service as part of the garrison of Fort Delaware, before mustering out on June 30th 1865.

Pennsylvania Independent Battery "B" started out as a company of the 77th Pennsylvania Infantry Regiment. During the early period of the war, there was a great deal of experimentation

---

[*] To avoid confusion in identifying specific organizations, these batteries are hereinafter identified by their letter designations even when referring to time periods prior to the assignment of those letter designations.

among volunteer units with respect to organizational structure. The 77th Pennsylvania Regiment was initially intended to have eight infantry companies and one artillery company, the artillery company to be commanded by Captain Peter B. Housum. The artillery company turned out to be undersized, so it was combined with Captain Charles F. Muehler's company from Erie County. When the 77th Pennsylvania Regiment was mustered into service on the 6th of November 1861, Housum was promoted to lieutenant colonel, and Captain Muehler became the commander of the artillery company. The 77th Pennsylvania Regiment was transferred to Camp Nevin, Kentucky in late 1861, and Captain Muehler's Artillery Company was severed from the regiment and outfitted as an independent battery of field artillery.

Pennsylvania Independent Battery "C" was raised in Pittsburgh by James Thompson in September of 1861 and immediately moved to Camp Lamon, near Williamsport, Maryland where it was mustered into U.S. service on the 6th of November. This battery started its career as part of a special brigade raised by General Ward H. Lamon. The units of Lamon's brigade were not raised as part of the usual system of state volunteers, and when the brigade was broken up in November of 1861 the individual units were not officially affiliated with their home states. Captain Thompson's battery was attached to the First Maryland Brigade and as a result was for a long time misleadingly referred to as the "Second Maryland Battery." On the 27th of June 1862, at the request of Captain Thompson, the Commonwealth of Pennsylvania retroactively recognized Captain Thompson's Battery as a Pennsylvania organization.

Pennsylvania Independent Battery "D" was organized at Doylestown on September 24th, 1861 (the same day Pennsylvania Independent Battery C left for Camp Lamon), under the command of Captain George W. Durell, from men of Berks and Bucks counties. On the 6th of November, Durell's Company was ordered to Washington where it was outfitted and trained as a battery of field artillery.

Pennsylvania Independent Battery "E" was raised by Charles A. Atwell and James D. McGill and was initially intended for service with the $63^{rd}$ Pennsylvania Regiment. In July of 1861, however, Lieutenant Joseph M. Knap of the $28^{th}$ Pennsylvania Infantry, which already had nearly double the number of men specified for a regiment, was authorized to raise a company of artillery for service with the $28^{th}$ Regiment, and persuaded Atwell and McGill to offer their company for that purpose. The company, which was enlarged by transfers from other companies of the regiment, mustered into service at Camp DeKorponay, Maryland in September of 1861 with Knap as captain and Atwell and McGill as lieutenants. The company was immediately detached and sent to Washington, where it was trained and equipped as a battery of field artillery before being returned to the $28^{th}$ Pennsylvania Regiment on the $24^{th}$ of November. The $28^{th}$ Pennsylvania Regiment was commanded by Colonel (later General) John W. Geary, whose son Edward was commissioned as a lieutenant in the battery, and Battery E would spend almost its entire term of service attached to various forces under John Geary's command.

Pennsylvania Independent Battery "F" was recruited in Pittsburgh and mustered into U.S. service on the $7^{th}$ of December 1861 under the command of Captain Robert B. Hampton. Battery F was immediately assigned to join a force commanded by General Nathan P. Banks on the upper Potomac.

## 4. Organization of a Field Battery

A full-strength Civil War field battery had one captain, four lieutenants, a first sergeant, a quartermaster sergeant, six other sergeants (chiefs of pieces), twelve corporals (six gunners and six chiefs of caissons), seventy cannoneers, fifty-two drivers, six artificers, two buglers, and one-hundred-and-ten horses. These men and animals were divided into three sections, each of which was equipped with two cannon, two caissons, and four limbers.

The captain was the commander of the battery and was responsible for all of those men, horses, and materiel. In a volunteer organization, the original captain and lieutenants were often elected by the men themselves and had usually played an important role in the organization's initial recruiting process.

The first sergeant (sometimes called an *Orderly Sergeant*) was the top enlisted man in the battery and was primarily responsible for the daily administration of the battery's affairs, including taking rolls, posting guards, and assigning work details. In the absence of a lieutenant, first sergeants could also temporarily command sections. The quartermaster sergeant meanwhile assisted the first sergeant by receiving, issuing, and inventorying the vast amounts of equipment held and used by the battery.

Each of a battery's three sections was commanded by a lieutenant who had a comparable responsibility over the men and materiel of his section as the captain had over the entire battery. The junior-most lieutenant served as *Chief of the Line of Caissons* and coordinated the rear area of the battery in battle while the other officers were busy at the front.

Each section was divided into two gun platoons, and each gun platoon had two detachments. One detachment served as the gun crew and the other detachment managed the caisson. A sergeant called the *Chief of the Piece* commanded each gun platoon. One corporal called a *Gunner* led the gun crew and aimed, or *sighted*, the cannon while a second corporal, called the *Chief of the Caisson*, supervised the detachment charged with managing the caisson.

A gun crew was usually comprised of six or more cannoneers, although in an emergency it was technically possible for as few as two men to fire a cannon. Each man on a gun crew was assigned a number and his duties corresponded with his number. The *one-man* swabbed the bore with a wet-sponge after each firing and rammed new rounds down the barrel with a rammer on the opposite end of the sponge staff. The *two-man* assisted with cleaning the barrel between shots by either dry sponging the bore or extracting debris with a tool called a *worm*; he also inserted the new round into the muzzle for the one-man to ram home. The *three-man* covered the touchhole, called the *vent*, with a leather strap, called a *thumbstall*, which was tied around his thumb (this prevented air from flowing through the cannon barrel and stirring up hot embers in the breech). The *four-man* handled the friction primers that were used to generate the spark that ignited the powder charge, and also actually fired the cannon by pulling a lanyard that was hooked to the top of the friction primer. The *five-man* was the runner who brought the rounds and powder charges from the ammunition chest on the limber up to the cannon and the *six-man* prepared each round for firing by unloading it from the ammunition chest and setting the fuses to the correct time.

Each ammunition chest held approximately thirty rounds, but the exact number varied with the model of cannon. Those rounds generally came in four types. *Solid shot* was just what it sounded like, a solid iron projectile. *Shells* were hollow, filled with gunpowder, and fused; they could be set to explode over the heads of the enemy by setting the fuse to go off after the correct amount of time had passed (a table of fuse-times-to-distances was usually placed inside the lid of each ammunition chest). *Case shot* were almost identical to shells, but contained over forty small iron balls mixed in with the powder to increase the destructive force. Although case shot had more striking power than shell, its increased weight reduced the range at which it could be used. It was nonetheless preferred because artillery rarely engaged at ranges too great for case shot. The last of the four main classes of artillery projectiles was *canister*. Canister rounds were thin tin cylinders filled with small iron balls with a wooden sabot attached to the rear between the projectile component and the powder charge. When a canister round was fired, the tin cylinder disintegrated inside the cannon barrel and the iron balls dispersed shotgun-like across a wide arc. The wooden sabot served much the same purpose as the wadding in a shotgun shell. Canister had a very short range, but was enormously destructive. In an emergency two canister rounds could even be loaded on top of a single powder bag to increase the amount of shrapnel ejected from the barrel (most artillery rounds produced during the Civil War held their powder charge in a cloth bag pre-attached to the rear of the projectile, so when firing double-canister the powder bag had to be cut off of the second canister round before it was loaded).

All of a battery's cannon and caissons were pulled by limbers. A limber was a two-wheeled vehicle with an ammunition chest that was pulled by a team of six horses. The horses were arranged in three teams of two, and one driver rode the left-side horse in each team (thus three drivers for each limber). Both cannon carriages and caissons had two wheels each and were hitched to limbers to produce quasi four-wheeled vehicles. A caisson was itself similar in design to a limber but with a spare wheel attached to the rear and two ammunition chests instead of one. That meant that each cannon had a total of four chests of ammunition available (one on its own limber, one on its caisson's limber, and two on its caisson).

With all of that specialized equipment, a battery relied very heavily on its artificers. Artificers were skilled craftsmen who maintained the battery's equipment while in the field. A combination of blacksmiths, carpenters, and leatherworkers, it was the artificers' job to keep all of the battery's cannon, limbers, caissons, and horse-tack in working condition.

The final specialists in a field battery were the buglers. A field battery took up a lot of space and made a lot of noise, and often spoken orders could not be heard above the din of battle. Most instructions were therefore given by an appropriate bugle call. The buglers remained close to the officers and translated their orders into high clear tones that carried above the general roar and let the officers give instructions far beyond the limited range of their own voices.

●○●

# II

## 1. First Shots

The first engagements fought by Pennsylvania batteries took place in the autumn and early winter of 1861. On October $4^{th}$ Batteries C and E, $1^{st}$ Pennsylvania Light Artillery (McCarthy's and Miller's), under the overall command of Major West, were with General W. F. Smith's Division at Great Falls, Maryland overlooking the Potomac River north of Washington. Major West was ordered to shell a barn on the south side of the river in which the Confederates were believed to be keeping military supplies. Major West ordered a single cannon forward and fired several rounds into the barn. A squad of Confederate cavalry immediately emerged from the barn and galloped away into the woods.

Two months later, on the $19^{th}$ of December, Pennsylvania Independent Battery E (Knap's) came under fire while stationed on the upper Potomac at Point of Rocks, Maryland. Three Confederate cannon positioned on the south side of the river began shelling Battery E's position, but Battery E returned fire and after a short but brisk exchange the Confederates withdrew.

At the Battle of Dranesville, Virginia, which took place the day after Battery E's brief artillery duel (and just under thirty miles to the southeast), a brigade-sized Confederate force of all arms under General J.E.B. Stuart was repulsed by a column of Union troops under General E.O.C. Ord. During the battle, Battery A, 1$^{st}$ Pennsylvania Light Artillery, under Captain Hezekiah Easton, engaged a Confederate battery at a range of five hundred yards and destroyed one of their caissons, as well as doing considerable other damage, while receiving no losses of their own. Battery A also captured a caisson and limber from the retreating enemy. Captain Easton reported the part his battery played in the action as follows:

> No appearance of the enemy was visible until we reached Thornton's house, near the junction of the Alexandria and Leesburg turnpike, when a heavy fire of artillery and musketry was suddenly opened from a thick woods on our left, the enemy evidently lying in large force in ambuscade, while their artillery was posted on the Centreville road, leading through the wood and coming into the Alexandria turnpike between Thornton's and Coleman's houses. My guns were immediately put into battery and opened fire. Having nothing to indicate the position of the enemy but the smoke of their guns, I opened a brisk discharge of shells into the woods occupied by the enemy, which was kept up until [the] order to cease firing. The examination of the ground afterward showed the successful and destructive effects of our artillery fire. The rebel battery, in my opinion, was unmanned by our third fire. They succeeded in drawing off their guns, but I captured one caisson and one limber, and one other was exploded and the horses fatally injured. The woods in which the enemy were concealed were found thickly strewn with dead and wounded. The mangled bodies of the dead showed the terrible execution of our fire. Besides the ordnance captured, a large quantity of clothing, blankets, knapsacks, haversacks, &c., was found, which the enemy had cast off in their hasty and thorough rout.
> 
> I have the satisfaction to state that, although the injury and loss of the enemy was so severe, in my battery there was not a man or horse lost and no injury done my guns. Our only casualty was the slight wounding of one of my men (Charles

Osborn), who was struck in the knee by a spent ball, which slightly harmed him ...[*]

Battery B, 1st Pennsylvania Light Artillery (Cooper's), was also present on the field at Dranesville but arrived too late to take part in the battle.

**Battery A, 1st Pennsylvania Light Artillery at the Battle of Dranesville. Engraving from *Frank Leslie's Illustrated Newspaper* (January 11, 1862).**

Several days prior to the Battle of Dranesville, a detached section (two cannon) of Battery F, 1st Pennsylvania Light Artillery (Matthews') under Lieutenant Charles B. Brockway had briefly engaged a small body of Confederates near Hancock, Maryland that was attempting to destroy a railroad line.

Throughout the month of December, a Confederate force under General Thomas "Stonewall" Jackson attempted to rupture Dam No. 5 on the Upper Potomac in order to drain the C & O canal and interfere with the flow of Union supplies from the West.

---

[*] From Bvt. Lieut. Col. Robert N. Scott, et al., ed., *The War of the Rebellion: A Compilation of the Official Records of the Union and Confederate Armies* (Washington: Government Printing Office, 1881-1901) (hereinafter cited as "O.R."), series I vol. 5, 488 (No. 9) 488-89.

From December 17$^{th}$ through the 21$^{st}$, Confederate soldiers waded out into the river with pickaxes, under enemy fire, and attempted to breech the dam.

On the 20$^{th}$, the same day as the Battle of Dranesville, another detached section from Battery F, 1$^{st}$ Pennsylvania Light Artillery (Matthews'), armed with two Parrott rifles and under the command of Lieutenant R. Bruce Ricketts, opened fire on a body of Confederate artillery and cavalry supporting the attack on the dam. Lieutenant Ricketts' section suffered several men killed and wounded, and one gun was dismounted. Pennsylvania Independent Battery F (Hampton's) was also engaged at Dam No. 5 on the 20$^{th}$, where Captain Hampton led a squad of men across the river and burned an old mill where the Confederates were storing equipment. Captain Hampton's squad captured a small supply of blankets and entrenching tools. Both batteries [Battery F, 1$^{st}$ Pennsylvania Light Artillery (Matthews') and Pennsylvania Independent Battery F (Hampton's)] were again engaged from January 4$^{th}$ through 6$^{th}$ in a protracted skirmish fought when Jackson's troops attempted to enter Hancock.

## 2. Armament and Rearmament

During this period, many field batteries were being re-armed with superior artillery pieces. Throughout 1861, many of the volunteer organizations were equipped with outdated cannon better suited to a Mexican War era battlefield, but as new weaponry became available, those pieces were rotated out of service and replaced with more modern weaponry.

For example, Battery B, 1$^{st}$ Pennsylvania Light Artillery (Cooper's) had originally been armed with four James rifles. The

James rifle, produced by the Ames Company of Massachusetts, was an early rifled cannon cast in bronze. Although less brittle than iron, bronze turned out to be unsuitable for rifled cannon because of its softness, and bronze rifles like the James rifle quickly broke down under the strain of active service.

### 14 Pdr. James Rifle

**Barrel Weight:** 918 lbs.
**Bore diameter:** 3.8 inches
**Inventor:** Charles James
**Manufacturer:**
The Ames Co., Mass.

In October of 1861, Battery B turned in two of its James rifles and received four new 10-pounder Parrott rifles. Parrott rifles, named for their inventor, Robert Parker Parrott, were manufactured by the West Point Foundry in New York. A Parrott rifle's barrel was made of cast iron, but had a wrought iron band heat-shrunk around the breech to provide added strength. The Parrott rifle was the first mass-produced and generally reliable rifled cannon in America.

### 10 Pdr. Parrott Rifle

**Barrel Weight:** 890 lbs.
**Bore diameter:** 2.9 & 3 inches
**Inventor:** Robert Parker Parrott
**Manufacturer:**
The West Point Foundry, NY.

On the 20$^{th}$ of February 1862, Battery F, 1$^{st}$ Pennsylvania Light Artillery (Matthews') replaced its four smoothbores and two Parrott rifles with six 3-in. Ordnance rifles. The 3-in. Ordnance rifle was produced by the Phoenix Iron Company of Pittsburgh, Pennsylvania using a technique pioneered by James Griffen. Griffen produced cannon barrels entirely from wrought iron. The barrels were created by beating sheets of wrought iron around a central mandrel in consecutive layers. Several years earlier, Griffen had developed a wrought iron smoothbore 6-pounder. The 6-pounder "Griffen Gun," heralded as "breech-proof," was not particularly popular and only about a dozen or so were produced, and these are believed to have been sold to the city of Philadelphia for use within the home defenses of Pennsylvania. It was not until 1860 when the first Ordnance rifle was produced that the true potential of Griffen's system was realized. The extreme strength of wrought iron made it perfect for rifled cannon. The 3-in. Ordnance rifle had at least the same range and firepower as the 10-pounder Parrott rifle, weighed about ninety pounds less, and was almost completely immune to cracking and breeching.

### 3-in. Ordnance Rifle

**Barrel Weight:** 800 lbs.
**Bore diameter:** 2.9 & 3 inches
**Inventor:** James Griffen
**Manufacturer:**
The Phoenix Iron Co., Penna.

Meanwhile, Captain Joseph Knap of Pennsylvania Independent Battery E had originally arranged for four 6-pounder cannon to be gifted to his battery by his family, which owned the Fort Pitt Foundry of Pittsburgh. The gesture seemed fitting since many of the men of Independent Battery E had been workers at the foundry before the war. The four cannon were custom-made for the battery, but due to an administrative error they were given to another battery instead, and Battery E was issued four 10-pounder Parrott rifles in their place.

The various other Pennsylvania batteries (and the batteries from other states as well) also tended to start the war with older pieces, like the James rifle, 6-pounder smoothbores, or the Model 1841 12-pounder field howitzer (a light piece from the Mexican War era), but soon saw them replaced by 10-pounder Parrott rifles and later by 3-in. Ordnance rifles.

## 3. A Pennsylvania Battery at Shiloh

Far from Maryland and Virginia, General Ulysses S. Grant's army was camped at Pittsburg Landing in Tennessee and was awaiting the arrival of reinforcements from General Buell's Army of the Ohio when a Confederate army under Generals Albert Sydney Johnston and P. G. T. Beauregard attacked on the 6$^{th}$ of April 1862. On the first day of the resulting Battle of Shiloh, Grant's army was beaten back badly, but during the night portions of Buell's army arrived, and on the next day the Confederate army was soundly defeated by the combined forces of Grant and Buell.

Although they did not arrive on the field in time to take part in the battle, Pennsylvania Independent Battery B (Muehler's) marched with Buell's Army of the Ohio and was a part of the relief column that came to Grant's aid.

After the battle, the two Union armies refitted and prepared for a joint advance under the personal command of General Henry W. Halleck (the commander of the Department of the Mississippi) against the defeated Confederates who had retreated to their base at Corinth, Mississippi (General Albert Sydney Johnston was killed during the Battle of Shiloh, leaving General Beauregard in command). Halleck, however, was an extremely cautious general and the advance was therefore quite slow. Before starting, Halleck waited for further reinforcements under General John Pope, and when he did finally move, his three-army advance was conducted more in the manner of a siege than of an active campaign. Meanwhile, a major campaign was already under way in the East under a general who also had a reputation for moving very slowly.

The Battle of Shiloh: Pittsburg Landing on the evening of April 6th.
Engraving from *Frank Leslie's Illustrated Newspaper* (May 17, 1862).

## 4. The Peninsula Campaign

In the spring of 1862, General George B. McClellan, commander of the Union Army of the Potomac, moved his forces by water down the Virginia coast to Fortress Monroe on the tip of the Virginia Peninsula between the York and James rivers. McClellan's plan was to march up the Peninsula and attack the Confederate capital at Richmond from behind, bypassing the fields of northern Virginia where the Union army had previously come to grief at Bull Run.

McClellan's advance up the Peninsula first met serious resistance along the line of the Warwick River on the 5$^{th}$ of April. Batteries C, D, E, and H of the 1$^{st}$ Pennsylvania Light Artillery, which served together throughout the Peninsula campaign, were attached to General Darius Couch's Division of the Fourth Corps. The Fourth Corps was on the left of the Union line, with a bend of the Warwick River to its left and front. In early through mid April, during the siege of Yorktown, the batteries attached to the Fourth Corps busily exchanged fire with their Confederate counterparts across the river. Prior to the Confederate evacuation of Yorktown, Battery H (Brady's) was called upon to shell an enemy encampment to its front, but received such a powerful return fire that it was compelled to temporarily withdraw to the far side of the James River aboard steamboats.

The Confederates were pushed back from the Yorktown and Warwick River line at the end of April and made their next stand at Williamsburg on the 5$^{th}$ of May. There, Battery D (Flood's) exchanged a severe fire with the enemy, who had previously measured the ranges to avoid delay and increase accuracy. After the battle, the Confederates again withdrew further up the Peninsula, but not without loss. The abandonment of the Warwick River line had made the capture of Norfolk inevitable, and the Confederates were forced to scuttle the dreaded ironclad *C.S.S. Virginia*. The Confederate capital was now vulnerable to an attack by water up the James River and the Confederates responded by building a heavy battery at Drewry's Bluff, overlooking the James River seven miles below Richmond. Several Union gunboats attempt to ascend the James but were repulsed by the battery at Drewry's Bluff.

When the Union army reached the swampy environs of the Chickahominy River just east of Richmond, which the first Union troops crossed on the 13$^{th}$ of May, sickness began to weaken many of the men, and Batteries D and H each lost a man to illness. Batteries D and E (Flood's and Miller's) were engaged on the 25$^{th}$ in the vicinity of Seven Pines, and afterwards Major West, with Batteries C, D, and E, was assigned the task of securing the portion of the Union line crossed by the Williamsburg Road.

By the end of May, portions of the Army of the Potomac were within twelve miles of Richmond. In order to facilitate a juncture with General Irvin McDowell's corps, which was approaching from overland across northern Virginia, McClellan's army straddled the Chickahominy River with two corps below and three above, the right flank extending far to the north. The Confederate commander, General Joseph E. Johnston, sought to take advantage of this division by attacking the southern half of the divided Union army and on May 31$^{st}$ initiated the Battle of Fair Oaks.

During the battle, Captain Brady of Battery H found that a body of Confederate infantry had approached to very near his position by moving through a wooded area to his left. A few rounds of canister fired in that direction caused the Confederates to fall back. Shortly thereafter, however, Battery H was forced to withdraw to a new position further back. From its new position Battery H repelled repeated advances by the Confederates. During the fighting, Captain Brady ran out of canister rounds for his cannon and Battery H was forced to fire shells without fuses instead. Without fuses, the shells exploded instantly when the cannon was fired, and produced an effect similar to canister. At the moment of desperation, reinforcements sent by General Darius Couch arrived and drove the Confederates from the field.

The three batteries under Major West (Batteries C, D, and E) were also severely engaged when the Confederates attacked their position astride the Williamsburg Road.

Johnston's attack at Fair Oaks failed to dislodge the advancing Union troops, and Johnston himself was wounded, but the shot that wounded Johnston soon turned the situation to the advantage of the Confederacy. Confederate President Jefferson Davis named General Robert E. Lee to replace Johnston as commander of the Confederate army defending Richmond, which was thereafter known as the Army of Northern Virginia. General Lee immediately began planning a new offensive designed to reverse the Army of the Potomac's advance against the Southern capital.

Battery C, 1st Pennsylvania Light Artillery at Fair Oaks.
Image from the P.R.V.C. Historical Society.

Unknown Union Battery at the Battle of Fair Oaks.
Image from the Library of Congress.

## 5. The Seven Days

In early June, Battery A, $1^{st}$ Pennsylvania Light Artillery (Easton's) joined the Union army on the Peninsula after having served uneventfully at various posts in central Virginia since their first experience of battle at Dranesville. Battery A was ordered to the vicinity of Mechanicsville, on the army's right. Battery B, $1^{st}$ Pennsylvania Light Artillery (Cooper's) arrived on the Peninsula on June $17^{th}$, and on the $20^{th}$ was placed near Battery A in advance and on the extreme right of the Union army. Battery G, $1^{st}$ Pennsylvania (Kern's) was also stationed at Mechanicsville, and all three batteries were assigned to the Fifth Corps.

On the $26^{th}$, Batteries A, B, and G were withdrawn to Beaver Dam Creek, a tributary of the Chickahominy. Easton's Battery A took a strong position overlooking a swamp and Cooper's Battery B established a position for defense in conjunction with the Pennsylvania Bucktails.* Kern's Battery G was positioned in support of Colonel Horatio G. Sickel's $32^{nd}$ Pennsylvania Regiment.

General Lee's plan was to strike the Union force's right flank along Beaver Dam Creek. The Union line was still divided down the center by the Chickahominy, and Lee hoped to destroy McClellan's right wing before reinforcements could be brought up from across the swollen river. Shortly after 3:00 p.m. the Confederates attacked.

---

* The $42^{nd}$ Pennsylvania Infantry Regiment ($13^{th}$ Pennsylvania Reserves) was called the "Bucktail Regiment" because the men decorated their caps with the tails of white-tailed deer.

Confederate attack at Beaver Dam Creek, from a contemporary sketch. Image from the National Park Service (Richmond National Battlefield Park).

Cooper's Battery B was able to prevent one Confederate battery from taking position to their front, but other enemy batteries, masked behind hills to the right of Battery B's position, were able to open fire on the Union lines. The artillery, in conjunction with the infantry, was able to repel wave after wave of Confederate attacks. Battery B suffered five men wounded during the fighting. Easton's Battery A, meanwhile, from its position above the swamp, was able to prevent a Confederate brigade from crossing to its front. After nightfall the Union forces fell back, but four of Cooper's Battery's six guns were left in position. On the morning of the 27th these four guns from Battery B fired at the enemy for almost an hour before retiring to the new Union line along Boatswain's Creek, another tributary of the Chickahominy. There was little time for rest, however, since the Confederates quickly renewed their assault in what would become known as the Battle of Gaines' Mill.

All day long on the 27th the Union lines faced wave after wave of Confederate attacks. At around 5 o'clock in the afternoon,

Batteries A and G faced a series of determined advances in which Confederate infantry came several times to within fifty yards of their front. Captain Kern was injured but continued in command of Battery G. Then a Union regular army cavalry unit attempted to charge the Confederates, but was repulsed and retreated directly through the position occupied by Captain Easton's Battery A. The fleeing troopers dragged Battery A's horse teams and limbers away with them, leaving Captain Easton's battery without ammunition. Battery A was quickly overwhelmed. In response to a demand that his battery surrender, Captain Easton shouted "No! We never surrender!" and was immediately killed, along with many of his men. Battery A's cannon all fell to the Confederates.

Captain Hezekiah Easton; Battery A, 1st Pennsylvania Light Artillery. Image from the Allison-Antrim Museum, Greencastle, PA.

Kern's Battery G nearly shared the fate of Battery A. Forced to retire after repelling repeated attacks, the wounded Captain Kern left behind two of his six cannon, and lost seven men killed and two other men wounded. Cooper's Battery B had been positioned to the right of the Watts house and was able to resist until nightfall, and retire under cover of darkness.

Batteries E and H, 1st Pennsylvania Light Artillery (Miller's and Brady's), had been ordered to a position in rear of the Union line after the Battle of Fair Oaks. After the Union right collapsed above the Chickahominy, these two batteries helped keep an important railroad and several important bridges open for several more days as the Army of the Potomac retreated across the river. On the 29th Captain Brady and Battery H were assigned the task of destroying a train loaded with supplies that could not be withdrawn southward. Captain Brady loaded the train with flammables (it already contained a considerable amount of ordinance), set it ablaze, and launched it over the edge of a previously destroyed bridge into the Chickahominy River, where it exploded. Meanwhile, Batteries C and D, $1^{st}$ Pennsylvania Light Artillery (McCarthy's and Flood's), repulsed a brigade of Confederate cavalry at Charles City Crossroads. On June $30^{th}$ Batteries C, D, E, and H were reunited and placed in reserve.

On June $30^{th}$, Batteries B and G (Cooper's and Kern's) were positioned in the center of the line at Charles City Crossroads during the Battle of Glendale. Battery B's guns had been declared unserviceable by the army's chief of artillery because intense use had caused the vent holes to burn out well beyond their proper size, but the emergency left the cannoneers with no choice but to position their well-used pieces in line and start firing. The cannoneers were forced to place one or two extra friction primers in the vent holes because of the increased diameter. Then the caissons were ordered rearward by General Truman Seymour to prevent their capture or destruction, and the artillery ran out of canister rounds. Some gunners began firing shells with the fuses removed. Attempts were made to have more ammunition advanced, but when no fresh supply was obtained, the batteries fired their last shots and retired from the field in good order. The Battle of Glendale claimed the life of Lieutenant Henry T. Danforth, who had previously resigned his commission as a Lieutenant Colonel in order to serve with Battery B.

The Army of the Potomac finally attained a position of relative safety along a series of heights overlooking the James River. The Union position encompassed Malvern Hill and Harrison's Landing, and supplies were forwarded to the army by ships on the James River. The Confederates attacked Malvern Hill on the $1^{st}$ of July and were repulsed, but the Union army withdrew entirely to Harrison's Landing during the night anyway. In one week General Lee had driven the Union army from the gates of Richmond to this final defensive position with its back to the water.

In the following weeks, Battery A, 1st Pennsylvania Light Artillery, which had lost all of its cannon at the Battle of Gaines' Mill, as well as its captain, was rearmed and reorganized under the command of Lieutenant John G. Simpson.

On the 4th of July, Battery B, 1st Pennsylvania Light Artillery (Cooper's) was issued four new cannon to replace the pieces that had previously been condemned. On that same day Battery D, 1st Pennsylvania Light Artillery (Flood's) was recognized with the honor of firing a national salute in observance of Independence Day.

The army remained in place throughout July, and that month brought several changes to the command structure of the 1st Pennsylvania Light Artillery regiment. On the 29th of July, Major Robert M. West was promoted to colonel. Captain Flood of Battery D was promoted to lieutenant colonel and Captain James Brady of Battery H was promoted to major. Lieutenant Michael Hall was promoted to captain and given command of Battery D in place of Flood, and Lieutenant Andrew Fagan was promoted to captain and given command of Battery H in place of Brady. Captain Miller of Battery E left that battery on the 4th of July to serve as an Assistant Adjutant General and was replaced as captain by Thomas G. Orwig. Batteries E and H were placed together under the direction of Major Brady and were designated as part of the reserve artillery of the Fourth Corps.

Battery H was also chosen for the distinction of being rearmed with Napoleons. The model 1857 12-pounder field howitzer was commonly known as the "Napoleon" because of its similarity to a French artillery piece of the same era. The Napoleon, a bronze smoothbore, was manufactured by the Ames Company and the

Revere Copper Company, both of Massachusetts. At 1,200 pounds, its barrel was several hundred pounds heavier than either the 10-pounder Parrott rifle, which weighed 890 pounds, or the 3-in. Ordnance rifle, which weighed 800 pounds. Although the Napoleon had enormous striking power at close range, it was unable to engage targets at anything like the distances that rifled cannon could reach. The Napoleon's great weight also made it difficult to handle and it was not particularly popular with the men required to service it. Needless to say, the cannoneers of Battery H did not consider it a particular honor to have to exchange their 10-pounder Parrott rifles for Napoleons. Nonetheless, despite the misgivings of the men of batteries like Battery H, the Napoleon was one of the mainstay artillery pieces of both armies during the war.

**The Napoleon**
1857 12 Pdr. Field Howitzer

**Barrel Weight**: 1,200 lbs.
**Bore diameter:** 4.62 inches
**Manufacturers:**
The Ames Co., Mass. &
The Revere Copper Co., Mass.

On August 6th, the day after a failed Confederate assault on Malvern Hill (which had been reoccupied several days earlier), Battery B, 1st Pennsylvania Light Artillery was ordered to cross the James River and join a force on the south shore under the command of General Daniel Butterfield. It remained there until ordered to proceed by water to Acquia Creek on the Potomac, where the forces on the Peninsula were being withdrawn to in order to participate in General John Pope's defense against General Lee's new movements in northern Virginia.

## 6. The Shenandoah Valley

While General McClellan's army was making its slow advance up the Peninsula, and its rapid retreat to Harrison's Landing, things had not remained quiet in north-central Virginia. Confederate General Stonewall Jackson had undertaken a campaign in the Shenandoah Valley that had scored the Confederacy a string of victories, confounded numerous Union columns sent to intercept him, renewed Northern fears of a Confederate attack on Washington, and forced President Lincoln to withhold large numbers of reinforcements which General McClellan had requested on the Peninsula. The latter may have played a significant part in making General Lee's success in the Seven Days campaign possible.

Throughout the spring and early summer of 1862, Pennsylvania Independent Battery F (Hampton's) operated in the Shenandoah Valley region as part of a force commanded by General Nathan P. Banks. By the 5th of April, General Banks had pursued Stonewall Jackson as far as Edinburg, where Battery F was involved in intermittent skirmishes through the 18th. During the subsequent reversal in which Stonewall Jackson pushed the Union forces back up the Shenandoah Valley, Battery F was engaged at Cross Keys on the 26th of April, at Middletown on the 24th of May, and at Winchester on the 25th of May.

The historian of Battery F later recorded that during the retreat from Winchester, "Some of the cannoneers of [Hampton's Battery F], seeing a little mulatto girl toiling along the dusty road trying to keep up with the retreating column, placed her on one of the limber chests and allowed her to ride there until they went into camp."*

This small act of kindness would probably have been forgotten if it had not come to the attention of Congress, which actually offered it as grounds for a rebuke against General Banks. A resolution was offered in the House of Representatives which complained that General Banks was inappropriately using military equipment to provide transportation northward for fugitive slaves, and the incident involving Hampton's Battery F and the little girl was cited as evidence against the general.

General Banks' classic response to the charge goes as follows:

> When a considerable distance on our march we overtook a small party on foot. My attention was attracted to a little girl about eight years old who was toddling along over the stones by the way-side, and I asked her how far she had traveled. 'From Winchester,' she said. We were then about twenty-seven miles from that place. I requested some cannoneers of the Hampton Battery [Battery F] to give her a lift and the gallant men who had hung on the rear of the column for its defense the greater part of the distance responded with alacrity. No efforts were made to ascertain her complexion, but it is not impossible that she belonged to the race referred to in the resolution [of Congress] and that her little limbs had been strengthened by some vague dream of liberty in that hurried night march.†

On the 23$^{rd}$ of May (the day before Independent Battery F was engaged at Middletown), Stonewall Jackson's command had attacked a 500-man Union force at Front Royal commanded by Colonel John R. Kenly of the 1$^{st}$ Maryland Infantry (U.S.). Attached to Colonel Kenly's force was Lieutenant Charles Atwell's section of Pennsylvania Independent Battery E (Knap's).

---

\* *Reproduced in* William Clark, *History of Hampton Battery F Independent Pennsylvania Light Artillery* (Akron and Pittsburgh: Werner Company, 1909), 18.
† Ibid.

The handful of Union troops made a rigorous resistance; Atwell's section did considerable damage to the advancing enemy, but in the end the superior numbers of the Confederates prevailed. Colonel Kenly was wounded and taken prisoner, and his command was forced to join the general retreat down the Valley towards Winchester. During the retreat, men and horses were overcome with exhaustion and Atwell's two pieces had to be spiked and abandoned just short of Winchester, but were later recovered when Stonewall Jackson withdrew back up the Shenandoah Valley.

In March of 1862, Pennsylvania Independent Battery C (Thompson's) (which had only received its cannon and horses on February 3rd) was operating in northern Virginia with General John J. Abercrombie's Brigade. On March 21st Battery C had been ordered, along with Abercrombie's Brigade, from Winchester to Alexandria, Virginia in order to embark for the Peninsula. En route, Battery C was diverted to Warrenton Junction and on the 18th of April 1862, fired its first shots in anger during a reconnaissance to the Rappahannock Bridge.

Meanwhile, after participating in an unopposed advance on Manassas Junction in March, Pennsylvania Independent Battery D (Durell's) was attached to General Irvin McDowell's Corps. During the months of March and April, Battery F, 1st Pennsylvania Light Artillery (Matthews') took part in a number of minor engagements in northern Virginia before it also joined General McDowell's Corps, which was then gathering near Falmouth for a move south to meet the right flank of General McClellan's force on the Peninsula. Stonewall Jackson's successes in the Shenandoah Valley forced General McDowell to move westward instead, towards Front Royal, where it was hoped his force would be able to converge with another Union force under General John C. Fremont in time to intercept Jackson. The convergence failed and the Confederates escaped, ultimately to join General Lee on the Peninsula in time to take part in the Seven Days. During the attempt, however, the artillery achieved no small accomplishment in rapidly moving their pieces from Falmouth over the Blue Ridge to Front Royal, on poor roads made even worse by inclement weather, in a mere six days.

●○●

# III

## 1. Cedar Mountain and Rappahannock River

Following the successes of Confederate arms in the Shenandoah Valley and on the Peninsula, General Lee decided the time was right to move his army northward. General McClellan's army was contained at Harrison's Landing, but a new Union army under General John Pope had been formed from the various smaller commands that had been operating in the Shenandoah Valley and in northern Virginia and was advancing along the Rapidan River. General Lee ordered Stonewall Jackson's command north to intercept it, soon followed by the remainder of the Army of Northern Virginia under General James Longstreet.

On the 9th of August 1862 the Confederates met a Union force under General Nathan P. Banks at Cedar Mountain. Early in the engagement, Pennsylvania Independent Battery E (Knap's) took position on an elevation overlooking the most severe fighting. They immediately came under fire from several Confederate batteries and after exhausting their ammunition, were forced to withdraw.

Pennsylvania Independent Battery C (Thompson's) arrived late in the evening and was immediately taken under canister fire by the enemy. Because of the presence of a line of Union infantry to their front, Battery C was not able to fire their own canister back. Instead, Captain Thompson ordered shell fired from his two

12-pounder field howitzers, and employed his four 10-pounder Parrott rifles with striking the Confederate infantry placed further back in support of the Confederate artillery. The Confederate batteries were silenced but Battery C continued firing well into the night.

Knap's Battery E at Cedar Mountain; sketch by Edwin Forbes (1839 – 1895). Image from the Library of Congress.

Lt. Henry L. Godbald; Battery F, 1st Pennsylvania Light Artillery. Image from the P.R.V.C. Historical Society.

After the Battle of Cedar Mountain, General Pope withdrew his army behind the line of the Rappahannock River. On the 21st of August, Battery F, 1st Pennsylvania Light Artillery (Matthews'), which was occupying a south-side bridgehead on a wooded knoll near Rappahannock Bridge, came under heavy fire from Confederate artillery. Pennsylvania Independent Battery C (Thompson's) was ordered to cross to the south bank of the river and assist Battery F. Battery F withdrew after the arrival of Battery C, having had two guns disabled (which were nonetheless successfully removed from the field), but Lieutenant Henry L. Godbald of Battery F was struck in the leg by an enemy shell and would die from the wound a month later on the 22$^{nd}$ of September.

**The Rappahannock Bridge. Image from the Library of Congress.**

Thompson's Battery C remained in position overnight until the 22$^{nd}$ of August, when they were ordered to return to the north shore of the Rappahannock. Battery C's two field howitzers crossed without incident, but just as the remainder of the battery was about to follow, the enemy appeared in force and Captain Thompson ordered his four Parrott rifles to unlimber and commence firing. Battery C continued firing until its ammunition ran low, at which time the battery completed the crossing of the river. When the Confederates attempted to occupy the position on the south shore that Battery C had just departed, Captain Thompson ordered his two howitzers to fire a few rounds across the river, and the Confederates were forced to pull back again.

On the 21st of August, the same day that Batteries C and F were first engaged at Rappahannock Bridge, Pennsylvania Independent Battery D (Durell's) saw action for the first time downriver at Kelly's Ford, where it fired about forty rounds at the enemy from another south shore bridgehead before retiring across the river at nightfall.

## 2. Second Bull Run

On the 25th of August, Stonewall Jackson's Corps of the Confederate army left the line of the Rappahannock on a long flanking movement around to the west and north to strike the Union supply depot at Manassas Junction. Three days later, on the 28th, a small Union force under General James B. Ricketts attempted to block General Longstreet's Corps from passing through Thoroughfare Gap as it attempted to join Jackson. Battery F, 1st Pennsylvania Light Artillery (Matthews') and Pennsylvania Independent Battery C (Thompson's) were both present and engaged in the resulting battle. The road through the Gap was obstructed by felled timber, but Lieutenant Charles Brockway's section of Battery F was moved forward by hand and opened fire on several buildings where Confederate sharpshooters were hiding. The sharpshooters withdrew and the Union infantry advanced until the buildings were brought within Union lines. Captain Thompson meanwhile took two of Battery C's guns forward across a small creek. Captain Thompson immediately came under intense fire from Confederate sharpshooters hiding in the woods a few hundred yards to his front, and was ordered to retire behind the creek. Battery C then took a strong defensive position and assisted in holding off Confederate attempts to force the gap until sundown. After dark, however, General Ricketts' force, which had been outflanked on both sides, withdrew from Thoroughfare Gap and moved towards New Market to rejoin the main Union force, leaving the door open for Longstreet to continue his march toward a junction with Jackson.

On the same day, the $28^{th}$, Stonewall Jackson's Corps, which had ransacked the depot at Manassas Junction on the $26^{th}$, struck a Union column on the Warrenton Pike near Groveton. During the attack, Battery B, $1^{st}$ Pennsylvania Light Artillery (Cooper's), which had been attached to the Third Division of the Third Corps of General Pope's Army of Virginia after returning from the Peninsula, was called up and ordered to relieve Captain Dunbar Ransom's Battery C, $5^{th}$ U.S. Artillery, which was stationed on the Warrenton Pike. Captain Ransom's battery was armed with outdated 12-pounder field howitzers and lacked the range to engage the enemy. Shortly after Battery B took position the enemy withdrew and Battery B advanced with General George Meade's Brigade of the Pennsylvania Reserves as far as Manassas Junction, and camped near the Conrad House on the field where the first major battle of the war had been fought the year before.

Pennsylvania Independent Battery F (Hampton's) was also engaged at Groveton. Hampton's Battery F, which was assigned to the Second Corps of General Pope's Army of Virginia, had just been enlarged to a full six-gun battery, having previously been only a four-gun battery. During the preceding week Independent Battery F had taken part in a series of minor engagements at Freeman's Ford on the $22^{nd}$, White Sulphur Springs on the $23^{rd}$ and $24^{th}$, and at Waterloo on the $25^{th}$. At Groveton, Battery F was sent forward to the aid of General Carl Schurz's First Corps of the Army of Virginia. In his report, General Carl Schurz describes the action of Hampton's Battery F at the Battle of Groveton as follows:

> [T]he battery of the First Brigade, under Captain Hampton, was ordered to march along the outer edge of the woods in which Colonel [Alexander] Schimmelfennig was engaged and to take position there, in order to protect and facilitate the advance of my right; but the crossfire of two of the enemy's batteries was so severe that Captain Hampton's battery failed in two successive attempts to establish itself until I sent Captain [Jacob] Roemer's [$2^{nd}$ New York Independent] battery to its support, the place of the latter being filled by a battery brought from the reserve....[*]

Later in the fighting, Independent Battery F was forced to fall back a short distance and lost a cannon which had gotten stuck on a tree stump. While firing its last shot before the battery retired, the left-most cannon recoiled against the stump and the handspike was driven forcefully into the wood. With the Confederates rapidly approaching and demanding the gun's surrender, Battery F was ordered to abandon the immobilized cannon.

Stonewall Jackson's attempt to destroy the passing Union column near Groveton failed when the federal forces simply refused to be driven away, and the fighting at Groveton faded out with the apparent withdrawal of the Confederates. General Pope then issued orders to concentrate his army for a unified thrust against Stonewall Jackson's detached corps. The battle that followed, the Second Battle of Bull Run, was the result of a serious misunderstanding by General Pope as to Stonewall Jackson's intentions. After the engagement at Groveton, General Pope believed that Stonewall Jackson was trying to escape and that the Union army could cut off and destroy his force before it could rejoin the other half of General Lee's army under General Longstreet. In fact, Stonewall Jackson had no intention of leaving, but rather was waiting for the arrival of Longstreet's Corps so that they could cooperate in destroying Pope. Lee and Longstreet were

---

[*] O.R., series I vol. 12 pt. 2, 296 (No. 16), 298-99.

already en route to join Jackson at Manassas after having passed through Thoroughfare Gap that same day.

On the 29th of August, General Pope launched a series of poorly coordinated attacks against Stonewall Jackson's line, and unbeknownst to Pope, General Longstreet's Corps arrived around midday and extended the Confederate line to the south by over a mile.

Batteries A, B, F, & G, 1st Pennsylvania Light Artillery and Pennsylvania Independent Battery C were all attached to General Irvin McDowell's Third Corps of the Army of Virginia, but Battery F, 1st Pennsylvania Light Artillery (Matthew's) and Independent Battery C (Thompson's) were still en route from Thoroughfare Gap and had not yet arrived on the field.

Battery A, 1st Pennsylvania Light Artillery (Simpson's) had been re-armed and re-equipped since losing all of its cannon and the life of Captain Hezekiah Easton during the Battle of Gaines' Mill on the Peninsula, and had rejoined the army in northern Virginia. Battery B, 1st Pennsylvania Light Artillery (Cooper's) was moved from its position near the Conrad House, which it had reached the day before after marching from Groveton, to near the extreme left of the Union line, where it relieved an Ohio battery. Battery B immediately came under fire from multiple Confederate batteries to their front and flank and in about twenty minutes lost four men killed and fifteen wounded. Battery B was soon ordered to pull back, but lost a caisson in the process. Battery G, 1st Pennsylvania Light Artillery (Kern's) was also placed on the army's left flank near Battery B.

Meanwhile, Pennsylvania Independent Battery D (Durell's) had been attached to General Hooker's Second Division of the Army of the Potomac's Third Corps on the 27th, and had followed up its first engagement at Kelly's Ford with a series of skirmishes between Bristoe Station and Manassas. When Battery D arrived on the field it was positioned near the overall center of the Union line but remained unengaged.

Pennsylvania Independent Battery F (Hampton's), which was still attached to General Franz Sigel's First Corps of the Army of Virginia, was heavily engaged supporting a failed attack against A.P. Hill's position in the middle of Jackson's line.

Pennsylvania Independent Battery E (Knap's), with General Nathan Banks' Second Corps of the Army of Virginia, was present on the field but does not appear to have been heavily engaged.

On the 30th, General Pope again misread the situation, and concluded that Stonewall Jackson's forces had abandoned their lines and were actually retreating. Pope therefore ordered a pursuit. General Pope was still unaware that General Longstreet's Corps had arrived on the field and overlapped the Union left flank by over mile. General Pope's "pursuit" of Jackson ended when Jackson's troops were found occupying the same positions they had held the day before. The Union army renewed its attack, further exposing its left flank, and Longstreet's Corps proceeded to swing around and crush the Union left.

Since Longstreet's presence on the field was still unknown to Pope, his unexpected attack was an almost complete success; the Union army was quickly thrown into dire confusion. Stonewall Jackson, seeing the collapse of the Union left and the resulting state of vulnerability, shifted his troops to the offensive as well and the Confederate assault became general.

Batteries B & G, 1st Pennsylvania Light Artillery (Cooper's and Kern's) were still in position supporting the Union left and took the full force of Longstreet's initial assault. Cooper's Battery B lost three men killed and another sixteen men wounded before being forced to withdraw. Battery B also lost all of its remaining caissons and the men and guns only narrowly escaped being captured as well. Kern's Battery G was overwhelmed and lost all four of its cannon to the enemy; Captain Kern was mortally wounded and had to be left on the field. In addition to Captain Kern, Battery G lost three men killed, twenty-two wounded, and eight captured.

Pennsylvania Independent Battery D (Durell's) was still positioned near the center of the Union line when the Union left flank collapsed, which exposed them to fire from their left. One of Battery D's cannon was dismounted from its carriage by an enemy shot and the battery was ordered to move back a few hundred yards. From its new position Battery D dueled with the enemy for about twenty minutes before being forced to join the general retreat northeast towards Centreville.

Pennsylvania Independent Battery C (Thompson's), which had finally arrived from Thoroughfare Gap, had spent the early morning engaged in counter-battery fire on the right of the Third Corps line, but was pulled back after Longstreet's attack and placed near Battery F, 1$^{st}$ Pennsylvania Light Artillery (Matthew's), near the Sudley Spring Road. The two remaining sections of Battery F, under Lieutenants Charles Brockway and T. Leroy Case, had also arrived on the field that day (the two guns of Battery F's third section had not yet been repaired from the damage received at Rappahannock Station, and Lieutenant R. Bruce Ricketts was away from the battery on recruiting duty).

When Stonewall Jackson's Corps joined in the general assault Thompson's Battery C met them with canister, but some of the supporting infantry mistook the advancing Confederates for federal troops, and failed to return fire until it was too late. The Union infantry was driven back, and the men of Captain Thompson's battery had to pull their guns backwards with prolong ropes in order to avoid being captured because there was not enough time to connect the guns to their limbers.

At one point during the retreat, one of Battery C's guns jammed between two trees and the approaching Confederates demanded that the gun crew surrender. The cannoneers briefly interrupted their efforts to free the stricken gun in order to answer the Confederates by firing a shot at them.

The men of Battery C eventually made enough headway to stop and get their guns limbered, but as the retreat continued both of their 12-pounder howitzers and one of their Parrott rifles were overtaken and captured when the battery was slowed while passing through a patch of thick woods and underbrush.

Battery F, 1st Pennsylvania Light Artillery was also heavily engaged during Jackson's attack and the subsequent Union retreat. Lieutenant Brockway's section was separated from Lieutenant Case's section early in the battle, and when the Confederate advance reached the Sudley Spring Road, Lieutenant Brockway's section became cut off. Lieutenant Brockway and a few of his men escaped, but his two guns were captured and most of his men were taken prisoner. Toward evening Brockway was reinforced with enough men borrowed from other units to form a full gun detachment, and he somehow acquired a new cannon (possibly a piece abandoned earlier during the general retreat). Brockway and his battered gun crew were stationed near the Henry House and, along with Thompson's Battery C, helped cover the retreat of the army across Bull Run, but Brockway himself was captured in the later stages of the withdrawal.

Lt. Charles Brockway; Battery F, 1st Pennsylvania Light Artillery. From the P.R.V.C. Historical Society.

During the battle, Battery C lost ten men wounded and captured, and three cannon left behind. Battery F suffered even more seriously; from its action at the Rappahannock nine days earlier through Second Bull Run, Battery F, 1st Pennsylvania Light Artillery lost eight men killed and fifteen wounded, as well as five men taken prisoner. Battery F also lost all but one of the cannon they had brought onto the field at Manassas. On the following day, September 1st, the remaining men of Battery F would take over the cannon and equipments of an Indiana battery.

General Ricketts commended Batteries C and F in his official report, declaring that: "Captains Matthews' and Thompson's Pennsylvania batteries and [two Maine batteries] deserve to be mentioned not only for their uniform attention to their duties, but for their efficiency throughout the 30th of August."*

On the morning of the 1st of September, General Pope's battered army continued its retreat to the northeast, passing through Germantown. Stonewall Jackson's Confederates moved parallel in pursuit, and occupied Chantilly (to the northwest), forcing Pope to send troops to meet him. This Union force, consisting mainly of troops from General Jesse Reno's Ninth Corps supported by elements of the Army of Virginia's Third Corps, advanced along the Little River Turnpike towards Chantilly. Pennsylvania Independent Battery C (Thompson's) went into position on the right flank along the crest of a ridge facing Ox Hill, where several Confederate batteries were placed. Pennsylvania Independent Battery D (Durell's), meanwhile, was placed to the west along the road connecting Centreville and Germantown.

During a severe afternoon thunderstorm, the Confederates launched a series of attacks against the Union lines, but the outnumbered defenders were able to hold their ground until evening. The Union army was then able to continue its retreat to the relative safety of the Potomac unmolested.

---

* O.R., series I vol. 12 pt. 2, 383 (No.35), 385.

## 3. Two New Batteries

Two new Pennsylvania batteries were raised in August of 1862. The "Keystone Battery" was organized on the 13$^{th}$ at Philadelphia under Captain Matthew Hastings. Technically speaking, the Keystone Battery was "reorganized" since Captain Hastings had raised a militia unit with the same name the previous year under the authority of the city of Philadelphia. That unit, a part of the city's defense forces, was never a recognized part of the state's system of volunteers. The new Keystone Battery, however, was a fully-fledged field battery acknowledged by the state of Pennsylvania and mustered into federal service (although the men enlisted for only one year's service instead of the more usual three year's service). Following its organization, the Keystone Battery was ordered to join the forces defending Washington, where it would remain until the following summer.

On the 22$^{nd}$ of August (a week before the Second Battle of Bull Run), Pennsylvania Independent Battery G, under Captain John J. Young, was organized at Harrisburg. Battery G was composed mainly of men from Allegheny County. Despite repeated requests by its commander to be sent to the front, Battery G would, like its predecessor Independent Battery A (Schaffer's), spend its entire term of service with the garrison of Fort Delaware.

The Keystone Battery at Drill. Image from the National Archives.

Fort Delaware on Pea Patch Island in the Delaware River.
From a painting by Seth Eastman (1808 – 1875).

## 4. South Mountain

The Second Battle of Bull Run was an enormous blow to the Union cause, and on the 2nd of September 1862, two days after the battle, President Lincoln removed General Pope from command and placed General McClellan in charge of all the Union troops in the Virginia theatre of war. General Pope's Army of Virginia was disbanded and its individual units were integrated into General McClellan's restored Army of the Potomac.

General Lee sought to follow up his victory at Bull Run with an invasion of the North. On the 4th of September, four days after the Second Battle of Bull Run, the Army of Northern Virginia began crossing the Potomac River into Maryland. On the following day, the Army of the Potomac began its pursuit.

On the 13th, Union forces found a lost copy of General Lee's Special Order 191, which outlined the Confederate plan for the capture of Harper's Ferry and revealed that the Army of Northern Virginia had been divided into three separate and far-flung columns. This information prompted General McClellan to move with uncharacteristic speed in order to strike the Confederates while they were still divided. On the following day, the Union army tried to force its way through three gaps cutting through South Mountain so as to place itself between the spread-out Confederate columns.

Batteries A and B, 1st Pennsylvania Light Artillery (Simpson's and Cooper's), now with the Third Division of the First Corps following the merger of the Army of Virginia and the Army of the Potomac,* both took part in the assault on Turner's Gap.

Captain Cooper reported the part played by his battery as follows:

> At 3.30 o'clock p.m., by order of General Hooker, the battery was placed upon a high hill to the right of the turnpike and near the base of the mountain. Immediately on coming into battery, 25 or 30 case-shot were thrown among the enemy on the slope of the mountain, scattering them, but, eliciting no reply from the enemy's guns, I ceased firing, by General Hooker's order, that the infantry might advance. The position of our lines prevented any further firing during the evening, no order to change position being received. No casualties attended the engagement.†

Pennsylvania Independent Battery C (Thompson's) and Battery F, 1ˢᵗ Pennsylvania Light Artillery (Matthews'), both with the Second Division of the First Corps, were also present at Turner's Gap but were not actively engaged. Several days earlier Battery C had received four 3-in. Ordnance rifles that were transferred to it from the 2ⁿᵈ Maine Battery, allowing Battery C to return several cannon it had borrowed from other batteries during the Second Battle of Bull Run. Battery F was also re-equipped with four 3-in. Ordnance rifles.

Lieutenant Samuel H. Rhodes of Independent Battery D (Durell's), which was with the Second Division of the Ninth Corps at Turner's Gap, described his battery's part in the action thus:

> At three P. M., on the 13ᵗʰ we went into position, near the top of South Mountain. We were very successful in this engagement, had good ammunition, twice silenced and drove off a rebel

---

* When the Army of Virginia was consolidated with the Army of the Potomac, the Third Corp of the Army of Virginia became the First Corps of the Army of the Potomac.
† O.R., series I vol. 19 pt. 1, 271 (No.34).

battery, and harassed the rebel infantry as they advanced on our troops on the right of our position, firing from our six guns about two hundred and fifty rounds.*

Batteries C and D, 1$^{st}$ Pennsylvania Light Artillery (McCarthy's and Hall's) were still with General Darius Couch's First Division of the Fourth Corps, which had been temporarily attached to the Sixth Corps and assigned a supporting role in the attack on Crampton's Gap. Neither of these batteries, however, nor their division, was engaged during the assault on the Gap.

Pennsylvania Independent Batteries E and F (Knap's and Hampton's) were both assigned to the Twelfth Corps, which was held in reserve and did not participate in the battle.

The Confederates were pushed hard at all three passes through South Mountain, and lost control of Crampton's Gap, rendering the entire position untenable. The Confederates withdrew during the night, but the Union army was unable to get between the divided sections of the Army of Northern Virginia as McClellan had planned. General Lee, recognizing the peril of his situation, ordered his forces to converge at Sharpsburg between Antietam Creek and the Potomac River. General McClellan was slow in his pursuit, and by the time the Army of the Potomac reached the creek the Confederates were already reunited and waiting on the opposite side.

---

* Bates at vol. 5, 876.

## 5. The Bloodiest Day – Antietam

General McClellan was not deterred. In the late afternoon of the 16th, the First Corps of the Union army, under General Joseph Hooker, crossed Antietam Creek above the Confederate positions. Batteries A and B, 1st Pennsylvania Light Artillery (Simpson's and Cooper's) were moving with the First Corps' Third Division towards Sharpsburg from the north. Battery B advanced with the Bucktails in the direction of the East Wood (one of two wooded groves above Sharpsburg that flanked the Hagerstown Pike) and took position near the north edge of Miller's cornfield, opposite the Confederate lines. Simpson's Battery A was meanwhile posted on Poffenberger's Ridge to the west of the Pike.

**Abandoned Limber and Confederate Dead in Front of the Dunker Church at Antietam. Image from the National Park Service.**

At dawn on September 17th, the First Corps attacked southward between the two woods and across the cornfield.

Cooper's Battery B was moved to the right and took a position near Simpson's Battery A and several other batteries on Poffenberger's Ridge. One of Battery B's sections, under Lieutenant Fullerton, crossed the Pike and maneuvered in conjunction with the infantry towards the front. Batteries A and B fired sporadically throughout the day whenever the enemy presented a target and Captain Cooper was nearly killed when his horse was struck by an enemy solid shot.

Battery F, 1$^{st}$ Pennsylvania Light Artillery (Matthews') and Pennsylvania Independent Battery C (Thompson's) were meanwhile engaged in severe fighting near Miller's cornfield. At around 5:45 a.m. Thompson's Battery C went into action targeting a Confederate battery to its right-front. After about ten minutes another Confederate battery to its left-front found their range and Captain Thompson shifted his fire toward this new enemy before advancing into a plowed field directly north of Miller's cornfield (in which plowed field Captain Matthews' Battery F was also positioned).

Battery C then advanced again, taking position on a knoll within the cornfield, which was by then in Union hands. Just before 7:00 a.m., however, the Confederates counterattacked. Captain Thompson was unable to fire with canister because Union wounded were retreating across his front, so he ordered shells fired with short fuses. Starting with three-second fuses, by the time the Confederates got to within seventy-five yards; Battery C was firing with one-and-a-half second fuses.

Captain Thompson ordered the battery to withdraw to a position approximately two hundred yards back in the plowed field they had previously occupied. This new position also proved untenable, and after a few minutes, it too was abandoned. One cannon was temporarily left behind because too many horses had been killed to pull it, but a team was quickly sent back and the cannon was retrieved. Captain Matthews' Battery F was meanwhile able to hold its ground in the rearward part of the plowed field throughout the Confederate counterattack, and repulsed repeated charges by the enemy with volleys of canister, but two of Battery F's cannon suffered serious damage.

During the engagement, the explosion of a Confederate shell lit the fuse of a round being carried by Private John Sullivan of Battery C. The round exploded and tore off most of Private Sullivan's clothing. Private Sullivan was wounded, but not fatally. Captain Matthews of Battery F, meanwhile, like Captain Cooper of Battery B that same morning, had his horse shot out from under him.

In his official report, General James B. Ricketts, commander of the Second Division of the First Corps, wrote of Batteries C and F that "Taking advantage of the ground, both batteries opened with destructive effect, officers and men displaying great coolness while exposed to a severe fire of artillery and infantry."[*] General Ricketts also commended the personal conduct of Captains Matthews and Thompson during the battle.

**Knap's Pennsylvania Independent Battery E at Antietam.**
**Image from the National Archives.**

---

[*] O.R., series I vol. 19 pt. 1, 258 (No.27), 259.

The Union Twelfth Corps under General Joseph K. Mansfield joined the attack from the east (skirting the East Wood to the Corps' north) just after 7:00 a.m. Pennsylvania Independent Batteries E and F (Knap's and Hampton's) were both assigned to the Twelfth Corps and joined the advance.

In his report of the battle, Captain Clermont L. Best, the commander of the Twelfth Corps' artillery, described the involvement of Captain Knap's Battery E as follows:

> I proceeded to the field, and found that General Mansfield and General [Alpheus S.] Williams, succeeding him, had already posted the rifled batteries of Knap and [Captain George W.] Cothran [Battery M, $1^{st}$ New York Light Artillery] in front of the infantry and near the enemy. Captain Knap commenced fire at 7 a. m. slowly and deliberately, the enemy advancing against him several times between that and 12 m., but each time repulsed with canister. At 12 m. one section of his battery, under Lieutenant McGill, was ordered by General [George S.] Greene forward to assist Colonel [Hector] Tyndale in holding a wood. Colonel Tyndale ordered one piece of this section to enter the wood, in the act of which it was met with such a destructive fire from the enemy, wounding 4 cannoneers and killing 3 horses, that the piece had to be abandoned and was lost. Captain Knap continued working the remaining five guns till 3 p. m., at which time he withdrew from the field, wanting ammunition.
>
> \*\*\*
>
> Captain Knap brought from the field on the 19th one iron 12-pounder howitzer and caisson abandoned by the enemy.[*]

Independent Battery F was meanwhile placed near the Dunker Church and spent the day mainly engaged at long range, keeping the enemy from massing artillery near that part of the field.

The Union drive down the Hagerstown Pike ground to a halt around the middle of the day, but further down the length of

---

[*] O.R., series I vol. 19 pt. 1, 482 (No.165).

Antietam Creek General Ambrose Burnside forced a crossing at the stone bridge that would forever after bear his name. Batteries C and D, 1st Pennsylvania Light Artillery (McCarthy's and Hall's), having been earlier attached, along with General Darius Couch's Division, to the Sixth Corps, were positioned throughout the day on a knoll overlooking the bridge, from which they exchanged fire with the enemy and supported the crossing. Pennsylvania Independent Battery D (Durell's) was then attached to General Burnside's Ninth Corps and joined the forces crossing the bridge.

Lieutenant Samuel H. Rhodes of Durell's Independent Battery D reported his unit's part in the action thus:

> On the morning of the 17th, we were shelled out of camp at daylight, and immediately went into position, and opened fire in reply. At nine A. M., we were ordered to the rear of Stone Bridge, No. 3 [Burnside's Bridge], nearly opposite Sharpsburg, and just before General [John F.] Hartranft took the bridge, our centre section moved near to the bridge, and followed closely the General's infantry across. This section was soon after joined by the rest of the battery, and the whole went into position at a point about nine hundred yards from the rebel guns opposed to us, which we engaged whenever they opened, at short intervals, for upwards of two hours, and only retired when we got out of projectiles, and were ordered back, the general commanding us, not deeming it advisable to allow our caissons to cross the bridge to bring up a supply of ammunition. This was the most desperate engagement, I think, and at shortest range, which our battery was in. Our loss was two men dangerously wounded; several of our horses dropped down in their harness from exhaustion, and had to be left on the field.[*]

This final Union advance was blocked by the last-minute arrival of Confederate reinforcements under General A.P. Hill, and the Battle of Antietam ended in a stalemate. The 17th of September 1862 had been the bloodiest day of battle in American history, with combined casualties of over 3,600 killed and over

---

[*] Bates at vol. 5, 876.

17,000 wounded. Among those fallen during the Antietam campaign were 1 killed and 3 wounded from Battery A, 1st Pennsylvania Light Artillery (Simpson's); 2 wounded from Battery B, 1st Pennsylvania Light Artillery (Cooper's); 4 killed from Battery F, 1st Pennsylvania Light Artillery (Matthews'); 1 killed and 3 wounded from Pennsylvania Independent Battery C (Thompson's); 1 killed from Independent Battery D (Durell's); 1 killed, 6 wounded, and 1 taken prisoner from Independent Battery E (Knap's); and 3 wounded from Independent Battery F (Hampton's).

Burnside's Bridge (Picture from September 1862).
Image from the Library of Congress.

## 6. The Autumn of 1862

Following the Battle of Antietam, General Robert E. Lee's Army of Northern Virginia re-crossed the Potomac into Virginia, bringing an end to the Maryland Campaign, and the Army of the Potomac began preparations for its next offensive.

Battery F, 1st Pennsylvania Light Artillery (Matthews') was in a particularly deplorable state. Captain Ezra W. Matthews was forced to leave the battery after the Battle of Antietam because of illness, and was never able to return. Lieutenant T. Leroy Case was also ill and absent from the command. Lieutenant Henry L. Godbald had lost a leg on August 21st at the Rappahannock River and died from that wound on September 22nd. In the same action the battery had lost two cannon disabled. At Second Bull Run, Battery F suffered severe losses in both men and materiel, including the loss of several more cannon and the gallant Lieutenant Charles Brockway, who was taken prisoner. Following Antietam, the total strength of Battery F was reduced to a mere two serviceable cannon.

Steps were, however, being taken to replace Battery F's losses. On the 23rd of September, less than a week after Antietam, Lieutenant R. Bruce Ricketts returned to the battery from recruiting duty in the North and assumed command. Shortly after his arrival the battery received two additional cannon and sufficient men and horses to make the new section operational.

On the 21st of October, a new Pennsylvania battery was organized at Pittsburgh. Pennsylvania Independent Battery H, under Captain John I. Nevin, briefly served with the Army of the Potomac in Maryland before being reassigned to duty in the defenses of Washington.

In early November, Pennsylvania Independent Battery D (Durell's), still with the Ninth Corps following Antietam, was briefly engaged at Amissville, Virginia on the 10th and at White Sulphur Springs on the 15th. At the latter battle Battery D fired over 300 rounds, and Lieutenant Howard McIlvaine and Private Henry B. Ives were wounded. Lieutenant McIlvaine would die on November 15th of the following year as a result of his wounds.

Batteries E and H, 1ˢᵗ Pennsylvania Light Artillery (Orwig's and Fagon's) had all this time remained on the Virginia Peninsula with the Fourth Corps after the rest of McClellan's army had been withdrawn by water to reinforce General Pope's Army of Virginia prior to Second Bull Run. The Fourth Corps had since then been holding position in the vicinity of Yorktown and Gloucester, but on the 11ᵗʰ of December they took part in a drive across the York River toward Gloucester Court House. The following day, Major Brady, who was still in general command over Batteries E and H, took a detachment of mounted artillerymen from the two batteries and led them in a cavalry-style raid that captured a herd of four hundred cattle from the enemy. By the 13ᵗʰ, the two batteries were at Urbana on the line of the Rappahannock, within possible marching distance of where the battle of Fredericksburg had already begun, but were ordered to proceed no further.

After Antietam, Pennsylvania Independent Battery F (Hampton's) was assigned to the Twelfth Corps, which was posted in the vicinity of Harper's Ferry. On the 9ᵗʰ of November the battery was engaged at Charlestown and on the 2ⁿᵈ of December they were again engaged at Winchester. Battery F was ordered on the 10ᵗʰ to proceed with the Twelfth Corps to where the main army was gathering opposite Fredericksburg, but did not arrive in time to participate in the battle. Pennsylvania Independent Battery E (Knap's), also assigned to the Twelfth Corps, likewise failed to rejoin the main army in time to take part in the battle of Fredericksburg.

Meanwhile, in the West, the autumn of 1862 had also been marked by the repulse of a Confederate invasion into the North. After the Battle of Shiloh, Pennsylvania Independent Battery B (Muehler's), which remained a part of General Don Carlos Buell's Army of the Ohio, had taken part in General Henry Halleck's three-army advance on Corinth, Mississippi. Corinth was occupied on the 30th of May, the Confederate defenders under General P. G. T. Beauregard having evacuated Corinth the previous night. Instead of pursuing, Halleck dispersed his force, and the Army of the Ohio moved into central Tennessee. In August, Confederate General Braxton Bragg, who replaced Beauregard shortly after Corinth, shifted his army eastward and struck north into Kentucky. Bragg's "invasion" culminated in the Battle of Perryville of the 8th of October, 1862. As had happened at Shiloh, Captain Muehler's Battery B arrived on the field too late to take part in the fighting. The battle was a tactical draw, but was followed by a Confederate retreat back into Tennessee. Shortly after Perryville, General Buell was replaced by General William S. Rosecrans, who renamed the Army of the Ohio as the "Army of the Cumberland."

## 7. Fredericksburg

On the 7th of November 1862, General McClellan was relieved of command of the Army of the Potomac, replaced by General Ambrose Burnside. On the 15th General Burnside ordered a movement towards Fredericksburg on the Rappahannock River. Two days later, the Union army was positioned on the opposite shore of the river facing their objective. Unfortunately, due to an administrative error, the pontoon bridges needed to cross the river

Private Harvey Bryant; McCarthy's Battery C, 1st Pennsylvania Light Artillery. Image from the P.R.V.C. Historical Society.

did not arrive until the 25th, by which time the Confederate army had occupied the hills that ringed the town and had heavily fortified themselves. Undaunted, General Burnside resolved to cross as planned and attack the enemy. On the 11th of December, engineers began assembling the pontoon bridges in the pre-dawn darkness.

Burnside had massed his artillery on Stafford Heights, a long eminence overlooking the river from the north bank. This forced the Confederates on the lower south bank to establish their lines further back from the river on the ridges behind the town.

Batteries C and D, 1st Pennsylvania Light Artillery (McCarthy's and Hall's), with the Sixth Corps, and Pennsylvania Independent Battery D (Durell's), with the Ninth Corps, were among the batteries posted on Stafford Heights, and spent the entire duration of the battle exchanging fire with the Confederate artillery opposite.

Batteries A and F, 1st Pennsylvania Light Artillery (Simpson's and Ricketts'), both with the First Corps, were initially posted along the river to cover the pontoons. The laying of the pontoons was challenged by Confederate artillery and sharpshooters positioned in the town of Fredericksburg, so the town was shelled. The shelling did not succeed in dislodging the sharpshooters, so at the suggestion of General Henry J. Hunt (who had succeeded William Barry as the Union chief of artillery) pontoon boats were used to ferry infantry across the river. These amphibious infantry were able to drive the sharpshooters out of the town so that the pontoon bridges could be completed.

The Army of the Potomac spent the evening of December 11th and the entire day of the 12th crossing the river and moving to its assigned jump-off positions for the attack which was finally launched at dawn on the 13th. The attack was massive in scale, but poorly planned and badly executed. Up and down the line, various commanders launched repeated piecemeal attacks carried out by individual units directly against the well-entrenched Confederates on the ridges above. Some units were not engaged at all, and the superior Union artillery was somewhat stymied by a heavy fog that limited its effectiveness.

Batteries B and G, 1st Pennsylvania Light Artillery (Cooper's and Amsden's) had crossed the river the day before with General George G. Meade's Third Division of the First Corps. Following the Battle of Second Bull Run, where it had taken such heavy losses, including the death of Captain Mark Kern, Battery G had returned to Washington to reorganize. Now under the command of Captain Frank P. Amsden and armed with four new 3-in. Ordnance rifles, Battery G had left Washington on the 9th of October and rejoined the army as it moved on Fredericksburg.

**Pontoon Bridges at Fredericksburg (Stafford Heights in the Background).**
**Image from the National Archives.**

On the morning of the 13th, the two batteries were near the left of the army and supported the first major attack of the day, which was spearheaded by their division. The attack was temporarily stalled by an ambitious section of Virginia Horse Artillery under

Major John Pelham that moved forward from the Confederate lines and attempted to disrupt the Union infantry as they marched to their assigned starting positions for the attack. Captain Cooper's Battery B took its own forward position on the left of the Union line and helped to drive off the enemy section and clear the way for the attack. General Meade's infantry finally started forward and Batteries B and G turned their attention to the main line of Confederate artillery above them. They destroyed several enemy limbers before becoming the subject of a concentrated fire from Confederate batteries on the ridge above. Two of the limbers of Battery B were destroyed by enemy fire, and the battery was forced to withdraw to a new position further back.

The infantry made an incredible effort to breech the Confederate line, but were ultimately driven back with extremely heavy casualties. Perceiving an opportunity, the Confederates counterattacked and tried to take the Union guns. They were met with shots of double canister, and with the support of the reformed infantry, the artillery were able to prevent their positions from being overrun. General John F. Reynolds, the commander of the First Corps, was present at the moment of crisis and said to the commander of Battery B, "Captain Cooper, you are the bravest man in the army."[*] Captain Cooper would report that "the battery ... expended 980 rounds of ammunition. The battery retained its position until about midnight, when we were relieved by Captain Thompson's battery [C], when we withdrew to a position near the Bernard house."[†] Battery B lost two men killed and two others wounded; Captain Amsden's Battery G lost one man killed, four wounded, and two cannon disabled.

---

[*] From an address by Lieutenant James A. Gardner at the dedication of the Cooper's Battery monument in Gettysburg on September 11, 1889. Bvt. Lt. Col. John P. Nicholson, ed., *Pennsylvania at Gettysburg...* (Harrisburg: Wm. Stanley Ray, State Printer, 1914), vol. 2, 906.
[†] O.R., series I vol. 21, 515 (No. 245), 516.

Pennsylvania Independent Battery C (Thompson's), which was now with General John Gibbon's Second Division of the First Corps, had supported the advance of that division, which likewise attacked and was likewise driven back. At one point they were caught in a crossfire of enemy artillery and infantry during the Confederate counterattack. Battery C focused its fire on the Confederate infantry until the enemy was driven back, and then turned its attention to the Confederate artillery and was able to destroy an enemy limber before retiring. During the night, Battery C relieved Cooper's Battery B in line but was not again engaged. Thompson's Battery C suffered two men wounded and one cannon disabled during the battle.

During the entire day's action, Batteries A and F, which were still positioned low along the north bank of the river covering the pontoons, came under a heavy enemy fire as they exchanged shots with the Confederate batteries above the town. The fire was so intense that after the battle every single cannon in Battery A was marked with damage from enemy shots.

The failed attack on the Confederates at Fredericksburg proved to be another disaster for the Union army, which suffered over 12,000 casualties while failing to dislodge the Confederates from the ridges above the town. Conceding defeat, General Burnside ordered the Union army to re-cross the Rappahannock on the 15$^{th}$ of December and had the engineers remove the pontoon bridges behind them.

## 8. Murfreesboro

Just over two weeks after Fredericksburg and six hundred miles to the southwest, another major battle was fought in

Tennessee. After succeeding General Buell as commander of the Army of the Ohio and renaming it the Army of the Cumberland, General William Rosecrans was assigned the task of driving General Braxton Bragg's Confederate Army of Tennessee out of the state from which it took its name. By late December in 1862 the two armies were facing each other across Stones River near Murfreesboro. The river was too shallow to be an effective obstacle, and each general planned to strengthen their left for an attack on the enemy's right to be launched on the last day of the year, but as it turned out the Confederates were a little quicker and their early morning assault forced the Army of the Cumberland onto the defensive.

Still with the Army of the Cumberland, Pennsylvania Independent Battery B prepared to do its part in the pending battle. Captain Charles F. Muehler had resigned from the service in November, and Lieutenant Alanson J. Stevens (who was the nephew of Pennsylvania Congressman Thaddeus Stevens) had been elevated to command of the battery as Muehler's successor.

Battery B crossed the river on the $31^{st}$ in support of Colonel Samuel Beatty's brigade of General Horatio P. Van Cleve's Division, as part of the force sent by Rosecrans to attack on the left, but as soon as they went into position on the opposite bank word arrived of the Confederate attack against the army's opposite flank, and they were ordered to re-cross and march south to reinforce the army's right wing.

Battery B attempted to follow Colonel Beatty's brigade towards the army's right, but was forced to separate from the infantry when they entered a wooded area in which the artillery could not effectively maneuver and fire. Lieutenant Stevens reported:

> We found everything there in confusion, and it was impossible to follow our brigade, and the battery nearly in the lines of the enemy. [Captain George R. Swallow (The Division Chief of

Artillery)] then gave me the permission to fight on my own hook, and do the best in my power. I then countermarched the battery and took position on the rising ground on the left of the old block-house, along the line of the railroad, and opened fire on the enemy, who were advancing through the woods on the right of the pike and in our front. ...*

Battery B helped drive the Confederates across the Nashville Pike, and then crossed over itself and took one position after another along a stretch of high ground in a cornfield to the right of the pike. The battery continued exchanging fire with enemy infantry and artillery until nightfall, when it was withdrawn a few hundred yards to refill its ammunition chests. They were also reinforced by the addition of several men from Battery C, 1$^{st}$ Illinois Light Artillery (Captain Charles Houghtaling). Houghtaling's Battery C had lost three of its guns during the day's fighting and Lieutenant John Van Dyke and some of the men of Battery C offered to fall in with Battery B for the duration.

The next day, New Year's Day, was mostly quiet. Battery B fired a few rounds towards the woods in their front during the morning, but was not otherwise engaged.

On the 2$^{nd}$ of January, Battery B exchanged fire intermittently with a Confederate battery in the woods to their front until shortly after 3:00 p.m., when an attack was made on the Union left flank, which still extended across the river. Battery B changed its front to the left and placed an enfilading fire on the Confederates on the far side of the river. The attack was repulsed, and Battery B ceased firing when the enemy fell back beyond its range. Battery B fell back itself in the evening when its infantry support withdrew, but returned the next morning when the infantry reoccupied the ridge. Battery B remained in place until 3:00 p.m. when it was ordered to relieve the 3$^{rd}$ Wisconsin Battery. At midnight Battery B was ordered to re-cross the river, presumably

---

* O.R., series I vol. 20 pt. 1, 580 (No.146).

for a renewal of the originally planned attack on the enemy right flank that had been interrupted three and a half days earlier by the enemy's attack on the Union flank.

The Confederate army, however, having done all the damage it could expect to do, and fearful that the Army of the Cumberland was being heavily reinforced, withdrew from the field that same night. Battery B lost two men killed and seven wounded during the battle.

## 9. The Winter of 1862-63

Following his defeat at Fredericksburg, General Burnside determined to make another attempt at crossing the Rappahannock. This time, he decided to make a sudden march northwestward and cross the river at Bank's Ford, above Fredericksburg, so as to outflank the Confederate army still entrenched on the ridges behind Fredericksburg.

The movement began on the $20^{th}$ of January 1863 in unusually warm weather. But it soon began to rain, and the rain became a deluge. For two days the Union army plowed through knee-deep mud that all but immobilized the men, horses, and artillery. Giving up, General Burnside ordered an end to the "Mud March" and the Union army returned to their starting point and went into winter quarters. On the $26^{th}$ of January, General Burnside was replaced as commander of the Army of the Potomac by General Joseph Hooker.

Soon thereafter, Batteries C and D, $1^{st}$ Pennsylvania Light Artillery, both of which were now well below the requisite strength for field batteries, were ordered to consolidate. The men of Battery C were integrated into Battery D, and the resulting composite organization kept the name of Battery D. Captain Hall of Battery D, being junior to Captain McCarthy, was mustered out, and Captain McCarthy assumed command of the whole. After the consolidation Battery D was a full six-gun battery.

*A Hard Pull*; sketch by Edwin Forbes (1839 – 1895).
Image from the Library of Congress.

On the 14th of March, Captain Matthews of Battery F, 1st Pennsylvania Light Artillery, who had left the battery the previous September on account of illness, was promoted to major. Lieutenant R. Bruce Ricketts, who had been leading the battery in his absence, was now formally given full command and was promoted to captain. The battery, which had never quite regained full strength after its extensive losses suffered throughout the autumn of 1862, was strengthened by the temporary attachment of men from several infantry regiments. Two days later on March 16th, Lieutenant Brockway, who had been exchanged and returned to the battery, was promoted to first lieutenant.

In late March, Pennsylvania Independent Battery D (Durell's) was transferred, along with the Ninth Corps, to the western theatre of war. Arriving in Kentucky, Durell's Battery D would spend the next several months stationed variously at Paris, Mount Sterling, and Crab Orchard, before being ordered to join General Ulysses S. Grant's army in Mississippi.

Meanwhile, Captain John I. Nevin of Pennsylvania Independent Battery H resigned on the 14$^{th}$ of February and was replaced by Captain William Borrowe, previously of the 2$^{nd}$ U.S. Artillery. Battery H continued to serve in the Washington defenses.

## 10. Chancellorsville

Having replaced General Burnside as commander of the Army of the Potomac after the defeat at Fredericksburg and the abortive Mud March, General Joseph Hooker began planning the Union army's next attempt to cross the Rappahannock and give battle to Lee's Confederates. In late April, Hooker ordered his army to leave its winter quarters and divide into two wings. Four corps were marched upstream for a crossing of the Rappahannock well above Fredericksburg, which would allow them to strike at the Confederate army's left flank and rear, and the three remaining corps stood ready to move directly against Fredericksburg from a crossing just downstream of the town. Simultaneous with this bold double envelopment, an independent column of cavalry under General George Stoneman would ride around the right flank and deep into enemy territory for a raid against the Confederate supply lines coming up from the south.

General Hooker personally led the Second, Fifth, Eleventh, and Twelfth Corps in their upstream march beyond the Confederate left flank. Meanwhile, General John Sedgwick was left in charge of the First and Third Corps, as well as his own

Sixth Corps, as they prepared to move against the Confederate works at Fredericksburg.

On the $27^{th}$ and $28^{th}$ of April, the columns above Fredericksburg crossed the Rappahannock and Rapidan rivers and converged in the vicinity of Chancellorsville, an almost abandoned crossroads in a hundred-acre clearing within an expanse of regrowth scrub forest called the Wilderness. Meeting little resistance, General Hooker halted his advance and changed his battle plans. He ordered General Sedgwick to send him additional troops from the First and Third Corps, which were ordered to march upstream and cross the Rappahannock above Fredericksburg and join Hooker at Chancellorsville.

General Sedgwick had already crossed the Rappahannock just south of Fredericksburg and had to countermarch the troops sent for by Hooker. Batteries B and F, $1^{st}$ Pennsylvania Light Artillery (Cooper's and Ricketts') and Pennsylvania Independent Battery C (Thompson's) had covered the crossing of the First Corps below Fredericksburg on the $29^{th}$, which once again had involved driving off enemy sharpshooters that fired on the engineers while they laid the pontoon bridges. The First Corps was preparing for its part in Sedgwick's advance against Maryes Heights above Fredericksburg when the order came from Hooker to join him at Chancellorsville. The First Corps re-crossed to the north bank and, accompanied by its artillery, marched upstream and crossed the Rappahannock yet again at United States Ford during the night of the $2^{nd}$ of May.

Meanwhile, disaster had struck the Union army a few miles to the west. The Confederates had withdrawn from their strong positions in the hills above Fredericksburg to face Hooker in the Wilderness. After making contact with the Union van just east of Chancellorsville, Lee sent Stonewall Jackson with his entire corps on a long march around Chancellorsville for a strike at Hooker's weakly guarded right flank along the Orange Turnpike.

General Oliver Howard's Eleventh Corps, which held the right flank, was caught completely by surprise. The charging Confederates struck the Eleventh Corps end-on and drove the Union troops before them, completely routed.

Next in line after Howard's Eleventh Corps was Henry Slocum's Twelfth Corps, to which Pennsylvania Independent Batteries E and F (Knap's and Hampton's) were attached. After having missed the Battle of Fredericksburg, the Twelfth Corps spent the winter guarding the line between Fairfax Courthouse and the landing at Acquia Creek on the Potomac. They had rejoined Hooker for his April $27^{th}$ crossing and had held the center of his line at Chancellorsville until Jackson's attack drove the remnants of the Eleventh Corps back on them.

The Twelfth Corps, although pressed back, was able to resist until nightfall ended the fighting. During the night, the Union line was reorganized to prepare for the renewal of combat the next day. The troops of the First Corps, who were still fresh, were sent to stem the rebel tide on the right. On reaching the south bank of the Rappahannock, the First Corps, along with its batteries, faced to the west and took position along Hunting Run. Hunting Run was a tributary that ran north into the Rapidan, and after the collapse of the Eleventh Corps, it became the army's new right flank. By occupying Hunting Run, the First Corps extended the Union right flank northward at a right angle to where it had previously been and anchored it on the river. The Twelfth Corps, meanwhile, continued to hold Chancellorsville, but now that the Union right had been pulled back towards the north, Chancellorsville itself had become a southward-pointing salient in the Union line.

On the morning of the $3^{rd}$, the Confederates renewed their attack and the Twelfth Corps was again heavily engaged. At one point in the fight, the Confederates captured Battery H, $1^{st}$ Ohio Light Artillery (James Huntington's) which was in an advanced position beyond the left of the corps' other artillery. The

Confederates turned the captured guns and began firing in enfilade against the other Twelfth Corps batteries.

Captain Hampton turned Battery F's guns to meet the new threat, but the terrain favored the Confederate-operated captured guns and the Twelfth Corps batteries were driven back with severe damage. Independent Battery F suffered heavy losses, including the loss of Captain Hampton, who was struck by a shell fragment that severed his left leg above the knee and mangled his horse. Hampton died several hours later.

Ultimately, the decision was made to abandon the salient encompassing Chancellorsville, and Independent Battery F withdrew with the Twelfth Corps behind the Union army's new defensive perimeter. Captain Knap's Independent Battery E, meanwhile, was temporarily transferred to the First Corps. During the fighting Lieutenant Charles A. Atwell was injured and Captain Knap had a horse shot out from under him. Battery E also suffered one man killed and several wounded.

The Union line was now shaped like a semicircle bulging towards the south. It started in the west where Hunting Run met the Rapidan River, proceeded southeast towards Chancellorsville without actually reaching it, and looped back around to the northeast behind Mineral Spring Run and anchored on the Rappahannock. The Army of the Potomac was therefore cornered with Hunting Run to its right, Mineral Spring Run to its left, and the juncture of the Rapidan and Rappahannock rivers to its rear. The Twelfth Corps, after withdrawing from the center, was moved to the left flank behind Mineral Spring Run.

In the evening, Captain Ricketts' Battery F was called forward to relieve Lieutenant Francis W. Seeley's Battery K, 4th U.S. Artillery, which had been heavily engaged all day. Battery K was assigned to the Third Corps, which was near the center of the line below the headwaters of Hunting Run. The position was critical to the integrity of the line, and Captain Ricketts received orders that he must hold the position no matter how heavily pressed. He therefore ordered all of Battery F's horses taken to the rear after the guns were pulled into position, and had ammunition stacked near the pieces to speed loading time. The Confederates were dug in only about 250 yards to the battery's front, and at 10:00 p.m., they attacked. Battery F was subjected to an incredible musketry fire but was able to repel the attack with double-shotted canister. The Confederates attempted several similar attacks during the night but were each time repelled.

Captain R. Bruce Ricketts; Battery F, 1st Pennsylvania Light Artillery. Image from the P.R.V.C. Historical Society.

The next day (the 4th), Battery F came under a heavy fire from enemy sharpshooters, who were eventually driven off by Union sharpshooters called forward for that purpose. No major attack came, however, until 10:00 p.m., when the Confederates repeated their attempt of the previous night, with similar result. The Confederate infantry advanced, brought the battery under heavy fire, and were driven back.

On the morning of the 5th, the Union center was struck again, this time in greater force than during the previous two nights, and with considerable artillery support. Battery F held its position, as it had since the evening of the 3rd, and this final major attack was also repulsed. In the evening, Battery F finally received the order to withdraw. With no other options, the Army of the Potomac retreated back across the Rappahannock. Captain Cooper's Battery B, Captain Thompson's Battery C, Captain Knap's Battery E, and Independent Battery F (the latter now without a captain), all took part in covering the retreat across United States Ford.

On the morning of the 6th the enemy reached the south bank of the ford from which the pontoon bridges had already been raised. The Confederates started placing guns on some high ground above the ford, and Thompson's Battery C and Knap's Battery E began exchanging fire with them. These batteries succeeded in destroying several enemy caissons and driving off the enemy's artillery, which was forced to leave behind several guns.

At the same time that the troops of General Hooker's reinforced right wing were fighting for their lives around Chancellorsville, the troops of the left wing under General Sedgwick made their own move against Fredericksburg, and were likewise repulsed. Battery D, 1st Pennsylvania Light Artillery (McCarthy's) had crossed the Rappahannock with the Sixth Corps at Bernard's House on the 2nd of May and had marched into Fredericksburg. On the morning of the 3rd, Battery D came under fire from the Confederate fortifications along the ridges encircling the town. Although the bulk of General Lee's army had withdrawn and marched west towards Chancellorsville, where Stonewall Jackson had already launched his devastating attack on General Hooker's right flank, a small force had been left behind at Fredericksburg to oppose Sedgwick. Battery D advanced against this force and opened with canister at a range of 300 yards. Battery D was soon repositioned and assigned the task of bombarding Maryes Heights, the scene of one of the previous December's bloodiest contests during the battle of Fredericksburg. Battery D succeeded in dismounting several pieces of enemy artillery along the heights and driving away their cannoneers. This success was soon followed up by a charge made by the battery's supporting infantry, which succeeded in capturing the enemy works. The battery advanced to the top of the heights and again went into position and exchanged fire with another enemy battery. That battery was also captured by the Union forces.

Battery D then joined in the westward pursuit of the retreating Confederates, stopping intermittently to fire upon the fleeing enemy rearguard. General Sedgwick's pursuit ended, however, in the vicinity of Salem Church, where the retreating Confederates from the Fredericksburg heights came upon reinforcements sent by Lee from Chancellorsville. There was a brief engagement, in which Battery D again went into action, but the Confederates were now so strong that Sedgwick's troops were themselves in danger of being cut off and surrounded. In fact, the Confederates even succeeded in recapturing the fortifications at Fredericksburg in Sedgwick's rear, which had been left unguarded. The tables were now turned, and Sedgwick decided that the only reasonable course of action was to withdraw back across the Rappahannock. Although their original route was now blocked, Sedgwick's troops were fortunate that their new position covered Bank's Ford, an alternative crossing near Salem Church. Sedgwick's troops conducted their retreat on the night of the 4$^{th}$ and reached the north bank without serious incident.

The battle of Chancellorsville had been a terrible setback for the Union cause. The Army of the Potomac had been soundly defeated by an enemy half its size. Part of the difficulty certainly arose from the challenges the terrain placed on the Union artillery. The claustrophobic re-growth woodland of the Wilderness limited the artillery to the immediate vicinity of roadways, and to the small clearing around Chancellorsville itself. The Union batteries were incapable of taking commanding positions, and when they did fight, they were generally forced to fight at very close range.

The battle did, however, result in one irreparable loss to the Confederates. Stonewall Jackson, who had been the author of so many Union setbacks, was accidentally killed by his own men while returning from a reconnaissance shortly after completing his devastating flank attack against the Eleventh Corps. It may have therefore been a small consolation to the men of the Army of the Potomac as they regrouped above the Rappahannock that they would never again have to face Old Stonewall.

Certainly some consolation was needed, for many brave men were lost at Chancellorsville. Among the Pennsylvania artillery, however, casualties were comparatively light. Battery B, 1st Pennsylvania Light Artillery (Cooper's) suffered five men wounded and two horsed killed. Battery D, 1st Pennsylvania Light Artillery (McCarthy's) lost one man killed and three wounded during the attack on Maryes Heights. Battery F, 1st Pennsylvania Light Artillery (Ricketts') reported no casualties. Pennsylvania Independent Battery C (Thompson's) lost one man killed and three wounded. Pennsylvania Independent Battery E (Knap's) lost one man killed and several who suffered minor injuries, including Lieutenant Atwell. On the 18th of May, two weeks after the battle, Captain Joseph M. Knap resigned his commission with Battery E to return to Pittsburgh and assume the superintendency of the Fort Pitt Foundry, which was owned by his family. Lieutenant Atwell succeeded him in command.

Captain Joseph M. Knap; Pennsylvania Independent Battery E. Image from the U.S. Army Heritage and Education Center.

Pennsylvania Independent Battery F suffered the loss of Captain Robert B. Hampton and one other man killed, four men wounded, and three caissons destroyed, as well as over thirty horses lost during the campaign.

General John Geary would write the following year that "The record of Captain Robert B. Hampton is such a brilliant one that no words of praise that we can now write would add any luster to it."* General Hooker was also an admirer of Captain Hampton, and described his late friend as "Genial, generous, strong and faithful in private life, and in his official character humorous, brave and noble. Of all who have fallen victims of the Rebellion, I know of no firmer spirit ..."†

As a final note on the campaign, the men of Pennsylvania's independent batteries returned from the battle to learn that they had been assigned letter designations in their absence. Prior to the battle, the independent batteries had usually been identified exclusively by the name of their commanding officer, or by some other nickname. On the $1^{st}$ of May, however, as the Battle of Chancellorsville raged, the Adjutant General of Pennsylvania promulgated a General Order which formally assigned letter designations of 'A' through 'H' to each of the Commonwealth's eight independent batteries.‡

● ○ ●

---

* Clark at 48.
† Ibid. at 49.
‡ As previously noted, in order to avoid confusion when identifying specific batteries within this narrative, the author has used these letter designations even when describing events that occurred prior to the letter designations being assigned.

# IV

## 1. The Invasion of Pennsylvania

General Lee decided that the best way to follow up the double Confederate victories at Fredericksburg and Chancellorsville was with another invasion of the North. But unlike the previous year's Maryland campaign, this time the objective would be a quick march into Pennsylvania. Lee realized that from the line of the Susquehanna he could threaten Harrisburg, Philadelphia, Baltimore, or even Washington. On June $3^{rd}$, 1863 the southern troops began evacuating their camps around Fredericksburg for a march around the Army of the Potomac's western flank. They moved up the Shenandoah Valley, keeping the Blue Ridge between them and their Union opponents, and crossed the Potomac River two weeks later. The Union troops pursued and reached the Potomac on the $25^{th}$. Three days later, on the $28^{th}$, General Hooker was relieved of command and was replaced by Pennsylvania native General George G. Meade. General Meade continued the rapid pursuit northward towards his home state, which had already been deeply pierced by advancing enemy columns; Stonewall Jackson's old corps, now under the command of General Richard Ewell, had reached the vicinity of Carlisle and was fast approaching the Susquehanna and the state capital.

General Meade approached the Maryland-Pennsylvania border with his army divided into two columns. General John Reynolds, also a Pennsylvanian, and the army's senior general, led a three corps van while General Meade followed with the remaining four corps.

As the Army of the Potomac's Pennsylvania batteries approached their native state, they probably had very little time to reflect on several major reorganizations that had been made over the course of the previous month. General Henry J. Hunt, the Chief of Artillery for the army, had carried out a top-to-bottom restructuring of the army's artillery service. Up until that point, the organization of the artillery branch above the battery level had been fairly haphazard, with individual batteries parceled out at the corps, division, or even brigade level more or less at the whim of inexpert infantry commanders. The main problem with that system, or rather lack thereof, was that artillery is most effective when massed together. The best way to employ artillery is to have as many guns as possible all concentrating their fire on a single target.

**General Henry J. Hunt; Chief of Artillery of the Army of the Potomac. Image from the Library of Congress.**

General Hunt's solution was to create artillery *brigades*. Each corps was assigned a single artillery brigade consisting of about half a dozen batteries. All of the batteries in each brigade took their orders from a single brigade commander who was himself an artillery officer, and he in turn reported directly to the corps commander. In addition, five entire artillery brigades were kept separate and designated as the "Artillery Reserve" of the entire army. Although batteries would continue to be detached from time to time to accompany particular infantry divisions when the situation warranted it, the artillery brigade system made it possible to quickly and efficiently bring large numbers of guns to bear on individual enemy targets. The brigade system also created new possibilities for promotion within the artillery service. Previously there had been few opportunities for skilled artillery officers to rise above the rank of captain because batteries took their orders directly from infantry commanders, but now it was possible for the best battery commanders to be assigned as brigade commanders, where their talents could be more effectively employed.

General Hunt also arranged to have numerous under-strength batteries merged together to create full-strength regulation batteries. Pennsylvania Independent Battery F, which had suffered heavy losses in men, horses, and equipment at Chancellorsville, including the loss of its captain, was consolidated with Captain Thompson's Independent Battery C. Twenty-four extra men from Battery F who were left over after the consolidation were assigned to temporary duty with Battery H, 1st Ohio Light Artillery (under Captain James Huntington). Consolidated Pennsylvania Independent Battery C & F was then assigned to one of the brigades of the Army of the Potomac's Artillery Reserve.

Captain Frank P Amsden; Battery G, 1st Pennsylvania Light Artillery. Image from the P.R.V.C. Historical Society.

Batteries F and G, 1st Pennsylvania Light Artillery (Ricketts' and Amsden's) were also consolidated. The remaining men of Battery G, now well below the proper strength for a battery, were attached as a section to Captain Ricketts' Battery F. Captain Amsden had resigned on the 25th of May, and Lieutenant Belden Spence took charge of the section of Battery F comprised of men from Battery G. Like Thompson's Battery C & F, Ricketts' Battery F & G was assigned to a brigade in the Artillery Reserve.

Battery B, 1$^{st}$ Pennsylvania Light Artillery (Cooper's) remained with the First Corps, but was now a part of Colonel Charles Wainwright's First Corps Artillery Brigade. Pennsylvania Independent Battery E (Atwell's) was meanwhile united with the other Twelfth Corps batteries as part of Lieutenant Edward Muhlenburg's Twelfth Corps Artillery Brigade.*

Despite its superiority over other systems, General Hunt's artillery brigade structure would be slow to catch on outside of the Army of the Potomac and would not be adopted in the West until the middle of the next year.

## 2. The Militia Batteries

Pennsylvania responded to the Confederate invasion by raising numerous new short-term militia organizations to meet the emergency. Captain E. Spenser Miller's Independent Militia Battery and Captain Robert J. Nevin's Independent Militia Battery were both organized at Harrisburg during the month of June, and Captain Benoni Frishmuth's Independent Militia Battery was raised on the 26$^{th}$ of June. Captain Joseph M. Knap, the former commander of Pennsylvania Independent Battery E, who had resigned in May to return to the superintendency of the Fort Pitt

---

* Lieutenant Muhlenburg was an officer of the 1$^{st}$ U.S. Artillery. At the time, none of the Twelfth Corps batteries was under the command of a captain. It is a telling example of the battered state of the army's artillery at that point in the war that a lieutenant was placed in command of an entire brigade.

Foundry, retook the field as commander of an independent militia battery raised at Pittsburgh on the 27th of June.

On the 20th of the same month, Miller's Independent Militia Battery had joined an advance of the militia westward from the state capital and had found Carlisle occupied by troops of General Richard Ewell's Confederate Corps. They withdrew back towards the Susquehanna as the Confederates followed, and on the 23rd Miller's Militia Battery shelled the Confederate vanguard when it reached the vicinity of Oyster Point (Camp Hill). The militia continued their withdrawal towards the river, but unbeknownst to them, General Ewell had received orders to march south for a concentration with the rest of the Confederate army near Gettysburg.

Captain Henry D. Landis' Militia Battery[*] was organized in Philadelphia, also on the 27th of June, and immediately proceeded to Harrisburg and crossed the Susquehanna to join the forces gathering along the west bank of the river. The Confederate advance towards Harrisburg was spearheaded by a cavalry force under Brigadier General Albert G. Jenkins. By the 28th of June, Jenkins' cavalry was in Mechanicsburg near the west bank of the Susquehanna and only a few miles south of the state capital, which was located on the opposite (east) bank. Opposing Jenkins was a federal force under Major General Darius Couch, who had resigned as a corps commander in the Army of the Potomac after the Battle of Chancellorsville and was now in command of the Pennsylvania defenses. Couch's troops occupied a position in and around Forts Couch and Washington, two hastily constructed

---

[*] Both Landis' Militia Battery and Miller's Militia Battery trace their origins to Philadelphia city militia organizations dating from April of 1861, but which were not mustered into the state service until the 1863 emergency.

earthworks atop Hummel Heights,* a medium-sized prominence overlooking the Susquehanna.

After making a feint against Oyster Point (Camp Hill) on the 29th, Jenkins remained in the vicinity of Mechanicsburg; he had not yet received word that Ewell's Corps was withdrawing southward or that the rest of the Confederate army was concentrating towards Gettysburg. On the 30th, the Union militia probed westward and made contact with Jenkins' rear guard at Sporting Hill. This rear guard, consisting of the 16th Virginia Cavalry Regiment, was occupying a barn on the north side of the Carlisle Pike and a nearby patch of woods. The Union militia was unable to drive the Confederates from these positions and the Confederates were soon reinforced by a section of Captain William L. Jackson's Charlottesville Virginia Artillery Battery.

Immediately thereafter an advance section of Landis' Philadelphia Militia Battery under Lieutenant Samuel C. Perkins arrived on the field and prepared to engage the enemy. One cannon was placed on the Carlisle Pike opposing the Confederates in the patch of woods and the other cannon was moved northward off the pike and into position to shell the barn. Lieutenant Rufus King, a regular army artillery officer who was serving with the militia as a staff advisor, saw the inexperienced gun crew of the latter cannon attempt to load a shell backwards. Lieutenant King intervened and corrected the error, and when the first shot struck the barn the Confederates within immediately abandoned their position. Shortly thereafter, the entire Confederate force withdrew and began the march southward to rejoin the main Confederate army.

---

* Hummel Heights is now known as Washington Heights.

## 3. Gettysburg – the First Day

After advancing through Pennsylvania to the very outskirts of Harrisburg, the Army of Northern Virginia turned around to meet the rapidly approaching Army of the Potomac. General Lee had underestimated the speed with which his army would be pursued and found it necessary to pick a central point at which he could concentrate his widely scattered columns. The town of Gettysburg, near the Maryland border, appeared to offer exactly what Lee was looking for. Lee ordered the two Confederate corps under Generals Longstreet and A. P. Hill to move towards Gettysburg from the west while General Ewell's corps descended from the north. Meanwhile, General Meade's army continued its rapid approach from the south.

On the 29th of June, Colonel Charles Wainwright's First Corps Artillery Brigade, to which Battery B, 1st Pennsylvania (Cooper's) was attached, camped at Emmitsburg, Maryland. On the 30th they advanced several miles up the Fairfield Road to the line of Marsh Creek, where General Meade intended to make his stand against the Confederates, but on that same day a division of Union cavalry under General John Buford occupied Gettysburg, which was still several miles further north. Buford recognized the strategic significance of the town, from which no less than ten roads radiated outward like the spokes of a wheel, and determined to hold his position against the Confederates until reinforcements could arrive. General John F. Reynolds, commander of the First Corps, sustained Buford, and General Meade sustained General Reynolds.

The artillery brigade of the First Corps was ordered on the morning of the 1st of July to march north with the infantry towards Gettysburg. The men were not informed that a battle was imminent, but the artillerists of Cooper's Battery B knew that they would very soon be fighting somewhere on the soil of their own state.

During the march, one of the sergeants of Cooper's Battery B cautioned the men of a nearby regular army battery, "Boys, don't forget that this is free soil! We are now about half a mile north of the Keystone State line!" After telling the regulars, who were mostly from the Midwest, that his own family's home was only a few miles away, the sergeant suggested that "maybe you [Midwesterners] don't know how a Pennsylvanian feels when he may have to fight to-morrow in his mother's dooryard!" To this the regulars replied that they "would stand by him until h—l froze over! And then, if necessary, perish on the ice!!"[*]

General John Reynolds; Commander of the First Corps, Army of the Potomac. Image from the National Archives.

When the First Corps was four miles below Gettysburg, General Abner Doubleday's Third Division, with Cooper's Battery B accompanying them, was detached from the main column and took a road veering off to the left.

They crossed Marsh Creek at White Bridge and proceeded up the west bank of Willoughby run. Hearing the sound of artillery to their front, they rejoined the Fairfield Road and hastened toward Seminary Ridge, a low ridge to the northwest of the town, where Cooper's Battery B went into action. The battery took a position to the south of a grove called McPherson's Wood and joined the battle around noon. General

---

[*] Augustus Buell, *The Cannoneer: Recollections of Service in the Army of the Potomac by a Detached Volunteer in the Regular Army* (Washington: The National Tribune, 1890), 62-63.

Buford's cavalry had succeeded in holding the town against the advancing Confederates of A. P. Hill's corps until the arrival of the General Reynolds' reinforcements, and by noon several brigades of the First Corps were already engaged along Seminary Ridge near McPherson's Wood. Early in the fighting General Reynolds was killed by a Confederate sharpshooter not far from where Battery B was positioned. The loss was deeply felt by the men of the battery, who held their fellow Pennsylvanian and corps commander in high esteem.

After taking position, Battery B commenced a heated exchange with Major W. J. Pegram's Battalion of Confederate artillery across the way on Herr's Ridge and kept it up until Pegram's artillery ceased firing. Soon, however, elements of General Ewell's Confederate Corps arrived from the north and struck the Union right flank to the north of Gettysburg, which was held by the recently arrived Union Eleventh Corps. Sometime in the early afternoon the Confederates reopened their fire against the First Corps artillery from batteries posted on Oak Hill, which was located to the right of the First Corps line and gave the Confederates an opportunity to fire in enfilade.

Battery B retired to a field between the crest of Seminary Ridge and the Lutheran Theological Seminary (from which the ridge took its name). The Union infantry then adjusted their lines to make an opening for the artillery, and Battery B changed front and commenced firing at the Confederates on Oak Hill. At around 2:30 p.m., General Robert Rodes' Division of General Ewell's Corps attacked the Union lines from the direction of Oak Hill and was repulsed, with many Confederates killed or captured.

Meanwhile the Confederates of Hill's Corps had massed to the west for another attempt against the Union line from that direction. Battery B withdrew to a position on the grounds of the Seminary behind a barricade of fence rails that had been constructed by other troops earlier in the day. After a short respite, Battery B came under fire from Captain T. A. Brander's Virginia Battery ("The Letcher Artillery"), which was positioned to the north on a hill overlooking a railroad cut. Battery B returned fire, and when the Confederate infantry attempted yet another attack, Battery B helped drive them back.

Having failed to break the First Corps line through frontal attack, the Confederates were extending their own lines southward, and the Union forces on Seminary Ridge began facing serious pressure on their left flank. After repulsing several more attacks, the troops along the crest of the ridge, including those of Battery B, were forced to withdraw to the southeast. They made their next stand behind another barricade of fence rails, where Battery B opened with double canister against the oncoming Confederates, but the Union left was overlapped again. The troops from Seminary Ridge retreated through Gettysburg and rallied on Cemetery Hill, a commanding elevation to the southeast. By this time Union reinforcements were rapidly coming up and the Confederates, satisfied with having secured the town, suspended their attacks for the day.

During the evening Colonel Wainwright lined up his batteries along the crest of Cemetery Hill and had his cannoneers hard at work building earthworks. Cooper's Battery B was positioned in front of the arched gatehouse of the town's cemetery with Battery I, 1st New York Light Artillery (Captain Michael Wiedrich) to the left and Battery L, 1st New York Light Artillery (Captain John A. Reynolds) to the right. During the first day of the battle, Cooper's Battery B had suffered one man killed and four men wounded, Lieutenant William C. Miller being among the latter.

## 4. Gettysburg – the Second Day

Elements of the Union Second, Third, Fifth, Sixth, and Twelfth Corps began arriving during the night and extended the flanks of the Cemetery Hill line in both directions. The Twelfth Corps, to which Pennsylvania Independent Battery E (Atwell's) was assigned, took position in reserve on Power's Hill to the east of Cemetery Hill, and within range to offer mutual support to the already-battered First Corps. A wooded elevation to the east called Culp's Hill was also occupied by Union troops. Other troops extended the Union left down the length of Cemetery Ridge, a long low eminence that stretched southward towards two large hills named Little Round Top and Big Round Top. These two hills anchored the new Union left flank, but neither hill was yet occupied in force.

Gettysburg Cemetery Gatehouse (July, 1863).
Image from the Library of Congress.

During the morning of July $2^{nd}$ the men of Battery B, $1^{st}$ Pennsylvania Light Artillery (Cooper's) improved the earthworks they had erected the previous night and exchanged occasional long-range shots with the enemy. At around 4 p.m., however, the Confederate artillery got their range and launched a major artillery barrage against Cemetery Hill.

One shell from a Confederate 24-pounder exploded directly under Battery B's 'Number Three' gun. Two men from the gun's crew were killed and another three were wounded, but replacement cannoneers took over and the cannon was back in action even before all of the wounded had been taken away. Another shell smashed the axle of the 'Number Two' gun, but that piece also remained in action, broken axle and all, until the carriage completely broke down and further firing was impossible.

At around 3:30 p.m., three guns from Independent Battery E, detached and under the command of Lieutenant Edward R. Geary, were sent from Power's Hill to the top of Culp's Hill where they took part in an artillery exchange with Confederate batteries on Benner's Hill. This helped relieve the pressure on Cemetery Hill by taking some of the Confederate artillery in enfilade. Towards evening these guns were withdrawn and rejoined the rest of the battery near Twelfth Corps headquarters on Power's Hill.

By early evening the firing on both sides had died down and Cooper's Battery B had expended most of its ammunition. Consolidated Battery F & G, $1^{st}$ Pennsylvania Light Artillery (Ricketts'), which had arrived in Gettysburg around midday but had been kept in reserve, was sent forward from the Artillery Reserve and took Battery B's place in front of the gate of the cemetery. Battery B reported to the camp of the Artillery Reserve behind Cemetery Ridge, where they could refit and refill their caissons. Colonel Wainwright informed Captain Ricketts that he was being assigned to a critical position and would not be permitted to withdraw under any circumstances.

No sooner did Ricketts' Battery F & G unlimber then it came under renewed fire from the enemy. The Confederates had massed infantry for an attack against the Union batteries in front of the cemetery, and Ricketts' Battery had arrived just in time to meet them. The charge, spearheaded by General Harry Hays' "Louisiana Tiger Brigade," swept up the hill towards the muzzles of the Union guns. Captain Ricketts met them with blasts of double canister, but the Union infantry support broke and ran and the enemy breeched the Union line just to the left of Ricketts' battery, where Battery I, $1^{st}$ New York Light Artillery (Wiedrich's) had been forced back. The Confederates immediately turned their fire towards Ricketts' left flank, fired a volley from behind a low stone wall, and charged the battery's left-most gun. They killed, wounded, or captured every man on that gun's crew and spiked the cannon.

The remaining guns of Battery F & G continued blasting away with canister at the enemy to their front even as their left-flank was being overrun. A Confederate officer attempted to seize the battery's guidon, which had been planted in the ground, but the guidon-bearer, James H. Riggin, shot the Confederate with his revolver and grabbed the guidon himself, only to be killed immediately thereafter as he clutched the colors he had died to defend. Its bearer fallen, the guidon again became the target of the enemy when a Confederate infantryman tried to take it up. This Confederate also tried to force the surrender of acting Sergeant Richard Stratford. Lieutenant Brockway struck the man with a rock, and Stratford wrested his musket from him, and shot the Confederate with his own weapon. Stratford was about to club the wounded Confederate with the captured musket when Captain Ricketts stopped him, saving the wounded Confederate's life.

The men of Battery F & G fought desperately, fighting the enemy hand to hand with rammer-staffs and other implements, Captain Ricketts shouting, "Die on your own soil boys before you give up your guns."[*] At this moment of desperation, Samuel S. Carroll's Brigade of Union infantry arrived and drove the Confederates back down the hill, restoring the Union line and saving the battery. Freed from the necessity of fighting hand to hand, the cannoneers resumed their posts and fired a blast of parting shots to speed the Confederates in their retreat.

Sketch of Cemetery Hill (July 3rd) by Alfred R. Waud (1828 – 1891).
The 5th Maine Battery in foreground; artillery, including Ricketts' Battery F & G, 1st Pennsylvania Light Artillery, in front of the Cemetery Gatehouse in background.
Image from the Library of Congress.

Meanwhile, near the opposite end of the long Union line, Consolidated Pennsylvania Independent Battery C & F (Thompson's) was also engaged in a desperate battle through the late afternoon and evening hours of the second day of the battle of Gettysburg. Thompson's Battery C & F was part of Lieutenant Colonel Freeman McGilvery's brigade of the Artillery Reserve, which arrived in Gettysburg around midday and was stationed behind the line of Cemetery Ridge and just to the north of Little Round Top.

The main Confederate attack on July 2nd was made by General James Longstreet's Corps and was intended to strike the Union left

---

[*] *Pennsylvania at Gettysburg* at vol. 2, 931.

flank on Cemetery Ridge, but unbeknownst to the Confederates the Union line had been extended west and south, encompassing a peach orchard to the east of the Emmitsburg Road, a rocky outcropping called Devil's Den, and even Little Round Top itself.

Confederate General Lafayette McLaws' Division of Longstreet's Corps therefore ended up striking the troops of General Daniel Sickles' Union Third Corps in the peach orchard. At around 4:30 p.m., Thompson's battery was rushed forward to relieve Battery G, 1$^{st}$ New York Light Artillery (Captain Nelson Ames'). Captain Ames' Battery had been severely engaged from its position in a salient angle held by the Third Corps. In front of the peach orchard the Union line turned back at a sharp angle with the troops above facing west across the Emmitsburg Road and the troops below facing almost perpendicularly to the south.

Thompson's battery took position in that angle with two sections facing south and one section facing west. Within twenty minutes of their arrival, a force of Confederate infantry attacked from the south and the two sections facing that direction engaged them. Minutes later, the advancing Confederates came within the field of fire of the westward-facing right section, and they too opened fire. No sooner did they do so then they began taking fire from several Confederate masked batteries that had been placed within a few hundred yards without being previously detected. The westward-facing right section was driven back by a fire so intense that it killed most of the horses used for pulling the guns. The other two sections were soon taking fire in enfilade and the entire battery was pushed back, along with its infantry supports. The advancing Confederate infantry captured one of the cannon of the right section, but the supporting Union infantry briefly rallied and recaptured the cannon before the entire force had to retire.

Captain Thompson described the capture of a second cannon as follows:

[A]s our infantry was again falling back, [the two western-facing guns were brought] into action again with the four guns that were in action facing to the south, and fired a few rounds, when we were driven back, having the horses in one of the gun's limbers killed, and also in one of the caisson's limbers, the enemy again capturing a gun and one caisson. I had the gun horses disengaged, and the piece was moved off some distance by hand, and as the enemy was gaining ground rapidly on us, the infantry that were assisting us left, and we were compelled to leave it ....[*]

Although one cannon was irretrievably lost, Private Casper R. Carlisle assisted Captain Thompson in saving another. The rest of the battery had fallen back, but a single cannon was trapped in the midst of a heavy crossfire. Most of the horses harnessed to that cannon's limber had been shot, so Carlisle and Thompson cut away the harnesses of the dead horses, brought up fresh horses, and pulled the cannon away to safety. Captain Thompson, whose horse had earlier been shot out from under him, was nearly left behind and had to run for several minutes to regain the relative safety of the retreating Union line and avoid being overtaken by the advancing Confederates.

The Union forces fell back through the peach orchard and eventually reformed at the foot of Little Round Top. The Confederate advance was stalled when it reached this new line, and Captain Thompson turned his attention to laying an enfilading fire on the Confederates who were now attacking the Second Corps line along Cemetery Ridge to the north. That attack was also driven back, and the approaching nightfall ended the day's fighting. Thompson's Battery had lost one man killed, nine wounded, and four missing during the day's fighting. Private

---

[*] O.R., series I vol. 27 pt. 1, 889 (No.323), 890.

Casper Carlisle would later be awarded the Medal of Honor for his roll in saving the cannon.*

Little Round Top as seen from below. Image from the Library of Congress.

# 5. Gettysburg – the Third Day

After two days of fighting, the Confederates had failed to achieve a breakthrough against either end of the Union line, and by the morning of the $3^{rd}$ of July, the third day of the battle, General Lee recognized that both Union flanks were too strong to make another attempt. By then the Union line stretched from Culp's Hill on the right, up and around Cemetery Hill, south along Cemetery Ridge, and was firmly anchored at the Round Tops on

---

* The Medal of Honor was issued to Carlisle on December 21, 1892. The citation reads, "Saved a gun of his battery under heavy musketry fire, most of the horses being killed and the drivers wounded."

the left. The best course of action, as General Lee saw it, was to attack what by now was the center of the Union line. Cemetery Ridge was a long low ridge running between Cemetery Hill to the north and Little Round Top to the south. A mile of open country stood between the opposing armies along this stretch of ground, but Lee believed that a massed artillery barrage could clear away enough of the defenders for his infantry to cross the expanse without unbearable losses and score a decisive breakthrough. General Longstreet was ordered to make the attempt and Colonel E. Porter Alexander, Longstreet's chief of artillery, spent the morning of the $3^{rd}$ positioning over one-hundred-and-fifty artillery pieces for the barrage that would precede the attack.

Meanwhile, however, fighting erupted along the Union right flank when the Twelfth Corps launched a dawn assault aimed at recapturing a line of works at the base of Culp's Hill that had been overrun by the Confederates the previous day. Consolidated Battery F & G, $1^{st}$ Pennsylvania Light Artillery (Ricketts') supported the assault from its position on Cemetery Hill by shelling the Confederates at the base of Culp's Hill and occasionally exchanging fire with various enemy batteries posted along the heights to the north and east of the town. During the morning, Captain Ricketts also advanced one piece towards a stone wall on the battery's left (facing north) and used it to shell Confederate sharpshooters out of a house in the town below.

The fighting on the Union right ended around 11:00 a.m. and silence fell over the entire field for the next two hours. Then, at 1:00 p.m., the Confederate batteries Colonel Alexander had been quietly massing all opened fire simultaneously, and were soon joined by other Confederate batteries from all over the field. The men of Captain Ricketts' battery, which occupied a part of the line that was effectively a salient, found themselves taking fire from both front and rear, and from their left flank. Captain Ricketts responded as best as he could by moving the two cannon of his center section to the stone wall on his left (where he had earlier posted the single cannon to engage the sharpshooters) and had them commence a counter-battery fire against Seminary Ridge.

The Confederate main effort, however, was aimed at Cemetery Ridge, not Cemetery Hill. General Longstreet's objective point was a small copse of trees about halfway down the length of the ridgeline. Battery B, 1$^{st}$ Pennsylvania Light Artillery (Cooper's) and Consolidated Pennsylvania Independent Battery C & F (Thompson's) were both nearby, having each been removed to Cemetery Ridge from their respective positions, near opposite ends of long Union line, where they had each fought so well the day before.

Thompson's Battery C & F had been on-line on Cemetery Ridge since dawn when it was ordered to take position at the point where the left flank of the Second Corps met the right flank of the Third Corps, just a few hundred yards below the copse of trees that, unbeknownst to them, was destined to be the Confederate objective point that day. They had spent the morning firing occasional shots towards the enemy in order to acquire their range, but had not yet otherwise been engaged. Captain Cooper's Battery B, meanwhile, had spent the morning at the camp of the Artillery Reserve, where they had gone the night before to refill their ammunition chests and repair their 'Number Two' gun, the carriage of which had been smashed by enemy fire the day before. Soon after the Confederate barrage began, General Hunt ordered Battery B forward to reinforce Colonel McGilvery's brigade of reserve artillery. Deploying under a heavy fire, they joined the other Union batteries along the ridgeline in answering the challenge of the Confederate artillery across the way.

General Hunt, who was concerned about the army's supply of artillery ammunition, quickly passed along an order for the Union batteries to cease firing and wait for the expected infantry assault. General Hancock, the commander of the Second Corps, was concerned that the morale of the infantry would be weakened if the counter-battery fire was abandoned so he countermanded General Hunt's order with respect to the batteries assigned to his section of the line. One by one, these batteries resumed their work, pleased with the opportunity to give as well as they received. Captain Thompson would later say that the men of his battery "were only too glad for the chance, for it is much easier to fight than lay idle under such a storm of shot, shell and missiles."[*]

After about two hours, the Confederate artillery ceased firing and the infantry attack got under way. Over 12,500 men in all, they emerged from the woods along Seminary Ridge opposite and advanced doggedly towards the Union center. The main attacking force was General George Pickett's Virginia Division, which marched across the low valley between Seminary and Cemetery Ridges with its right flank exposed to the south. Now was the opportunity for which General Hunt had wanted to make sure there would be enough ammunition. Battery C & F met the advancing infantry with case shot, and switched to canister when the range was close enough. The Union fire was so effective that no Confederates reached that section of the Union line except as prisoners.

Cooper's Battery B, meanwhile, struck General Pickett's advancing infantry almost end-on from their position to the south, but had to shift their line of fire when a Confederate battery (Eshelman's Battery of the Washington Artillery of New Orleans) advanced in their front and opened fire against the Union line just to the right of Battery B. Battery B's counter-battery fire forced the Confederates back, but after a short lull, a brigade of Confederate infantry (General Wilcox's Alabama Brigade) appeared in front and began advancing directly towards Battery B. As Thompson's Battery C & F and the other Union batteries to the north were doing, Cooper's Battery B met the advancing infantry

---

[*] *Pennsylvania at Gettysburg* at vol. 2, 921.

with case shot, which was switched to double canister when the range got close. The fire was extremely destructive, and the Confederates were driven back. The artillery repulsed the Confederates in front of Battery B so effectively that the assistance of the supporting infantry was not even required.

To the north, the Confederate infantry reached the Union line in front of the copse of trees, but their breakthrough was short-lived. Smashed by overwhelming fire and flanked on both sides, the remnants of Pickett's Division ether surrendered or fled back across the valley to Seminary Ridge. The repulse was total, and the Union victory was complete.

Pickett's Charge from *The Battle of Gettysburg* by Paul Dominic Philippoteaux (1846-1923). Image from the National Park Service.

The failure of Pickett's Charge was a disaster for General Lee's army, and there was no longer any question of the Confederates continuing operations in Pennsylvania. Escape to the south became Lee's sole concern, provided Meade would let him get away without forcing another battle. Believing that Lee himself had demonstrated the futility of attacking across such open ground, Meade attempted no counterattack and contented himself with preparing for the inevitable pursuit southward (and savoring the well-earned Union victory). The victory had not, however, come without a severe price. The Army of the Potomac has suffered over 23,000 casualties. During the three days of fighting, the losses among the Pennsylvania batteries were 3 killed and 9 wounded from Battery B, $1^{st}$ Pennsylvania Light Artillery (Cooper's); 3 wounded from Pennsylvania Independent Battery E (Knap's); 2 killed, 23 wounded, and 3 missing from Consolidated Pennsylvania Independent Battery C & F (Thompson's); and 6 killed, 14 wounded, and 3 missing from Consolidated Battery F & G, $1^{st}$ Pennsylvania Light Artillery (Ricketts').

An appendix must be made of the part played by Captain William D. Rank's Company H, $3^{rd}$ Pennsylvania Heavy Artillery during the battle of Gettysburg. The road that led Captain Rank's heavy artillery company to Gettysburg, where they served as a field battery, began nearly two years earlier in Philadelphia. The $3^{rd}$ Pennsylvania Heavy Artillery Regiment started out in 1861 as a two-company battalion of so-called "marine artillery" under Colonel Hermann Segebarth. In late 1862 the organization was re-designated as heavy artillery and Colonel Segebarth was ordered to recruit new men until the unit reached regimental strength. Four new companies were soon recruited, including Company H.

The men of Company H were organized in September of 1862 across the Delaware River at Camp Camden, New Jersey. Most of the men came from Lebanon County, but the company also included men from Allegheny, Armstrong, Crawford, Dauphin, and Luzerne Counties, as well as from Philadelphia. A misunderstanding about the bounty to which the men of Company H were entitled led to a near mutiny, and the entire company was separated from the rest of the battalion and sent in arrest to Fort Delaware. After reaching Fort Delaware, they explained the situation to the military authorities. It was found that they had a valid grievance, and Colonel Segebarth was dismissed from the service for his role in the affair. Segebarth's command was subsequently merged with a heavy artillery battalion commanded by Major Joseph Roberts, previously of the 4th U.S. Artillery Regiment, and Roberts was promoted to Colonel and given command of the whole. The unit was re-designated as the 3rd Pennsylvania Heavy Artillery (also known as the 152nd Pennsylvania Regiment). Company H, however, was immediately detached and sent to Baltimore, never to be reunited with the rest of the regiment.

They remained at Baltimore until May of 1863, when they were issued with a battery of 3-in. Ordnance rifles and otherwise outfitted as field artillery, and sent with the 1st Delaware Cavalry to secure the bridge were the Baltimore and Ohio Railroad crossed the Monocacy River. The Confederate advance through Maryland forced them to abandon their position, and Battery H was nearly enveloped and captured by enemy columns as they fell back. They were present but not engaged during several small skirmishes at Hanover Junction and Westminster on the 30th of June, and reached the vicinity of Gettysburg with two guns on the 2nd of July. They were placed in battery three miles outside of Gettysburg on the Hanover Road and called on to fire a few shots at a small Confederate force to their front, which immediately withdrew. At sundown they were ordered towards the town and parked with the Artillery Reserve behind Cemetery Ridge. On the 3rd, Battery H was ordered to relieve a Second Corps battery and was caught in column along the crest of the ridge when the Confederate artillery barrage commenced. Battery H was not able to engage the enemy, but from their position they witnessed the entire action, including the infantry charge and its repulse. Their entire loss for the battle was a single man who was captured during the night when he accidentally strayed into enemy lines.

## 6. The Pursuit Southward

Following their disastrous repulse on the $3^{rd}$ of July, the Confederates were in no condition for further offensive operations, and were only concerned with withdrawing back to the relative safety of northern Virginia. After taking a day to secure as many of the wounded as could safely be carried southward in wagons, General Lee had his army begin the long march back to Virginia on July $5^{th}$. The Army of the Potomac pursued them through heavy rain as far as Williamsport, Maryland where General Lee's retreating army was cornered with its back to a swollen river. General Meade's troops circled their foes and prepared for an assault that they hoped would finally crush the Army of Northern Virginia, and with it the rebellion, but the Confederates were able to improvise a bridge and escape to the south bank unmolested and continue their march.

**Pursuit of Lee's Army. Near Emmitsburg, Maryland on July $7^{th}$.**
**Painting by Edwin Forbes (1839 – 1895); from the Library of Congress.**

An early result of Lee's attempted invasion had been a renewed apprehension for the safety of the national capital. To meet this threat, some of the units along the lower Rappahannock, including Battery H, 1st Pennsylvania Light Artillery (Fagan's), had been ordered to Washington to join in the defense of that city. When Lee crossed into Pennsylvania and it became clear that his target was not Washington, Battery H was ordered to join Meade's army in Pennsylvania with all possible speed. Battery H left Washington on the 1st of July, not knowing that a major battle was already in progress. Battery H did not arrive at Gettysburg in time to participate in the battle, but it did skirmish with a small detachment of the enemy in route. As Lee's army retreated, Battery H was ordered to return to Washington where it was assigned as a reserve battery at Camp Barry.

Pennsylvania also raised a few last emergency militia batteries during and after the battle of Gettysburg. Captain George R. Guss' "Chester County Artillery" battery was organized on the 1st of July; Captain W. C. Ermentrout's Independent Militia Battery was raised on the 3rd of July; and three days after the battle, on the 6th of July, a battery commanded by Captain Edward Fitzki and known as the Keystone Independent Militia Battery (or sometimes the "Second Keystone Battery" to differentiate it from Captain Hastings' command) was raised in Philadelphia. Captain W. H. Woodward's militia battery was raised on the 9th of July, and Captain Horatio K. Tyler's militia battery was raised on the 16th of July. Guss' Battery and the Second Keystone Battery mustered out on the 24th of August, and Ermentrout's Battery mustered out on the 26th. Woodward's and Tyler's militia batteries would muster out on the 4th of November and the 28th of January, respectively.

Four of the earlier emergency militia batteries had already been discharged -- Knap's Independent Militia Battery on the 15th of July, Miller's Independent Militia Battery on the 25th of July, Landis' Independent Militia Battery on the 27th of July, and Frishmuth's Independent Militia Battery on the 1st of August -- and the last, Nevin's Independent Militia Battery, was ordered from Harrisburg to Philadelphia where it remained until November, when it was transferred to Harper's Ferry. Nevin's Independent Militia Battery remained in service at Harper's Ferry until recalled to Harrisburg in January, 1864 at which time enough of the men were willing to sign three-year enlistments to convert the organization from militia into a full volunteer field battery.

Meanwhile, the original Keystone Battery under Captain Hastings saw action for the first and only time while taking part in the pursuit of the Army of Northern Virginia after the battle of Gettysburg. Shortly before the battle, the Keystone Battery had been ordered to leave its longstanding post in the Washington defenses and join the Army of the Potomac en route to Pennsylvania. The battery did not reach the army until after the battle, but accompanied the Third Corps, under General William H. French,[*] during the subsequent pursuit.

**Men of the Keystone Battery. Image from the National Archives.**

After the Confederates escaped across the Potomac at Williamsport, they began retiring up the Shenandoah Valley.

---

[*] General French, who along with William F. Barry and Henry J. Hunt had authored *Instruction for Field Artillery* (1861), was assigned to lead the Third Corps after its previous commander, General Daniel Sickles, lost a leg at Gettysburg.

General Meade attempted to intercept and cut off the Confederate column by sending the Third Corps through the Manassas Gap. The Keystone Battery went into position and shelled the enemy during the resulting action at Wapping Heights on the 23$^{rd}$ of July, but the attempt to interfere with the Confederate withdrawal was a failure. The Army of Northern Virginia was able to continue its escape southward and return to the relative safety of the line of the Rappahannock. The Keystone battery mustered out shortly thereafter at the expiration of its term of service on the 20$^{th}$ of August.

## 7. Chickamauga

With Lee's invasion of Pennsylvania successfully repulsed and the old stalemate resumed in Virginia, the attention of both sides shifted temporarily to the West. After the Confederate retreat from Murfreesboro, General Rosecrans had taken his time before launching a campaign against the Confederate Army of Tennessee. Once he started, however, he successfully drove the Confederates all the way beyond Chattanooga, mainly through skillful maneuvering, before finally meeting serious resistance just to the east of Chattanooga in the valley of Chickamauga creek.

On the 15$^{th}$ of September, Pennsylvania Independent Battery B, under Alanson J. Stevens (who had been promoted to captain after leading Battery B during the Battle of Murfreesboro), went into camp two miles beyond Crawfish Spring in the Chickamauga valley and remained there for the next three days. Battery B was still assigned to General Horatio Van Cleve's Division of the Twenty-first Corps. On the morning of the 18$^{th}$, the battery received orders to prepare for rapid movement but had no sooner hitched its horse teams then a Confederate attack was launched against Battery B's position. The battery unlimbered and went into action under enemy artillery fire, and the men watched as the Union infantry to their front were at first pushed back, but then regained their original line.

Reinforcements soon arrived and Battery B was relieved and ordered back to Gordon's Mills, where they remained until the following morning. At dawn on the 19th they were shifted towards the right and came under fire from a Confederate battery in the woods opposite them. Battery B returned fire and the Confederate battery was quickly silenced. At noon, Battery B was ordered towards the front and placed behind a line of slowly advancing infantry. Captain Stevens held his fire because he believed that there was another line of Union infantry somewhere to the front of the first line, and he did not want to risk hitting them. Captain Stevens decided to advance his four 6-pounder smoothbore cannon (his other two guns were James rifles) up into line with the infantry. After having done so, he discovered that they were the front line after all, and that there was no danger of hitting friends further forward.

The Confederate infantry soon attacked and Battery B met them with canister, but the Union infantry on the battery's right panicked and fell back through the battery's position. Captain Stevens tried to withdraw and take a new position further back, but one limber was destroyed by enemy fire and so many horses were killed that three cannon could not be pulled off, and a fourth was lost when its limber pole was smashed by a Confederate artillery round, making it impossible to pull. Captain Stevens himself was killed during the action and Lieutenant Samuel M. McDowell had to assume command of the battery.

Battery B, which was no longer in fighting condition, was ordered to return to Chattanooga where its losses were partially balanced by the acquisition of two smoothbore cannon captured from the Confederates on another part of the field. On the next morning, September 20th, the battery returned to the front and was met by yet another Confederate infantry assault. Lieutenant McDowell fired canister until he ran out, then limbered up and attempted to retire from the field. But Battery B once again suffered the loss of so many of its horses that maneuvering became impossible and two of the four cannon that the battery had taken onto the field that day had to be abandoned. There was very little open ground, and of the two cannon that did escape, one only made it through the thick underbrush with the assistance of a detachment of infantry who pulled the gun along with a prolong rope. Battery B returned to Chattanooga having lost two men killed (including its captain), fourteen wounded, one missing, as well as four of their original six guns on the 19th, two more guns on the 20th, a limber, several wagons, and a total of thirty-seven horses.

**The Battle of Chickamauga from a Contemporary Lithograph.
Image from the Library of Congress.**

The Confederate attacks had succeeded in breaking the Union line, and the Army of the Cumberland retreated through the mountain passes to their base at Chattanooga. The Confederates pursued and occupied the heights surrounding the town, apparently content to settle down for a siege in which they hoped to starve out the Union soldiers below.

●○●

# V

## 1. The Autumn of 1863

By the autumn of 1863, over a dozen batteries of Pennsylvania field artillery were serving at various posts from the Delaware to the Mississippi River:

Battery A, 1$^{st}$ Pennsylvania Light Artillery (Simpson's) had been detached from the Army of the Potomac after the battle of Fredericksburg and sent to Fortress Monroe at the tip of the Virginia Peninsula, and from that place was forwarded to Norfolk where it joined the various forces operating in southeastern Virginia below the James River.

Battery B, 1$^{st}$ Pennsylvania Light Artillery (Cooper's), following its rigorous service in the Gettysburg campaign, continued south with the First Corps across the Potomac and back to the line of the Rappahannock. In October the Army of Northern Virginia again advanced around the flank of the Union army in what appeared to be another attempt to invade the North, but General Lee's actual purpose was merely to throw his opponents off balance and delay a return of the Army of the Potomac to the offensive. On the 11$^{th}$ and 12$^{th}$ of October, Battery B covered the crossing of the Union army at Kelly's Ford on the Rappahannock, but was not otherwise active in the campaign. After a month of maneuvering and limited engagements between the two armies, the Confederates returned to the south side of the Rappahannock with General Meade's army in close pursuit.

Battery D, 1$^{st}$ Pennsylvania Light Artillery (McCarthy's), into which Battery C had been permanently consolidated after the battle of Fredericksburg, had returned to Camp Barry in the Washington defenses after the battle of Chancellorsville. Captain McCarthy fell seriously ill in June, forcing his retirement from the service, and command of the battery was transferred to Lieutenant William Munk. In August, Battery D was reassigned to duty at Harper's Ferry in West Virginia, where it would remain until the following year.

Battery E, 1$^{st}$ Pennsylvania Light Artillery (Orwig's) had continued to serve on the Virginia Peninsula with the Fourth Corps following its advance on Urbana the previous winter. In July, the battery was assigned to the garrison at Yorktown and would remain posted in that vicinity for most of the next year.

Consolidated Battery F & G, 1$^{st}$ Pennsylvania Light Artillery (Ricketts') was transferred from the Army of the Potomac's Artillery Reserve to the artillery brigade of the Second Corps nine days after the Battle of Gettysburg (on July 12$^{th}$). The battery was heavily engaged during the Battle of Bristoe Station on the 14$^{th}$ of October, when the Second Corps laid a trap for General A. P. Hill's Corps by hiding behind an embankment of the Orange & Alexandria Railroad as the Confederates advanced past them to attack what they thought was the Union rear-guard. Ricketts' Battery F & G was ordered up in support after the trap was sprung, but had to cross a wide open field under heavy enemy fire before taking position. They opened with case and canister, and did severe damage to the enemy. After the battle, which saw the Confederates severely mauled and repulsed, Battery F & G (which suffered nine casualties during the brief action) was given the honor of presenting five captured cannon to General Meade.

Battery H, 1st Pennsylvania Light Artillery (Fagan's), following their skirmish in route to Gettysburg, returned to Washington where they would remain as a reserve battery at Camp Barry until the following May.

The regimental staff of the 1st Pennsylvania Light Artillery also underwent a slight change during this period. Lieutenant Colonel Edward H. Flood left the service on the 22nd of September and Major James Brady was promoted to lieutenant colonel on the 13th of November to succeed Flood. Because the regiment's individual batteries served independently of each other, the staff officers were all detailed out on other assignments. Colonel West, the commander of the regiment, was serving on the Peninsula as the commander of the Yorktown garrison. Brady, meanwhile, had been serving as the Chief of Artillery in the Department of the Susquehanna, where he had helped organize the defense of Harrisburg during the Gettysburg campaign. Following his promotion, Lieutenant Colonel Brady was given command of the First Brigade of the Artillery Reserve of the Army of the Potomac.

Pennsylvania Independent Battery A was still serving as part of the garrison at Fort Delaware. Captain Schaffer had resigned on the 28th of February of the previous year, and Lieutenant Stanley Miotkowski had been promoted to captain. Despite the loss of many of its original men who chose not to re-enlist at the expiration of their terms (which had ended during the summer) the company was nonetheless successfully enlarged by the addition of recruits until it reached a strength of one hundred and fifty men.

Pennsylvania Independent Battery B (McDowell's) was meanwhile besieged with the Army of the Cumberland at Chattanooga, where the Union forces were suffering severely from want of supplies, particularly food. General Rosecrans was relieved of command after the battle of Chickamauga and General George H. Thomas, who had stood firm during the battle and covered the retreat, was named as the Army of the Cumberland's new commander. Meanwhile, General Grant was en route to Chattanooga, along with substantial reinforcements from both the East and the West, and was laying plans to break through the Confederate ring surrounding the town, establish a supply line, and end the siege.

Consolidated Pennsylvania Independent Battery C & F (Thompson's) was engaged at Mitchell's Ford in Virginia on the 14$^{th}$ of October, the same day that Ricketts' Battery F & G fought at Bristoe Station. The headquarters of General Gouverneur K. Warren had come under enemy artillery fire and Captain Thompson was ordered to respond. After taking position, the men of Battery C & F realized that they were opposing Hardaway's Alabama Battery (Captain William B. Hurt), which was armed with two British-built breech-loading Whitworth rifles. These weapons had a fearful reputation; they were loaded through a mechanism in the breech for greater speed and had a longer range than the 3-in. Ordnance rifles of Thompson's Battery. Whitworth rifles also used an unusual twisted hexagonal shell design that produced an unnerving shriek as they blasted through the air towards their targets. Battery C & F, with the support of two other nearby batteries, was nonetheless able to drive off the Confederate Whitworths after about twenty minutes, despite their advantages.

Pennsylvania Independent Battery D (Durell's) had been sent west with the Ninth Corps in March, before the battle of Chancellorsville, and was stationed at various points in Kentucky before being sent to join General Ulysses S. Grant's besieging force around Vicksburg, Mississippi in early June. The battery was posted in the line of contravallation twelve miles in rear of Vicksburg to guard against attacks from the direction of Jackson, Mississippi, where Confederate General Joseph E. Johnston was massing a force in the hope of extricating the surrounded Vicksburg garrison. After the Vicksburg garrison surrendered on the 4th of July, Battery D took part in an advance against Jackson led by General William T. Sherman. Arriving before Jackson on the 10th, the battery spent the next several days shelling the Confederates at long range until General Johnston's forces retreated from the town, after which the Union force, including Battery D, returned to their camps above Vicksburg. The Vicksburg campaign took a serious toll on the health and fighting strength of the battery, which lost ten men killed and forty others either wounded or too ill to serve in the field. Of those who remained with the battery, only about two dozen were truly in good health, and most of the battery's horses were either dead or unfit for service. In August, the battery returned to Kentucky, where it was placed in camp at Covington to recuperate and regain the fighting strength it had lost down in Mississippi.

Pennsylvania Independent Battery E (Atwell's) was transferred in late September, along with the Twelfth Corps, to the Tennessee theatre of war to assist in the relief of Chattanooga. After traveling by rail from Washington to Murfreesboro, Battery E moved south to Bridgeport, Alabama and prepared for a march northward toward the besieged Army of the Cumberland. Charles Atwell, who had succeeded to command of the battery after the resignation of Joseph Knap in May, had been promoted to captain in July.

Pennsylvania Independent Battery G (Young's), like its sister organization, Independent Battery A, would spend its entire term of service uneventfully at Fort Delaware. In the summer of 1863, however, one of the officers of Battery G took a leading role in a unique experiment. On the 27th of July, Lieutenant George W. Ahl of Battery G was promoted to captain and given command of a newly raised company of Delaware heavy artillery. "Ahl's Heavy Artillery Company" (as it was called) was one of the most unusual units in the Union army. Delaware's only heavy artillery company, the men were actually recruited from among the

Confederate prisoners being held at the fort. Under the authority of the U.S. government, prisoners who had been conscripted into the Confederate army (as opposed to volunteers) could be released from captivity if they enlisted in the Union army. Ahl's company was the only unit raised expressly from Confederate prisoners during the entire war. Ahl's company would, like its "parent" organization, Battery G, spend its entire term of service at Fort Delaware.

Pennsylvania Independent Battery H (Borrowe's) had been transferred in March from the Washington defenses to join the garrison of Alexandria, Virginia under General John P. Slough. The battery was assigned to provost duty and would spend most of its remaining term of service guarding Union installations against Confederate raiders and guerillas.

Battery H, 3$^{rd}$ Pennsylvania Heavy Artillery (Rank's), after its brief field service during the Gettysburg campaign, returned to the vicinity of Baltimore and resumed its prior role as guardian of the Monumental City, where it would remain until mustered out of service on the 25$^{th}$ of July, 1865.

## 2. The Relief of Chattanooga

The situation in eastern Tennessee was critical. The Army of the Cumberland was trapped in Chattanooga with the guns of General Bragg's victorious army frowning down on them from the surrounding heights. To meet the emergency, General Grant personally took charge of the multi-pronged relief expedition. His available force included much of his old command, the Army of the Tennessee (now under General William T. Sherman), and the two corps that had been sent from the Army of the Potomac.

These would of course be supplemented by whatever help the Army of the Cumberland could provide from inside the town. One of Grant's first acts had been to replace the commander of the latter. General Rosecrans was relieved and replaced by General George Thomas, who was already being called "the Rock of Chickamauga" for his stubborn resistance during that battle.

Grant's first challenge was to get supplies past the Confederates and into the town. On the 28$^{th}$ of October, General John W. Geary's division of the Twelfth Corps, to which Pennsylvania Independent Battery E (Atwell's) was still attached, began marching from Bridgeport, Alabama towards Chattanooga. They were part of a three-division force under General Joseph Hooker that Grant had sent to help open a line of supply along the base of Lookout Mountain towards the Tennessee River and Chattanooga to the north. General Geary's division was immediately detached and ordered to guard the Nashville and Chattanooga Railroad from Confederate interference while the rest of General Hooker's force moved north through Lookout Valley towards Brown's Ferry.

General Geary's column reached Wauhatchie Station at the foot of Lookout Mountain late on the 29$^{th}$, and Battery E went into camp. Just after midnight, a large Confederate force attacked, and Battery E brought their guns online and joined the fight. The fighting was severe, and Battery E suffered heavy casualties, including Captain Atwell, who was mortally wounded.

Also killed during the battle was Lieutenant Edward R. Geary, the son of General John W. Geary. Lieutenant Geary was only eighteen years old, but had already been promoted to the rank of first lieutenant on July 16$^{th}$ (just two weeks after the battle of Gettysburg) and had been slated to take command of Pennsylvania Independent Battery F, which was scheduled to be separated from Independent Battery C and reconstituted. Geary's father was carrying his son's captain's commission in his pocket during the battle, but Lieutenant Geary was killed before the commission could be delivered. Lieutenant Geary was struck and killed immediately after sighting one of his guns on the enemy and giving the command, "Fire!" Major John A. Reynolds, the Chief of Artillery for the Twelfth Corps, described Lieutenant Geary as "a brave and efficient officer, and a noble-hearted and courteous gentleman[,]" and said that "[t]hough young in years he possessed rare and natural qualifications as an officer[.]"* Having just missed attaining a captaincy in life, he would be posthumously promoted to lieutenant colonel in 1865.

Despite his grief over the death of his son, General Geary was able to lead his division through a successful repulse of the Confederate attack. In part, this was achieved through the accidental release of several dozen mules, which in their panic rushed towards the Confederates and were mistaken in the dark for Union cavalry. Meanwhile, the rest of General Hooker's force and several other cooperating Union columns were able to break through the ring of Confederates around Chattanooga and open up the "Cracker Line," through which supplies could be forwarded to the hungry Cumberlanders within.

Battery E received much praise for their service at Wauhatchie Station; Colonel George A. Cobham, Jr. of the 111th Pennsylvania Regiment, who commanded General Geary's second brigade that night, wrote in his official report that he "cannot omit paying tribute to the gallant conduct of the officers and men of Atwell's battery; the deplorable loss sustained by them and their crippled condition sufficiently attest the gallantry with which their guns were worked, and the heavy fire to which they were exposed."†

---

* O.R., series I vol. 31 pt. 1, 134 (No.35), 135-36.
† O.R., series I vol. 31 pt. 1, 121 (No.25), 122.

**Captain Charles Atwell;
Pennsylvania Independent Battery E.
Image from the U.S. Army Heritage
and Education Center.**

**Lieutenant Edward R. Geary.**

**General John W. Geary.**

Image of Lieutenant Edward R. Geary from *History of Hampton Battery F Independent Light Artillery* by William Clark; Image of General John W. Geary from the Library of Congress.

## 3. Lookout Mountain and Missionary Ridge

With communications reestablished with Chattanooga and the troops within, General Grant was ready to swing back over to the offensive and drive the Confederates from their lines along the surrounding ridges. Grant's plan was for General Hooker's troops to strike at the Confederate left on Lookout Mountain while General Sherman's troops launched the main assault against the Confederate right at the north end of Missionary Ridge. General Thomas' Cumberlanders, meanwhile, would demonstrate against the Confederate center, and keep Bragg from shifting reinforcements to his flanks.

Lieutenant James D. McGill assumed command of Pennsylvania Independent Battery E after the deaths of Captain Atwell and Lieutenant Geary, and the battery was soon called upon to take part in General Hooker's attack on Lookout Mountain. On the 24$^{th}$ of November, the troops began moving forward, Battery E still accompanying the grieving General Geary's division. The terrain was difficult, and the battery was split up into sections during the assault, each section advancing with a different part of the division. In the midst of a thick fog, Hooker's troops successfully forced their way up the mountain, driving the Confederates from their positions in what would thereafter be remembered as the "Battle above the Clouds." McGill's battery suffered no losses during the attack.

Meanwhile, at the opposite end of the Confederate line, General Sherman's attack was far less successful. The troops from the Army of the Tennessee found, to their dismay, that their designated objective point was not actually part of Missionary Ridge, but was actually a completely detached hill that was separated from the ridge by a steep valley. After occupying this hill with little resistance, they found themselves facing the actual enemy flank, which was well guarded by the troops of General Patrick Cleburne's Division, who held a very strong position.

Pennsylvania Independent Battery B, which had been under the command of Lieutenant Samuel M. McDowell since the death of Captain Stevens during the battle of Chickamauga, was in position near the left of the Army of the Cumberland, and took part in shelling the enemy's lines in front of General Oliver Howard's troops at long range.

On the 25th, Sherman ordered his men forward, but the enemy position was too strong and too well defended, and the Army of the Tennessee was unable to make a lodgment. Believing that Bragg was drawing off troops from the rest of his line to meet Sherman's threat from the north, General Grant ordered General Thomas to move the Army of the Cumberland forward to the base of Missionary Ridge and capture the first line of enemy rifle pits. Grant still hoped that a demonstration against the Confederate center would stop Bragg from reinforcing his flanks. Grant did not, however, order a full-scale attack because Missionary Ridge was an extremely strong natural defensive position and it seemed almost impossible that such an attack would be successful.

The Confederate defenses were three lines deep, with the first line consisting of rifle pits near the base of the ridge. The other two lines were more heavily defended and were halfway up and along the crest of the ridge, respectively. The Cumberlanders quickly captured the rifle pits as ordered, but found themselves subject to a galling plunging fire from the lines above. Without orders, the men instinctively pressed forward, trying to get under the fire coming down on them from above. First in small groups, then in larger groups, the army pushed its way up the incline. It soon reached and overwhelmed the second line, and kept moving towards the third. Without any sanction from the commanding generals, the Army of the Cumberland was launching an all-out assault against the Confederate center.

The Confederate works on top of the ridge were very poorly surveyed. The bulk of the Confederate artillery was along the actual crest of the ridge, from which position the pieces could not be depressed enough to fire on the approaching Union infantry. The Cumberlanders were literally able to advance *under* the fire of the enemy's guns.

*Battle of Missionary Ridge*; sketch by Alfred R. Waud (1828-1891).
Image from the Library of Congress.

The Union troops pierced the third defensive line just as they had pierced the two below, and the Confederates were thrown into full retreat. General Bragg's army was effectively cut in two and he had no choice but to withdraw whatever forces he could still save and flee southward.

Following the collapse of the Confederate center, General Hooker was able to follow up his success of the day before by pushing from Lookout Mountain towards the south end of Missionary Ridge, where he struck the remnants of the Confederate left. During the movement, Battery E went into position and engaged the Confederates as they withdrew from the ridge.

On the 26th, the pursuit of the beaten enemy continued and Battery E advanced with the van beyond Rossville. On the following day, they reached Ringgold towards the end of a brutal fight with the Confederate rear-guard. This rear-guard, led by General Cleburne (who had thwarted Sherman the day before), not only refused to budge, but was even threatening to outflank and counterattack the pursuing Union troops. Battery E went into position and began firing shells over the heads of the Union infantry fighting to their front. Their fire was not only effective; it also had an electric effect on the men around them. Colonel James C. Lane of the 102nd New York Infantry reported "when Knap's battery [Battery E*] opened on the rebels, sending shells over our heads into the rebels, it was difficult to keep the men from rising and cheering."†

The Battle of Ringgold Gap halted the Union pursuit, and allowed Bragg to escape with the remnants of his army. Shortly thereafter, the onset of winter ended the campaign season and General Sherman began making plans for his spring offensive, an offensive that would be aimed at Atlanta.

## 4. The Mine Run Campaign

Eager to follow up his recent successes against the Army of Northern Virginia, most notably at Bristoe Station, where Consolidated Battery F & G, 1st Pennsylvania Light Artillery

---

\* Artillery batteries were often called by the name of their original commander even after subsequent changes in command.
† O.R., series I vol. 31 pt. 2, 443 (No.125), 445.

(Ricketts') had assisted in doing so much damage to A. P. Hill's Corps, General Meade decided he was willing to risk another confrontation in the Wilderness region to the south of the Rapidan River (where Hooker had previously come to grief). Meade concentrated his entire army for a rapid crossing at Ely's, Germanna, and Jacob's Fords, all downstream of where General Lee's army was waiting. The crossing began on the on the 26$^{th}$ of November, but was delayed when General French's Third Corps, which crossed at Jacob's ford, found the river bank too steep for artillery. French reacted by sending his artillery downstream to Germanna Ford, which quickly became congested with the extra traffic.

Upon reaching the south bank, Meade marched his army west towards Lee's right flank, but the delays in crossing had given Lee time to change his army's front to the east, where he took up a strong position behind Mine Run, a minor tributary that ran northward into the Rapidan.

On the 27$^{th}$, Pennsylvania Independent Battery C & F (Thompson's) reached the Mine Run line with the Second Corps and was briefly engaged at Robertson's Crossroads. Battery B, 1$^{st}$ Pennsylvania Light Artillery (Cooper's) crossed the Rapidan that same day with the First Corps, and early the next morning took position to the left of a road that traversed Mine Run. From there they compelled the withdrawal of a Confederate battery to their front. Battery B remained in position until 8:00 a.m. on the 30$^{th}$, when it joined in a general bombardment of the Confederate lines. This bombardment was intended as a diversion in support of General Warren's Second Corps, which was ordered to strike the Confederate right flank. The planned attack was cancelled, however, when General Meade concluded that the enemy's lines were too strong to be breeched. Concerned over the precarious position of his army, Meade decided to withdraw, and over the course of the next two days the Union army returned to the north bank of the river.

The engagement was inconclusive, and marked the end of active campaigning in the Virginia theatre for 1863. After re-crossing the Rapidan, the Army of the Potomac went into winter quarters and began the long wait until spring weather would allow a renewal of hostilities.

The new year was ushered in by the formal addition of the last of Pennsylvania's "independent" batteries. Nevin's Independent Militia Battery, which had enlisted for six months during the Confederate invasion of Pennsylvania the previous June, had been transferred first to Philadelphia and then to Harper's Ferry before being recalled to Harrisburg at the end of the year to be discharged. Since many of the men were willing to reenlist for a term of three years, the battery was reorganized as Pennsylvania Independent Battery I. The battery was mustered into service on January $7^{th}$, 1864 with Captain Robert J. Nevin retaining command. It then moved to Philadelphia and was strengthened by the addition of recruits before being sent to Washington, where it was equipped with six 3-in. Ordnance rifles and assigned to duty in the Washington defenses.

Although the army was in winter quarters, the early months of 1864 were not entirely devoid of action for Consolidated Pennsylvania Independent Battery C & F (Thompson's), which had re-enlisted during December and January. On the $6^{th}$ of February, the battery was called forward to take part in a demonstration at Morton's Ford on the Rapidan River. The objective was to draw attention away from simultaneous operations on the Virginia Peninsula. The battery remained on the north bank while a column of infantry attempted to force a crossing and establish a bridgehead on the other side. The action lasted until the following day when the feigned assault was suspended and the troops returned to their winter quarters.

## 5. The Spring of 1864

In the spring of 1864, soldiers on both sides waited for the return of good weather and firm roads that would signal the start of campaigning season. But as they waited, significant changes were afoot in the organization of the Union army. The biggest change was the appointment of a new General-in-Chief. Ulysses S. Grant was promoted to Lieutenant General on the 12th of March and given command of all the Union armies. He went straight to work reorganizing the forces under his command for the heavy service he had in mind for them. At all levels from companies to corps, units were transferred, consolidated, reconstituted, and dissolved, all in order to make the army a more efficient fighting force.

In March, the First Corps was broken up and Battery B, 1st Pennsylvania Light Artillery (Cooper's), which had re-enlisted and received about forty new recruits and two new cannon (bringing their total back up to six) was reassigned to the Fifth Corps. That same month, Consolidated Pennsylvania Independent Battery C & F (Thompson's) was transferred from the Second Corps to the capital defenses. On the 25th, Battery F was detached from Battery C and reconstituted as a separate field battery with Nathaniel Irish as its captain. Battery F remained in the Washington defenses along with Battery C until July.

On April 3rd, Battery G, 1st Pennsylvania Light Artillery was detached from Ricketts' Battery F and also reconstituted. Lieutenant William Jennings took the men of Battery G to Camp

Barry where they were issued six new Napoleons and otherwise fully equipped for service as an independent six-gun battery. Belden Spence, who had commanded the men of Battery G during their tenure as a section of Battery F, had been promoted to captain in January but appears to have been separated from the battery during this period because Lieutenant Jennings remained in command. From Camp Barry, the battery crossed back into Virginia and joined the capital defense forces on the south side of the Potomac.

The men of Pennsylvania Independent Battery D (Durell's) had completed their recuperation in Kentucky after their service in Mississippi, and in November the battery had been sent temporarily to Johnson's Island on Lake Erie, near Sandusky, Ohio. Johnson's Island was home to a prison camp where Confederate prisoners of war were being kept, and a rumor had circulated that a breakout was being planned with help from Confederate agents already in the North. The men of Battery D bolstered the garrison until other reinforcements arrived. In April, Battery D was moved to Washington and armed with six new 10-pdr Parrott rifles and recruited back to full strength. From there they were assigned to General Ambrose Burnside's Ninth Corps, which was preparing to re-join the Army of the Potomac for service in Virginia.

In May, Battery H, 1$^{st}$ Pennsylvania Light Artillery (Fagan's), which had been stationed at Camp Barry since the previous July, was dismounted and ordered to report to Lieutenant Colonel Brady as garrison troops. Brady was serving as Chief of Artillery for a section of the Washington defenses on the south side of the Potomac, and used the men of Battery H to replace the garrison of Fort Whipple, which had been reassigned to duty in the field.

Meanwhile, in the Western theatre of war, Pennsylvania Independent Battery E (McGill's) had reenlisted on the 6$^{th}$ of January and took part in an unusual amphibious expedition during the first month of 1864. Shortly after the men returned from their reenlistment furloughs, General Geary loaded a select detachment of infantry and a single section of Battery E aboard the Steamboat *Chickamauga* for a run down the Tennessee River. Their mission was to destroy all boats between Bridgeport and Decatur to prevent their use by the enemy. The *Chickamauga* departed on the 12$^{th}$ of April, and at Guntersville encountered a force of Confederate cavalry along the shoreline. When the ship approached, the Confederates took the ship under fire. Some of the Union infantry were landed, and the two cannon from Battery E opened fire on the enemy from the deck of the steamer. The Confederate cavalry faded back from contact and the *Chickamauga* continued its mission as far as Triana, where it learned that a much larger enemy force was waiting to intercept them. General Geary decided that it would be too dangerous to proceed further and gave the order to turn back. Upon their return, they learned that the Twelfth and the Eleventh Corps had been consolidated and re-designated as the Twentieth Corps, under the command of General Hooker. General Geary's division became the Second Division of the Twentieth Corps and Battery E remained assigned to General Geary's division.

The Steamboat *Chickamauga*. Image from the
Hamilton County Tennessee Genealogical Society.

## 6. The Overland Campaign

At the beginning of May, the Army of the Potomac left its winter camps and began a new southward advance. General Grant's initial plan was very similar to General Hooker's plan from the Chancellorsville campaign or General Meade's plan from the Mine Run campaign. The Union troops would cross the Rapidan and advance through the Wilderness, turn General Lee's troops out of their defenses, and force them to fight in open country. Unfortunately for Grant, General Lee was once again able to re-deploy his forces quickly enough to meet the Union army while still confined in the tangles of the Wilderness.

Battery B, 1st Pennsylvania Light Artillery (Cooper's) crossed the Rapidan River at Germanna Ford with General Gouverneur K. Warren's Fifth Corps on the 4th of May, and Battery F, 1st Pennsylvania Light Artillery (Ricketts'), with General Hancock's

Second Corps, crossed at Ely's Ford on the same day. That night Ricketts' Battery F camped, as chance would have it, at the very same position it had occupied the previous year during the battle of Chancellorsville. The next day Pennsylvania Independent Battery D (Durell's) crossed Germanna Ford with General Ambrose Burnside's Ninth Corps, which was acting as a general reserve for the entire army.

The thick woods and underbrush throughout the region south of the Rapidan interfered with the use of artillery, and most of the army's batteries were only intermittently engaged during the ensuing Battle of the Wilderness. Ricketts' Battery F, however, played an important role in countering a major Confederate attack near the extreme left of the Union line.

**Artillery crossing the Rappahannock at Germanna Ford (Spring 1864).
Image from the Library of Congress.**

On May 5$^{th}$, General Hancock ordered Battery F to support General George W. Getty's Division of the Sixth Corps. Owing to the terrain, only a single section could be deployed at any time, and that by advancing along the Orange Plank Road behind the line of infantry. Shortly after 4:30 p.m. the van met the enemy, and Lieutenant Brockway's section began exchanging fire with a Confederate battery to their front. The Confederate battery was armed with Napoleons and was firing canister, which proved less effective than the percussion rounds Brockway was firing from his two 3-in. Ordnance rifles. The Confederate battery withdrew, but only after one of its limbers exploded under Brockway's fire. Shortly thereafter, the enemy infantry attacked the Union troops, and for two hours the lines swung back and forth while Brockway's guns met the Confederates with shell and canister. Lieutenant Francis H. Snider's section was advanced to relieve Brockway, but one of Snider's guns burst at the muzzle on its very first shot and was rendered unserviceable.* The Confederates were then able to push the Union infantry back and one gun of Battery F, which had lost most of its horse team and could not retire, was left behind. It was soon recovered, however, when the 14$^{th}$ Indiana and 8$^{th}$ Ohio Infantry Regiments, both of Colonel Samuel S. Carroll's brigade of the Second Corps, made a charge and pushed back the Confederates. Shortly thereafter Battery F was withdrawn by order of General Hancock.

---

* This is the only recorded instance during the entire war of a 3-in. Ordnance rifle breeching its barrel while in service.

Lieutenant Francis H. Snider, Battery F, 1st Pennsylvania Light Artillery, and a view of the Wilderness. Image of Lieutenant Snider from the P.R.V.C. Historical Society; Image of the Wilderness from the National Archives.

After three days of brutal fighting in the maze of the Wilderness, during which time neither side was able to gain a decisive advantage over the other, the Army of the Potomac began a sidling movement around the Confederate right flank towards Spotsylvania Courthouse about a dozen miles to the southeast. On the 8th of May, Cooper's Battery B reached Laurel Hill and took position on a knoll to the right of the road leading down to Spotsylvania, where it took part in a heavy exchange of fire with the enemy.

On the 9th, Battery B was shifted to the army's right to support an attack by the Second Corps and fired about forty rounds at the enemy across the Po River. On the 13th, Battery B was placed on the picket line near the Beverly House (General Warren's headquarters) on the Fredericksburg-Spotsylvania Road and faced toward the left flank. In the afternoon they assisted in repelling two attacks aimed in the direction of the Myer's house, but there was little cover available and the enemy's fire was so intense that the cannoneers had to work on their knees while loading their pieces.

Battery B was withdrawn during the night and reunited with the Fifth Corps. On the morning of the 14th they went into line and opened fire on the enemy to their front, but were not heavily engaged that day.

Two days later, in compliance with an order from General Grant to lighten the army of surplus artillery, the batteries of the Fifth Corps, including Battery B, were reduced from six to four guns apiece, although they were each permitted to retain all six of their caissons and as many serviceable horses as they then had with them.

On the 18th, General Grant launched another attack against the Confederates entrenched around Spotsylvania, and Captain Cooper supported the advance of the Second Corps (to his right) at the head of an improvised artillery brigade consisting of his own battery, Lieutenant George Breck's Consolidated Battery E & L, 1st New York Light Artillery, and Captain Charles A. Phillips' 5th Massachusetts Battery. The artillery exchange was one of the severest of the war, and several of Battery B's cannon took direct hits to their carriages. This attack, like the ones before it, failed to decisively break the Confederate line and General Grant decided to attempt another sidle around the enemy's right flank, this time towards the North Anna River. The army reached the north bank of that river on the 23rd of May, but the Confederates had beaten them there and were already in position on the south bank.

Pontoon Bridge over Jericho Mills (May 24th 1864).
Image from the Library of Congress.

General Grant ordered crossings both above and below the enemy flanks, and Battery B supported the Fifth Corps' upstream crossing at Jericho Mills by going into position on the north bank. Captain Cooper was placed in charge of another ad hoc artillery brigade, this time consisting of Lieutenant James Stewart's Battery B, 4th U.S. Artillery (also of the Fifth Corps) and Captain Patrick Hart's 15th New York Independent Battery, which had been forwarded from the Artillery Reserve. Lieutenant William C. Miller led Battery B in Captain Cooper's absence. All of these batteries were posted on the north bank of the river and engaged the enemy batteries to the south. A Confederate counterattack stalled the Fifth Corps below the river, and the action shifted to the downstream attempt.

Ricketts' Battery F had all this time been posted on the left of a railroad bridge located downstream of the Confederates and had fired over 200 rounds across the river in the course of the day. On the 24th Battery F crossed the river with the Second Corps as part of General Grant's downstream effort. This attack was also met with heavy resistance, and just like the previous day's upstream attempt it ended by stalling without achieving any breakthrough. The Ninth Corps, to which Durell's Battery D was attached, also failed in a simultaneous attempt to cross at Ox Ford, directly opposite the Confederate center.

General Grant now recognized the danger of his position, half above and half below an enemy who held excellent interior lines and could strike out in either direction, and he reacted with yet another sidling movement around the enemy's right flank. The Army of the Potomac crossed the Pamunkey River and moved towards Totopotomoy Creek. Finding the line of the Totopotomoy blocked, the sidling movement was extended towards Old Church and Old Cold Harbor.

By the 1$^{st}$ of June the two armies were facing each other at Cold Harbor, on the same field where many of these same men had met in battle two years earlier at the Battle of Gaines' Mill during the Seven Days campaign.

Battery B, 1$^{st}$ Pennsylvania Light Artillery was soon heavily engaged with the enemy near the Mechanicsville Pike, but not under Captain Cooper, who left temporarily on the last day of May to escort about forty of his men to Harrisburg for discharge after their terms of service had expired. Lieutenant Miller continued in command in Cooper's absence and led the battery through two days of terrible fighting on the 2$^{nd}$ and 3$^{rd}$ during which the Union troops attempted to break through the Confederate lines. The main assault was launched on the morning 3$^{rd}$ and resulted in one of the most complete repulses of the war. In a matter of minutes, thousands of Union men were either killed or wounded while the Confederates suffered extremely light casualties. During these two days of fighting at Cold Harbor, Battery B fired more rounds than the combined total from all of their previous actions since crossing the Rapidan the previous month. Ricketts' Battery F meanwhile fought at Cold Harbor in support of the Eighteenth Corps, to which they had been temporarily assigned, and fired over 230 rounds on the 3$^{rd}$ and suffered three men wounded.

Unable to decisively break the Confederate line by direct assault, here as in all of his previous attempts of the campaign, General Grant again resorted to a flanking maneuver. This time the Army of the Potomac moved toward the James River down the same path McClellan had used to fall back during the Seven Days battles. Grant's plan was to cross the James, and using that river as an impervious line of supply and communication, launch an assault on Petersburg to the south of Richmond.

## 7. The Atlanta Campaign

At the same time as the Army of the Potomac was fighting its way southward across the Virginia landscape from the Rapidan to the James, the armies of the West under General Sherman were likewise advancing from their base at Chattanooga towards Atlanta, driving the Confederate Army of Tennessee before them. Shortly after the battles of Chattanooga, Confederate General Braxton Bragg was relieved of command and General Joseph E. Johnston replaced him at the head of the Army of Tennessee.

Pennsylvania Independent Battery B (McDowell's) joined Sherman's advance with General David S. Stanley's First Division of the Fourth Corps, to which they had been assigned, and Pennsylvania Independent Battery E (McGill's), which had just received a new issue of 3-in. Ordnance rifles, continued to march with General Geary's Second Division of General Hooker's new Twentieth Corps.

The campaign began in early May. On the 3rd of the month McDowell's Battery B broke camp in Blue Springs, Tennessee and on the following day McGill's Battery E left its camp in the Wauhatchie Valley, where Captain Atwell and Lieutenant Geary had both fallen during the previous autumn's action at Wauhatchie Station.

On May 8th both batteries reached Rocky Face Ridge where the enemy was entrenched and waiting for them. General Sherman's plan was to demonstrate against the Confederates along the ridge while General James McPherson's Army of the Tennessee passed around the enemy right flank and through Snake Creek Gap for a strike at the Confederate forward supply base on the Oostanula River at Resaca. Battery B went into position and shelled an enemy force along the ridge and Battery E was called on to cover the withdrawal of Geary's Division after an unsuccessful assault on Dug's Gap. The next day Battery E advanced to a knoll between Tunnel Hill, the sight of General Sherman's attack the previous November, and Rocky Face Ridge, and exchanged fire with the Confederate batteries opposite.

On May 10th, Battery B continued shelling Rocky Face Ridge, but General McPherson had given up his flanking movement the day before in fear of being cut off and overwhelmed, and his column had retired to Snake Creek Gap. General Sherman decided to disengage from the fight at Rocky Face Ridge and move most of his forces to join McPherson for a renewed advance towards the Oostanula. General Johnston observed the movement and withdrew his own troops from Rocky Face Ridge on the 11th for a rapid concentration at Resaca.

On the 13th, Battery E reached the vicinity of Resaca, but was held in reserve and was not engaged. Battery B, however, was engaged on both the 14th and 15th in shelling the enemy in support of repeated Union attacks against the Confederates around the town. Unable to make any headway by direct assault, General

Sherman launched another flanking movement across the Oostanula beyond the Confederate left flank.

Facing this new threat to their rear, the Confederates abandoned Resaca on the night of May 15$^{th}$ and retired across the Oostanula, and on the following day the Union troops followed towards Adairsville where the Fourth Corps encountered the Confederate troops of General William Hardee's Corps entrenched above the town. General Thomas decided to delay the attack until more troops could be brought up, but in the meantime the Confederates continued their withdrawal southward.

After taking part in an assault on General Hardee's rearguard on the 20$^{th}$, Battery B moved with its corps to Dallas on the 23$^{rd}$. On May 25$^{th}$ Battery E was at Vine Creek and four of the battery's men strayed from the Union lines and were captured by the Confederates. These four men were later reported as deserters. On the 10$^{th}$ of June Battery B reached Pine Mountain and was placed near the Marietta road. Four days later, on the 14$^{th}$, Battery B began firing towards enemy emplacements on the mountain. On that same day Battery E shelled the Confederates at Pilot Knob.

General Johnston evacuated Pine Mountain during the night in order to contract his overextended lines, and on the following day Battery B was advanced to within 500 yards of the new Confederate lines. Battery B pounded these new lines throughout the day with a heavy fire of canister, case, and shell.

On the 17$^{th}$, Sherman began another sidling movement around the Confederate left flank. Battery B advanced on Cassville and Battery E shelled the enemy at Noyes' Creek. On the 18$^{th}$, Battery B fought at New Hope Church, which General Sherman mistakenly believed was only lightly guarded, but which in fact General Johnston had heavily reinforced. During the action, Battery B advanced to within 250 yards of the Confederate works, and from an exposed position the battery helped drive off a Confederate force that was threatening part of the Union line. The

Union troops ultimately failed to break the Confederate lines at New Hope Church, but Johnston realized that his troops would be in danger of being enveloped unless they were quickly withdrawn. He reacted by pulling back and moving his army to Kennesaw Mountain.

McDowell's Battery B was again called to the front on June $19^{th}$, and drove an advanced force of the enemy back on their new main lines along the mountain. On the $20^{th}$ of June, Battery B shelled the Confederates at long range during the afternoon and on the $22^{nd}$ they were taken out of line and sent, along with their division, to reinforce General Daniel Butterfield's division of the Twentieth Corps at Kolb's Farm.

General John Bell Hood's Confederate corps had just struck Butterfield's division in an attack designed to preempt another flanking movement by Sherman. McGill's Battery E, which was part of the Twentieth Corps, was already engaged and was busily exchanging fire with General Hood's Confederates. Battery B soon joined the fight and assisted in repelling General Hood's attack.

Although Hood's troops were driven back, the attack did succeed in blocking another attempt by General Sherman to move around the Confederate left flank. Sherman became convinced that Johnston must have significantly weakened his center at Kennesaw Mountain in order to strengthen his flanks, and so he decided to launch a direct assault against the Confederate center.

On morning of June $27^{th}$, the assault was made, but it was a complete failure. The Union troops were unable to make any headway against the well-entrenched Confederates, and suffered very heavy casualties. Among them was Captain McDowell of Battery B, who was killed when his battery joined in the massive artillery barrage that accompanied the attack. Lieutenant Jacob Zeigler succeeded McDowell in command.

*Battle of Kennesaw Mountain*; from a Lithograph by L. Prang & Co., 1887; by Bror Thure de Thulstrup (1848 – 1930). Image from the Library of Congress.

On the 1st of July, Battery B joined in a general bombardment of the enemy lines that began at 6:00 p.m. and continued through the next day. Once again finding his position untenable, General Johnston withdrew his army and retreated across the Chattahoochee River to Peach Tree Creek.

On July 3rd, the march was resumed and both Batteries B and E marched through Marietta to near Neal Dow Station, where Battery B was engaged on the left side of the railroad. On the 4th, Battery B participated in a long-range exchange with the enemy's artillery near the Chattahoochee River. On the 5th, Battery B entrenched on the north bank of the river at a position commanding the ferry crossing near Vining's Station, and assisted in the capture of an enemy pontoon bridge. On July 10th, the battery crossed the river and was placed near Power's Ferry, eight miles above the Vining's Station crossing.

On the 8th of July, Captain McGill of Battery E left the service and Lieutenant James Dunlevy succeeded him in command, but

Captain McGill decided to remain in the field with Battery E unofficially as a civilian volunteer.

Battery E followed Battery B south across the Chattahoochee on July 17th, and on the 18th Battery B marched to Buckhead. On the 19th Battery E went into position along Peach Tree Creek and shelled the enemy along a wooded ridge on the opposite bank while the men of General Geary's division crossed over. On the 20th of the month Battery E followed them across the creek.

Meanwhile, the Confederate army had lost its commanding general. General Johnston's retreat across the Chattahoochee had angered the authorities in Richmond, and he was relieved of command and replaced by General Hood. General Hood was an aggressive adversary, although a somewhat clumsy one. Although heavily outnumbered, Hood decided to swing immediately over to the offensive. On the afternoon of July 20th, he launched a major attack against the Union forces on the near side of Peach Tree Creek. The fighting was intense, and Battery E was hotly engaged, but after two hours of fighting the Confederates were repulsed. Captain McGill was wounded during the battle.

With the Confederates driven back to the very gates of Atlanta, General Sherman's army began shifting to the west to encircle the city in anticipation of the final lunge. As the ring of the attackers grew tighter and tighter around the defenders, the Union artillery began shelling the city. Through the remainder of July the Union army's field batteries shelled Atlanta at long range.

At this juncture in the campaign, the Army of the Cumberland finally adopted the artillery brigade system devised by General Hunt for the Army of the Potomac during the previous year. On the 26th of July, Battery B and the other batteries of the Fourth Corps were removed from their respective divisions and assigned to the new Fourth Corps Artillery Brigade.

Likewise, Battery E became part of the Twentieth Corps Artillery Brigade. When the Twelfth Corps had been transferred from Virginia to Chattanooga the previous autumn, its artillery brigade had been disbanded and Battery E had been re-assigned to General Geary's division. When the Twelfth Corps was later combined with the Eleventh Corps to create the Twentieth Corps, Battery E had remained attached to Geary's division. Now the batteries of the Twentieth Corps readopted the brigade system that had proven so effective for many of them the year before in Pennsylvania. The artillery brigade system was very popular and received favorable comment from the officers entrusted with its execution. The Fourth Corps Chief of Artillery, Captain Lyman Bridges, would, for example, laud the "new" system in his official report for the campaign:

> The organization of the Artillery Brigade has been an era of good in this corps; although organized upon an active campaign good results have already resulted. The batteries can be more promptly equipped and supplied, all unnecessary marches avoided, the labor equally distributed, and all the artillery of the corps used to advantage. The animals of the corps are in much better condition than when the brigade was organized.*

Meanwhile, the bombardment of Atlanta continued throughout the first two weeks of August. On the 5$^{th}$ of the month, Battery B received orders to fire into the city every fifteen minutes between noon and sundown, and starting the next day the artillery regularly began their barrages at 4:00 p.m. and would continue late into the night or early morning of the next day. Also on August 6$^{th}$, Lieutenant Dunlevy resigned from Battery E and Lieutenant Thomas S. Sloan took over command.

Battery E was withdrawn in late August to the Chattahoochee River where it was kept in reserve for the remainder of the month. On the 25$^{th}$ of August, Battery B, along with the other batteries of the Fourth Corps, were withdrawn from their positions between

---

* O.R., series I vol. 38 pt. 1, 480 (No. 78), 486.

the Augusta Railroad line and Peach Tree Creek, and shifted to a new position near Proctor's Creek. Battery B was kept on the move with the advance all during the next week, reaching Utoy Creek on August $26^{th}$, Red Oak on the $28^{th}$, and Cobb's Mills on the $31^{st}$. On the $2^{nd}$ of September Battery B was placed in position at Lovejoy's Station, but word soon came that the Confederates had abandoned Atlanta the night before.

General Sherman's snakelike counter-clockwise encircling of the city had force General Hood to either retreat or risk being completely surrounded and cut of from his lines of supply. Union troops immediately entered and occupied the city, including Battery E, which returned from its reserve assignment on the Chattahoochee.

Battery B and the rest of the Fourth Corps artillery withdrew from Lovejoy's Station on September $5^{th}$ and marched to a position two miles north of Jonesborough. On the $7^{th}$, Battery B marched to Rough-and-Ready and on the following day entered Atlanta at noon. General David S. Stanley, who commanded the First Division of the Fourth Corps during the campaign, commended Battery B for their conduct in his official report: "I must also make honorable mention of [Battery B and the $5^{th}$ Indiana Battery] ... They rendered excellent service daily, and always courted exposed positions, never slackening fire, however much exposed, either to the artillery or musketry of the enemy."[*] During the campaign Battery B lost one officer and one man killed, one officer and thirteen men wounded, and twenty-two horsed killed or disabled.

●○●

---

[*] O.R., series I vol. 38 pt. 1, 219 (No. 14), 227.

# VI

## 1. The Siege of Petersburg

One unfortunate consequence of the organization of the artillery branch of service during the Civil War was that many excellent officers on the staffs of volunteer artillery regiments were not employed to their full potential. When early in the war the U.S. Army decided to deploy batteries individually, rather than as full regiments, the staff and field officers of already-existing volunteer artillery regiments found themselves without responsibilities commensurate with their rank.

Colonel Robert M. West; 1st Pennsylvania Light Artillery. Image from the U.S. Army Heritage and Education Center.

For the preceding two and a half years before the Siege of Petersburg, the 1st Pennsylvania Light Artillery had continued to exist as a paper organization, but its eight batteries were widely scattered throughout the army and operated completely independently of each other.

On the 29th of May, Colonel Robert M. West left his nominal post as head of the regiment to take command of the 5th

Pennsylvania Cavalry, where his talents could be more actively employed in the field. West had already spent most of the preceding two years on detached service commanding various brigade-sized forces on the Virginia Peninsula, including the combined-arms garrisons at Yorktown and Williamsburg.

Lieutenant Colonel James Brady had been similarly detailed out. Brady had issued the original call for volunteers in Philadelphia in 1861 that had led to the creation of the regiment, and had served as the captain of Battery H until July of 1862, when he was promoted to major. During the Gettysburg campaign, Brady was in Pennsylvania as Chief of Artillery for the Department of the Susquehanna and had assisted in the defense of Harrisburg. In recognition of his services, in November of 1863 he was promoted to lieutenant colonel and briefly commanded the First Brigade of the Army of the Potomac's Artillery Reserve before being reassigned as Chief of Artillery for a section of the Washington defenses. On the transfer of Colonel West, Lieutenant Colonel Brady acceded to the command of the regiment, but continued to actually serve in the Washington defenses with his headquarters at Fort Corcoran.

Meanwhile, the Army of the Potomac proceeded with General Grant's plan to break the latest stalemate at Cold Harbor by rapidly crossing the James River and attacking the Confederate supply lines at Petersburg.

Battery F, $1^{st}$ Pennsylvania (Ricketts') reached Wilcox's Landing on the James River by the $13^{th}$ of June and crossed to the south shore on the $15^{th}$. During the next day, the battery marched to the vicinity of Petersburg and fired ten rounds into the Confederate works around the city. On the $17^{th}$, Pennsylvania Independent Battery D (Durell's) crossed the James at Powhatan Point and also advanced on Petersburg. On the $18^{th}$ Ricketts' Battery F fired 362 rounds into the Petersburg works, and on June

25th two sections of Battery D occupied a fort to the right side of the Norfolk road.

Despite the rapidity of General Grant's latest attempt to move around the Confederate right flank, General Lee was again able to concentrate his forces between the Union army and its objective. As additional units from both sides came on line the situation once again became a stalemate, and the opposing forces began digging in to the soft Virginia mud. In the weeks that followed, massive earthworks began appearing on both sides and the campaign took on the form of a siege.

In late June, General Burnside approved a plan presented by Lieutenant Colonel Henry Pleasants, commander of the 48th Pennsylvania Infantry, to end the siege. Pleasants' plan was to dig a mine under the Confederate works and lay a massive explosive charge that would literally blow a hole in the Confederate line so the Union infantry could launch an assault through the gap. Colonel Pleasants had been an engineer before the war and most of his men were former coal miners from Schuylkill County. They began work immediately and completed the mine by the end of July. General Burnside designated General Edward Ferrero's Division of United States Colored Troops, to which Pennsylvania Independent Battery D (Durell's) was attached, to spearhead the attack.

At the last minute, Generals Grant and Meade ordered another division to take the place of Ferrero's division in leading the attack. Never having shared General Burnside's enthusiasm for Colonel Pleasants' plan, these two generals feared that if the attack failed, the army would be accused of recklessly exposing green black troops to more than their fair share of danger in a long-shot experiment.

Before dawn, on the morning of the 30th of July, the fuse was lit on several thousand pounds of gunpowder just twenty feet under a section of Confederate line known as Elliot's Salient.

After a short delay caused by a failure of the fuse (which had to be spliced and relit), a massive explosion broke the silence and sent many tons of rubble into the air. A Confederate fort was completely destroyed and a trench-like crater twenty feet deep and nearly two hundred feet long was left in its place.

The Union infantry rushed forward and Battery D commenced firing in support of the attack. Lieutenant George Silvis, who was in command of the battery during the temporary absence of Captain Durell, reported the following of the battery's limited involvement in the action:

> As soon as the mine exploded we commenced firing; most of the firing was directly toward the crest of the hill in the rear of the crater. Owing to the limited field of firing from the part of the work in which we were stationed, and the danger of firing with our troops so near the enemy, after about half an hour's firing we ceased. At intervals during the morning we fired a few more rounds, expending in all during the day eighty-four rounds of ammunition.[*]

The spearhead infantry that replaced General Ferrero's division had not been properly instructed to round the outer edges of the crater, and instead jumped straight into it, perhaps thinking that the mine had created the penultimate trench-line for them. The problem was that the twenty-foot deep crater was too deep to fire out of, and quickly became a trap when the Confederates counterattacked. General Ferrero's troops advance in support, but the advantage of surprise had passed and they too were driven into the crater, where many of the attackers were killed or forced to surrender. Despite the best hopes of the Union participants, the Battle of the Crater failed to break the Confederate line and ended in defeat.

---

[*] O.R., series I vol. 40 pt. 1, 610 (No. 224).

Meanwhile, in the early summer of 1864, Joseph Knap returned to the service at the head of a new artillery organization. The original captain of Pennsylvania Independent Battery E (now under the command of Lieutenant Thomas S. Sloan), Knap had resigned his commission in May of 1863 to become superintendent of the Fort Pitt Foundry, but had briefly returned to the field during the Confederate invasion of Pennsylvania as the commander of an emergency militia battery. Apparently not content to sit quietly by as the war continued, Knap accepted a major's commission and took command of a newly raised two-battery artillery battalion that was raised in Pittsburgh during the months of May and June for three months' service. This new organization, which served under the name "Knap's Independent Light Artillery Battalion," would serve uneventfully in the Washington defenses until mustered out on the 5th of September.

**Officers of the Keystone Battery. Image from the National Archives.**

In July of 1864 Captain Matthew Hastings also retook the field by reconstituting the Keystone Battery, which had been disbanded the previous autumn at the end of its men's short one-year enlistment terms. This time the terms were even shorter, with the men signing up for only one hundred days. This newest "Keystone Battery" was assigned to the Department of the

Susquehanna and would spend its entire three-month existence within Pennsylvania defending various important points from potential Confederate incursions. Such incursions seemed less and less likely as time went by, but nonetheless required the presence of garrison troops throughout the region in case a renewed threat were to materialize.

Battery B, 1st Pennsylvania Light Artillery in action at Petersburg.
Image from the National Archives.

As the siege of Petersburg stretched on through late summer and autumn, three of the Pennsylvania batteries in the trenches lost their veteran captains. On the 8th of August, Captain James H. Cooper of Battery B, 1st Pennsylvania Light Artillery, who had already overstayed the end of his original term of service by over two months, turned his battery over to Lieutenant William McClelland and returned home. Captain Cooper had led his battery from shortly after its creation in 1861 (when he took command upon Henry T. Danforth's promotion to major) and had served with distinction ever since. During the Battle of Fredericksburg, his fellow Pennsylvanian, General John Reynolds, had called Captain Cooper "the bravest man in the army," and in the recent Overland Campaign and siege operations Captain Cooper was several times employed as the commander of ad hoc battalions of artillery. The month after he left the army Captain

Cooper was awarded with a brevet to the rank of major, but had already returned home and never mustered in under that rank.

On the 21$^{st}$ of August, Captain John G. Simpson of Battery A 1$^{st}$ Pennsylvania Light Artillery also left the service. Battery A had been on the Virginia Peninsula for over a year serving with the forces around Yorktown, and had been variously stationed at Black Water, Deep Bottom, Fort Darling, and Seven Pines. After the departure of Captain Simpson, Lieutenant William Stitt took command of Battery A, and was promoted to captain on the 17$^{th}$ of September.

On the 23$^{rd}$ of September Captain George W. Durell of Pennsylvania Independent Battery D also left for home, his term of service having ended. The original captain of Battery D, Captain Durell had led his battery through the bloody Virginia and Maryland campaigns of 1862 before taking them west to join Grant and Sherman in Mississippi at the capture of Vicksburg and the assault of Jackson. After brief sojourns in Kentucky and Ohio, his battery returned east and joined in the Overland campaign that had brought the army to the gates of Petersburg. Lieutenant Samuel H. Rhoads was promoted to captain and succeeded Captain Durell in command of Battery D.

## 2. Cedar Creek

As the siege continued at Petersburg, the attention of both armies turned west toward the Shenandoah Valley. The Confederates were diverting whatever forces they could spare to the Valley in the hopes of threatening Washington from behind the cover of the Blue Ridge. General Grant was likewise hoping to use the Valley as an avenue of invasion into Virginia's interior behind the lines of the Army of Northern Virginia. General Jubal Early, whom General Lee had sent to take command in the Valley, crossed the Potomac into Maryland on the 5th of July on a massive raid aimed at the national capital. Although Early's raid failed and he was forced back into Virginia and up the Valley, in large part due to reinforcements sent up from the Army of the Potomac, one of its immediate effects was to convince the civil and military authorities that several threatened points along the Potomac needed to be strengthened.

Positioned at the northern outlet of the Shenandoah Valley, at the junction where the Shenandoah and Potomac rivers meet, Harper's Ferry was an obvious target for the Confederates (the town had already changed hands eight times during the war) and an important base of operations for any Union forces operating in the Valley. Pennsylvania Independent Battery F (Irish's) was transferred from Washington to Harper's Ferry on the 4th of July, and reached that post three days later. Upon arrival, the men were rearmed and equipped as infantry and assigned to duty as pickets and train guards, and guards of prisoners, until October 5th, when they were reissued a battery of cannon and assigned to the garrison on Maryland Heights, which overlook Harper's Ferry.

Meanwhile Battery G, 1st Pennsylvania Light Artillery, under Lieutenant Jennings, had also been forwarded from Washington in response to the renewed threat from the direction of the Valley. On the 3rd of July Battery G was ordered to Frederick, Maryland where, like Independent Battery F at Harper's Ferry, the men were given muskets and re-equipped as infantry. From Frederick they marched to Point of Rocks on the Potomac where they would remain on picket from the 6th of July through the 12th of December.

After the withdrawal of General Early's troops from Maryland, General Grant had put General Philip Sheridan in charge of operations in western Virginia with instructions to pursue and destroy General Early's army. Sheridan consolidated his forces and began advancing up the Shenandoah Valley.

In August, Battery D, 1$^{st}$ Pennsylvania Light Artillery (Munk's) left Harper's Ferry, where it had been stationed since the previous August, and joined Sheridan's campaign as part of General George Crook's "Army of West Virginia," in reality a single corps of General Sheridan's "Army of the Shenandoah."

As the Army of the Shenandoah drove the Confederates up the Valley, Battery D was engaged at Berryville on the 3$^{rd}$ of September, Winchester (Opequon) on the 19$^{th}$, and Fisher's Hill on the 22$^{nd}$. By the end of the month the Confederates had been driven back towards Brown's Gap, and General Sheridan decided to withdraw part of the way back down the Valley so that he could send reinforcements to Grant and the Army of the Potomac. The army marched back towards Middletown and took a defensive position along Cedar Creek.

General Sheridan did not expect Early to attack, believing that the Confederates lacked the strength to move against his significantly superior force. Early, however, saw an opening for a surprise strike on the exposed and unprepared Union left flank.

On the 16$^{th}$ of October, Munk's Battery D made camp on a hill to the east of a bridge that carried the Valley Turnpike across Cedar Creek. Battery D camped behind a line of entrenchments being prepared by the infantry. The rest of Sheridan's forces were camped to the west of the Turnpike, and General Crook's command, including Battery D, was therefore directly in the path of Early's intended flank attack.

Before dawn on the 19$^{th}$, Crook's Chief of Artillery, Captain Henry A. DuPont, heard the sound of light picket fire from beyond the lines and ordered reveille sounded immediately. The cannoneers of Battery D had been trained to report at reveille to their assigned positions on the guns, but as yet had no reason to believe that a major attack was already in progress. They first learned otherwise when a Confederate battle line emerged from the woods and brush only twenty yards away. Battery D immediately opened with canister, and managed to fire about fifteen rounds from their six 10-pounder Parrott rifles before the Confederates fired a massed volley and charged the battery with bayonets and clubbed muskets. The supporting infantry had fallen back in the first rush and Battery D, with its horse teams unharnessed and picketed to rear, was unable to draw off its guns when the cannoneers were driven from their posts. Lieutenant Munk managed to harness enough horses to pull off three of his caissons, but the other three were taken along with the guns. In just a few minutes, Battery D lost six men killed, six wounded, eighteen captured (including one lieutenant), all six of its guns, six limbers, three caissons, eleven horses, a battery wagon, a traveling forge, three army supply wagons, eighteen mules, and a wide assortment of harness and tack.

Battery D was effectively removed from the battle by the loss of their guns, but the Confederate attack, after sweeping through most of the camps of the Union army, was eventually slowed, stopped, and reversed. Union counterattacks broke the enemy line and General Early's army was ultimately driven from the field with great loss, including the recapture of all eighteen of the Union cannon previous taken, including the six guns of Battery D, as well as twenty-five cannon that the Confederates themselves had brought to the field.

The battle resulted in the near destruction of General Early's army as a fighting force and firmly secured the Shenandoah Valley in Union hands. Although the losses on the Union left, where men were thrown straight from their sleep into an unexpected battle, were extremely heavy, the stubborn resistance of these troops was credited with delaying the Confederates sufficiently to save the army and the battle. Captain DuPont, for example, was later awarded the Medal of Honor for leading the artillery of Crook's corps during the surprise attack.

Following the battle, Battery D returned to Harper's Ferry for reequipping and was reassigned to garrison duty on Maryland Heights, where it remained for rest of its term of service. Lieutenant Munk was promoted to captain on the $9^{th}$ of March, 1865.

## 3. The March to the Sea

Following the capture of Atlanta, General Sherman began preparing for one of the boldest campaigns of the war. His plan was to march straight across the state of Georgia from Atlanta to Savannah. Along the way he would destroy Confederate communications, supplies, and infrastructure in a region that was critical to the support of the Confederacy's remaining armies in the field.

Before starting, however, Sherman needed to make sure that enough troops were left behind to deal with the remnants of General Hood's Confederate Army of Tennessee, which was hovering to the west of Atlanta near the Alabama border. Sherman divided his forces and left half with General George Thomas to keep Hood in check while using the rest for the Savannah expedition. Pennsylvania Independent Battery B (Ziegler's), with the Fourth Corps, was part of the force left with Thomas, and Pennsylvania Independent Battery E (Sloan's), with the Twentieth Corps, was assigned a place in Sherman's column.

Before the campaign began, there were preparatory matters that needed to be taken care of. In September, General Sherman ordered that his batteries be reduced from six to four guns each, just as Grant was doing in the East, in order to promote mobility. Sloan's Battery E was thereby reduced to four 3-in. Ordnance rifles.

On the 16th of October, Battery E joined Colonel James S. Robinson's 82nd Ohio Infantry Regiment in a foraging expedition to Flat Rock Shoals on the South River, and on the 26th one section of the battery accompanied a force under General Geary on a similar expedition towards Lithonia. These expeditions were highly successful in bringing in supplies for the army and fodder for the artillery horses.

On the 15th of November, with everything ready, General Sherman's Savannah force left Atlanta and began its march across Georgia. They met almost no resistance in their march across the Empire State of the South, and reached the outskirts of Savannah on the 11th of December. Battery E had not gone into action, or even had to unlimber and take position, during the entire course of the nearly month-long march.

Upon reaching the objective, Battery E was immediately placed in position overlooking the Savannah River. On December 12th, Battery E fired several long-range shots at a downriver steamer, and a few more towards the fortified city itself. On the 20th, a Confederate gunboat came upriver and began a nuisance fire against a detachment of Union troops occupying Hutchinson's Island; Battery E opened fire and drove the gunboat off.

The Confederates withdrew from Savannah during the night without a fight, and the city was occupied the next day. General Sherman wanted to avoid any unnecessary destruction to civilian property and so assigned General Geary (who was a former mayor of San Francisco) and his division of eastern troops the task of occupying the city. Battery E accompanied Geary and went into position on the 21st at the end of Bay Street.

A Confederate ironclad ram, also named "Savannah," was berthed across the river on the South Carolina shore and men were spotted working on its decks, apparently trying to unload supplies. Battery E opened fire and drove the work crews away, but Battery E's 3-inch field guns were too small to do any damage to the ironclad ship itself. During the night, however, the Confederates blew up the ram themselves in order to prevent it from being captured. The next day, Battery E moved to West Broad Street and went into camp with their guns in park, awaiting, with the rest of the army, General Sherman's orders for their next movements.

Destruction of the Confederate ram *Savannah* on November 21$^{st}$, 1864.
Image from *Harper's Weekly* (February 4, 1865).

# 4. Franklin and Nashville

When General Sherman left Atlanta to begin his campaign across Georgia, he left a substantial force behind under General George Thomas to deal with General Hood's weakened Confederate Army of Tennessee. General Hood, relieved by his recent defeat of the necessity of keeping between the Union troops and any fixed point, shifted his army west through northern Alabama and prepared to strike northward. General Thomas meanwhile pulled the bulk of his troops back into Tennessee and prepared to face the threat. Despite this precaution, when the Confederates finally crossed the Tennessee River on the 31$^{st}$ of October, the Federals were not yet prepared to challenge them.

General Thomas decided to concentrate his army at Nashville, but his columns were still widely scattered through southern Tennessee when Hood made his move. Pennsylvania Independent Battery B (Ziegler's), still with the Fourth Corps, was part of a detached force under General John Schofield that found itself in Hood's path. Too weak to go against Hood alone, but too closely pursued to avoid battle, General Schofield was forced to fight a number of small battles as he rushed to join Thomas at Nashville.

On November 28$^{th}$, Battery B went into position north of Columbia, but was not engaged. On the following day they moved in the direction of Spring Hill and went into line on the army's extreme right. General George Wagner, the commander of the Second Division of the Fourth Corps, to which Battery B was temporarily assigned, ordered one of Ziegler's sections to take a forward position and open fire on the enemy. An infantry regiment advanced in support of Ziegler's detached section, but soon after the cannoneers opened fire, the enemy charged, and the supporting infantry was driven back.

Orders immediately came from General Wagner to fall back as quickly as possible, and the detached section rejoined the other two sections and the entire battery opened fire. The enemy charge was broken, and when night fell Schofield broke off contact and started moving towards Nashville again.

On the 30$^{th}$ the men of the battery turned out at 2:00 a.m. and continued the march northward. An attack by Confederate cavalry forced Battery B to unlimber and take position around 9:00 a.m., but the cavalry withdrew and the battery re-limbered without having fired and resumed the march. They reached Franklin around 10:00 a.m. and were placed near the right of the Twenty-third Corps. The town of Franklin was located in a bend of the Harpeth River, and General Schofield formed his line in a half circle around the town with each flank anchored on the riverbank. His intention was to fight a holding action until nightfall and cross the river to his rear under cover of darkness.

The Confederates reached Franklin shortly after the Union troops, and General Hood had no intention of waiting until dark and letting the federals escape. Hood ordered a massive attack, and sometime between 3:30 p.m. and 4:00 p.m. the Confederates struck out toward the Union lines.

As the Confederates approached Franklin, they found General Wagner's troops in an advanced position nearly half a mile in front of the main Union line. Wagner had been given orders to withdraw if any large force of Confederates approached, but the order was misunderstood and Wagner's exposed division briefly stood its ground before being driven back with the Confederates right behind them. The failure of Wagner's division to withdraw sooner made it possible for the Confederates to practically follow them into the Union works, since the troops already there could not fire through Wagner's retreating men.

The Confederates briefly breeched a section of the Union center along the front of the Twenty-third Corps, which was to the left of Battery B's position, but were driven back when reserves were brought forward. The battle ended with the total and bloody repulse of the Confederates.

General Nathan Kimball praised the service of Battery B during the battle, reporting that "Captain Zeigler's battery on this, as on former occasions, did splendidly, inflicting severe punishment upon the enemy, and, in fact, at one time prevented the enemy penetrating our line near the right of the Second Division, Twenty-third Corps. Too much praise cannot be awarded this battery."[*] Battery B lost three men wounded, three horses killed, and four horses disabled during the battle.

Schofield withdrew that evening as planned and the victors of Franklin reached Nashville on the 1st of December. Like Franklin, Nashville was positioned within the bend of a river, and the defensive dispositions were very similar. General Thomas, who had been awaiting the arrival of Schofield, formed the Union line in a semicircle around the city with one flank anchored on the Cumberland River above the city and the other flank anchored on the river below.

When Hood's battered army arrived in front of Nashville on December 2nd, it was clearly in no condition to assault the well-manned works around the city. The Union forces were entrenched behind heavy earthworks, and now that Schofield's forces were reunited with General Thomas' troops, the Federals actually outnumbered the Confederates. Unwilling to withdraw, but unable to advance, General Hood decided to besiege the Union forces instead.

But when Hood began deploying his units, he did not have enough men to completely surround the city. Instead he entrenched along the widest arc he could manage and waited for General Thomas to come out and attack him. Unfortunately for General Hood, that is exactly what General Thomas intended to do.

General Thomas took his time in making preparations, and on the 8th of December a severe ice storm struck and halted major operations on both sides for several days. On that same day (before the ice storm began in earnest), the Confederates rushed and temporarily overran an advanced section of the Union line in General Schofield's sector, and Battery B assisted in retaking it.

The Union attack commenced on the 15th. It began with General Thomas' left wing striking out at General Hood's right

---

[*] O.R., series I vol. 45 pt. 1, 177 (No. 13), 178.

flank, but this was only intended as a diversion. Thomas' main assault was aimed at the other end of the line.

Battery B was ordered in the pre-dawn darkness to report to General Nathan Kimball's First Division of the Fourth Corps, and at 6:00 a.m. moved about 500 yards to the right of the Granny White Pike and was placed in rear of Kimball's infantry. At 9:00 a.m. Battery B began advancing with the division and at 2:00 p.m. it went into position in front of a hill near the Hillsborough Pike and opened fire on the Confederate works to its front. Two hours later Battery B advanced closer to the enemy's works and again opened fire. Battery B continued firing until 9:00 p.m. when it was recalled to its camp within the Nashville entrenchments, having suffered no casualties.

Col. Isaac M. Kirby of the 101$^{st}$ Ohio Infantry Regiment, who commanded the 1$^{st}$ Brigade of General Kimball's division during the action, said of Battery B:

> I was surprised to see Ziegler's battery again on my right in the open field and within easy musket-range of the enemy, and throwing shot into him thick and fast. This battery, together with one placed in position by General Kimball, near the left of my brigade, soon worked confusion in the ranks of rebeldom ....

At 7:00 a.m. on the 16$^{th}$, Independent Battery B advanced two and a half miles down the Franklin Pike before following in rear of the division into a cornfield to the right of the pike. Battery B unlimbered in the cornfield and opened fire on a group of Confederate batteries about 1000 yards to their front. Battery B soon came under enfilade fire from two different enemy batteries and began taking serious damage. Both guns of the left section were disabled when the axle of the section's right gun was smashed and an enemy shot broke off the trail of the section's left

---

* O.R., series I vol. 45 pt. 1, 184 (No.14), 185.

gun. One man was killed and two others were wounded in the exchange, and the disabled left section was withdrawn from the field. The right section, however, remained in position until relieved by Battery M, 4$^{th}$ U.S. Artillery (Lieutenant Samuel Canby's) at 1:00 p.m.

General Hood's army was completely defeated by the two-day Union attack and was driven from the field in total disarray. On the 17$^{th}$ of December the Union advance became a pursuit of the remnants of the Confederate army and Battery B moved out at daylight and camped opposite Franklin on the Little Harpeth River that night. The pursuit continued for a full week until the Confederates were chased all the way beyond the Duck River by December 24$^{th}$.

## 5. Triumph and Tragedy

As the campaign season of 1864 ended, a feeling began to permeate the army that the end of the war was finally approaching. In the Western theatre General Thomas had decisively smashed General Hood's Confederate Army of Tennessee and General Sherman was marching through the heart of the south without meeting any serious resistance. In Virginia, General Grant had cornered General Lee at Petersburg and was holding him in a death grip from which escape seemed impossible. It appeared that victory was finally within sight.

Battery E, 1$^{st}$ Pennsylvania Light Artillery (Orwig's) had been operating in eastern Virginia since 1862 and joined the siege operations at Petersburg in July of 1864. The battery was attached to General Benjamin Butler's "Army of the James," which occupied the center section of the Union line. After two years in command of Battery E, Captain Thomas G. Orwig resigned his commission on the 21$^{st}$ of September 1864. Lieutenant Henry Y. Wildey of Battery H was promoted to captain on the 1$^{st}$ of November and transferred to Battery E to replace Orwig.

During the winter months of late 1864 and early 1865, all of the batteries of the 1$^{st}$ Pennsylvania Light Artillery Regiment were recruited back to full strength and afterwards enough recruits were left over to form two new batteries. A new Battery C, 1$^{st}$ Pennsylvania Light Artillery was organized in December under Captain Sharp L. Richards. This battery replaced the original Battery C, which had been merged with Battery D back in October of 1863. The new Battery C was sent to West Virginia and spent its entire term of service in the vicinity of Harper's Ferry and in the Shenandoah Valley. The rest of the extra recruits were used to create Battery I, 1$^{st}$ Pennsylvania Light Artillery, under the command of Captain Sylvester B. Cameron. Battery I was organized on the 2$^{nd}$ of March and spent its entire term of service in the defenses of Washington.

In December of 1864 the men of Battery G, 1$^{st}$ Pennsylvania Light Artillery (Jennings') were ordered to leave Point of Rocks and march to Maryland Heights above Harper's Ferry, where they turned in the muskets they had been carrying since July and received a full new battery of cannon. Battery G remained at Maryland Heights until April, when they were ordered to return to the defenses of Washington. In March, Lieutenant Jennings' term expired and Lieutenant Eugene C. Moore acceded to the command of the battery. Moore was promoted to captain on the 15$^{th}$ of May, 1865.*

On the 1$^{st}$ of December 1864 Captain R. Bruce Ricketts of Battery F, 1$^{st}$ Pennsylvania was promoted to acting major and

---

* Captain Belden Spence of Battery G had mustered out on the 4$^{th}$ of December 1864. Captain Spence's status and assignment after the separation of Battery G from Battery F is not clear.

placed in charge of several batteries of the Second Corps. Battery F, which had been transferred from the Second Corps to the Artillery Reserve in September, was left under the command of Lieutenant John F. Campbell, who was promoted to captain on the 17th of April. Major Ricketts was soon transferred to the Ninth Corps where he served first as Inspector of Artillery and then as Chief of Artillery. On the 15th of March, Major Ricketts was again promoted, this time to colonel,* and was made Inspector of Artillery for the Artillery Reserve.

Also in early 1865, Captain Borrowe left the service and Lieutenant Edwin H. Nevin Jr. succeeded him in command of Pennsylvania Independent Battery H. Nevin would be promoted to captain on the 3rd of April.

At Petersburg General Grant kept his vise-grip on the Army of Northern Virginia all through the winter and spring of 1865. Since the beginning of the siege, the Union line was gradually extended further out in both directions. In the north, Richmond itself was encircled, and in the south, the last supply lines between the Confederate capital and the south Atlantic states were on the verge of capture.

Realizing that the pressure on the Confederate lines was at the snapping point, General Lee ordered the last major offensive that the Army of Northern Virginia would attempt during the war. Designed to throw the Union army off balance so that the Confederates could attempt a withdrawal from their lines around Petersburg and Richmond (which General Lee now accepted must both be abandoned), the attack was launched on the 25th of March against Fort Stedman, on a section of line near the upper side of

---

* Although Ricketts never mustered in under the rank of colonel, he was frequently referred to as "Colonel Ricketts" after the war, so presumably he did accept the promotion.

Petersburg and below where the opposing lines crossed the Appomattox River to the north.

The pre-dawn attack was initially successful in overrunning the forward Union works, but the Confederates were quickly pinned down by crossfire from the surrounding fortifications. Pinned down with them were a number of Union prisoners taken during the initial attack, including Major Theodore Miller, formerly the captain of Battery E, 1$^{st}$ Pennsylvania Light Artillery. Miller had left Battery E in 1862 to become an Assistant Adjutant General, and a month prior to the attack on Fort Stedman had been promoted to major and reassigned as Inspector of Artillery for the Ninth Corps.

The attack was a failure, and the choice for the Confederates was between returning to their own lines under fire or surrendering where they were. The Union artillery fire was too intense for the Confederates who captured Major Miller to even attempt a withdrawal, and Miller convinced them all to surrender to him instead. Miller was able to personally lead between 250 and 300 Confederates into the Union lines as his prisoners.

Meanwhile Pennsylvania Independent Battery D (Rhoads'), still serving with the Ninth Corps, was lightly engaged in repulsing the Confederate breakthrough, which took place to the north of Battery D's position. Immediately following the attack, Major Ricketts ordered Captain Rhoads to have his battery harness its horses and limber its guns in case they needed to move out quickly. Lieutenant Henry Sailor's section, which was on detached duty in nearby Fort Meikel, fired six rounds towards an enemy battery after receiving a few incoming rounds from them. Four of Sailor's rounds struck the embrasures of the enemy's guns and the Confederates ceased firing towards Fort Meikel. The Confederate attack, which began around dawn, was completely repulsed by 10:00 a.m. and Battery D unhitched its horse teams and returned its guns to their prior positions in the fortifications.

On the 1st of April, Battery B, 1st Pennsylvania Light Artillery (McClelland's) was ordered to report to Captain John C. Tidball, the Chief of Artillery of the Ninth Corps. A section of Confederate works had just been captured along the Jerusalem Plank Road, and Lieutenant Thomas C. Rice of Battery B was sent forward with two detachments to take charge of captured ordnance. The men from Battery B turned around several captured artillery pieces and began firing them at their previous owners. After Lieutenant Rice opened fire with the captured cannon, Captain McClelland went forward himself to assist in the operation. The next day a detachment from Pennsylvania Independent Battery D (Rhoads') was sent forward on a similar mission. Under the overall direction of one of Battery D's gunners, the men from Battery D supervised and assisted as several improvised gun crews taken from the infantry worked artillery pieces that had been captured from the enemy.

The 2nd of April was also the day that the Confederate lines were finally breeched and the remaining Confederate units withdrew from around Richmond and Petersburg. Batteries A & E, 1st Pennsylvania Light Artillery (Stitt's and Wildey's) entered Richmond on the 3rd with General Godfrey Weitzel's Twenty-fifth Corps. Both batteries were assigned to Lieutenant Colonel James Brady, who had come down from Washington, and were assigned the task of securing all of the captured Confederate ordnance in the city. The task was a very difficult one, since most of the remaining ordnance was heavy artillery pieces mounted at difficult to access locations throughout the city. The men of Batteries A and E succeeded, however, in shipping all salvageable materials northward and destroyed the rest without accident or loss.

Battery B, 1st Pennsylvania Light Artillery (McClelland's) was meanwhile taking part in the pursuit of the remnant of General Lee's army through the interior of Virginia. Battery B was engaged at Rice's Station on the 6th of April and reached Appomattox Courthouse by the 9th, on which date General Lee surrendered his army to General Grant.

**Captured Confederate Siege Artillery at Richmond, Spring 1865.
Image from the Library of Congress.**

By the time General Grant was accepting the surrender of the Army of Northern Virginia near the headwaters of the Appomattox, Pennsylvania Independent Battery C (Thompson's) had been serving in the Washington defenses for over a year. On the 14th of April, Good Friday of 1865, privates John Corey, Jabez Griffiths, William Sample, and Samuel Soles went into the city on leave for a little relaxation. They ended up at Ford's Theater where they took their seats for a performance of *Our American Cousin*, starring Miss Laura Keene.

Halfway through the first act, the play was interrupted by the arrival of President Lincoln, the first lady, and several of the President's guests, who took their places in a private box just above where the small party of Pennsylvania artillerists was seated. The play resumed, but was interrupted in the middle of Act III by a muffled explosion in the Presidential box. Immediately thereafter, a man later identified as John Wilkes Booth leapt from the box to the stage and shouted either "sic semper tyrannis" or "the South is avenged," or both (depending on the witness).

Booth ran from the stage as screams rang out from the box above. President Lincoln had been shot in the head. An army surgeon named Doctor Charles Leale was in the theater and rushed to the aid of the President. After a brief examination, Doctor Leale asked for help in carrying his unconscious patient out of the theater. Privates Corry, Griffiths, Sample, and Soles, along with two other men, went up to the box and lifted the prostrate form of Abraham Lincoln in their arms. Laura Keene led them downstairs and outside where an officer named Lieutenant James Bolton cleared the way through a crowd by brandishing his sword and cursing those who got too close.

The four artillerists carried their charge to the nearby home of William Petersen at 453 Tenth Street, where the unconscious and mortally wounded President was placed on a bed in a small room. The four men from Battery C stepped outside, their personal role in the national tragedy having ended. President Abraham Lincoln, who had led the United States of America through the Civil War, died a victim of that war several hours later.

Five days after the assassination, on the 19th of April, a select detachment of mounted men from Pennsylvania Independent Battery F (Irish's) were selected as an honor guard when the catafalque bearing Lincoln's coffin was taken from the White House to the train that would carry it across a mourning nation to the President's final resting place in Illinois.

In April and May, the terms of the original members of Pennsylvania Independent Battery F (Irish's) ended, and they mustered out. The remainder of the battery was returned to the Washington defenses. Battery G, 1st Pennsylvania (Moore's), meanwhile, was once again issued muskets for duty as improvised infantry and would spend the rest of their service moving from post to post within the fortifications around the nation's capital.

## 6. The Guns Fall Silent

With the surrender of the Army of Northern Virginia, the various Confederate department commanders realized that the war was effectively over, and one by one they surrendered to their Union army counterparts. Pennsylvania Independent Battery E (Sloan's) had marched north with Sherman through the Carolinas after leaving Savannah on the 27th of January. They faced hard marching over poor roads, but reached Raleigh, North Carolina by the 13th of April without serious incident, although one man had been wounded and two others captured while on foraging details. An improvised force under the command of Sherman's old adversary, Joseph Johnston, was lurking to the north, but after receiving word of General Lee's surrender to Grant, General Johnston surrendered to Sherman.

On the 10th of May, President Andrew Johnson declared "armed resistance to the authority of this government may be regarded as virtually at an end." With the war officially concluded, the victorious Union armies converged on Washington, and on the 23rd and 24th of May, they paraded through the city in a final Grand Review before setting out for their home states and a return to civilian life. Their last task completed, one by one

Pennsylvania's field batteries turned in their guns to the military authorities and returned home to muster out:

Battery A, 1st Pennsylvania Light Artillery (Stitt's) mustered out on July 25th in Harrisburg. In addition to Captain Hezekiah Easton, who was struck down at the Battle of Gaines' Mill, Battery A lost during its term of service sixteen enlisted men killed or mortally wounded and twenty enlisted men who succumbed to disease.

Battery B, 1st Pennsylvania Light Artillery (McClelland's) mustered out on June 9th in Harrisburg. Their losses included two officers killed, nineteen enlisted men killed or mortally wounded, and seventeen enlisted men who succumbed to disease. Battery B therefore lost more men killed in battle during the war than any other volunteer field battery in the Union army.

Battery C, 1st Pennsylvania Light Artillery (Richard's), the second battery to bear the name, mustered out on June 30th in Harrisburg. Their total losses included two enlisted men killed and twelve enlisted men who succumbed to disease.

Battery D, 1st Pennsylvania Light Artillery (Munk's), into which the original Battery C had been consolidated in 1863, mustered out on June 29th in Harrisburg. The battery's total losses included eleven enlisted men killed or mortally wounded, and eighteen enlisted men and one officer who succumbed to disease.

Battery E, 1st Pennsylvania Light Artillery (Wildey's) mustered out on July 20th in Philadelphia. Their losses included two enlisted men killed or mortally wounded, and twenty-one enlisted men who succumbed to disease.

Battery F, 1st Pennsylvania Light Artillery (Campbell's) mustered out on June 10th in Harrisburg. Lieutenant Henry L. Godbald, who was mortally wounded at Rappahannock Station, was the only officer in Battery F to die in service. Seventeen enlisted men, however, were killed during the war and thirteen succumbed to disease.

Battery G, 1st Pennsylvania Light Artillery (Moore's) mustered out on June 29th in Philadelphia. Captain Kern, who was killed at the Second Battle of Bull Run, was the only officer from Battery G to fall during the war. The battery's enlisted losses totaled sixteen men killed or mortally wounded and fourteen who succumbed to disease.

Battery H, 1st Pennsylvania Light Artillery mustered out on June 27th in Philadelphia. Captain Andrew Fagan had left the battery on the 1st of May and Lieutenant Lord B. Richards had been promoted to captain as his replacement on the 5th of June, only twenty-two days before the battery mustered out. Battery H lost one enlisted man killed in action and one officer and eighteen enlisted men who succumbed to disease.

Battery I, 1st Pennsylvania Light Artillery (Cameron's), youngest of the regiment's batteries, mustered out on July 1st in Philadelphia, with no losses.

Pennsylvania Independent Battery A (Miotkowski's) mustered out on June 30th in Philadelphia. Their entire term of service had been spent at Fort Delaware and their total losses were one officer and sixteen enlisted men who succumbed to disease.

Pennsylvania Independent Battery B (Zeigler's) was sent to Texas after the surrenders of the two principle Confederate armies under Lee and Johnston. At the time, the Government was concerned about events in Mexico, where the French had sent troops to support the puppet-emperor Maximilian I, and a force was sent under General Sheridan to reassert federal authority along the line of the Rio Grande. Nothing came of this, and Battery B mustered out on October 12th in Victoria, Texas. Battery B had lost two captains killed in action during the course of the war. Captain Alanson J. Stevens fell at the Battle of

Chickamauga, and his successor, Captain Samuel M. McDowell, was killed at Kennesaw Mountain. The battery's losses among enlisted men totaled to eight killed or mortally wounded and twenty-five who succumbed to disease.

Pennsylvania Independent Battery C (Thompson's) mustered out on June 30th in Pittsburgh. The battery lost two enlisted men killed and twenty-one enlisted men who succumbed to disease.

Pennsylvania Independent Battery D (Rhoads') mustered out on June 13th in Philadelphia. Battery D's losses included one officer mortally wounded, Lieutenant Howard McIlvaine, who died of wounds received at White Sulphur Springs, and two enlisted men killed or mortally wounded and twenty-one enlisted men who succumbed to disease.

Pennsylvania Independent Battery E (Sloan's) mustered out on June 14th in Pittsburgh. Battery E lost two officers during the war, Captain Charles A. Atwell and Lieutenant Edward R. Geary, who were both killed at the Battle of Wauhatchie Station. The battery's enlisted losses were twelve killed or mortally wounded and eleven who succumbed to disease.

Pennsylvania Independent Battery F (Irish's) mustered out on June 26th in Washington, D.C. Its original captain, Robert B. Hampton, was killed at the Battle of Chancellorsville, and Lieutenant Joseph L. Miller was mortally wounded at the Battle of Gettysburg (while the battery was attached to Independent Battery C). The battery's enlisted losses were eight killed or mortally wounded and fourteen who succumbed to disease.

Pennsylvania Independent Battery G (Young's) mustered out on June 15th after spending its entire term of service at Fort Delaware, having lost nine men to disease.

Pennsylvania Independent Battery H (Edwin H. Nevin's) mustered out on June 18th in Pittsburgh. Battery H had spent its entire term of service in the Washington defenses and lost seven men to disease.

Pennsylvania Independent Battery I (Robert J. Nevin's) mustered out on June 23$^{rd}$ in Philadelphia, having suffered no losses.

●○●

# Epilogue

With the war ended, the men of both armies returned to their homes. Pennsylvania's veterans resumed their earlier lives as farmers, laborers, miners, businessmen, artisans, preachers, lawyers, shoemakers, blacksmiths, or whatever other vocation they had pursued before the war. Most of the men who served in the Pennsylvania field artillery soon faded into the general obscurity of civilian life in peaceful times, but a few figures would re-emerge to add new footnotes to the history of the Commonwealth and of the world.

Robert Bruce Ricketts, who had set aside a plan to study law at Yale in order to join the army in 1861, returned home and was highly successful as a land speculator and partner in a lumber concern. In 1886 he was on the ballot as the Democratic Party's nominee for Lieutenant Governor of Pennsylvania, but the Democrats lost to the Republicans that year. After his death, the Colonel's family transferred his sprawling estate to the Commonwealth of Pennsylvania and it became the nucleus of "Ricketts' Glen State Park," which was named in his honor. The park draws many visitors each year with its scenic waterfalls and other natural wonders.

**Colonel R. Bruce Ricketts.
Image from the Sullivan
County Historical Society.**

William McClelland, the captain of Battery B, 1st Pennsylvania Light Artillery, was more successful than Ricketts in his political ambitions. McClelland was elected to Congress in 1870 and served a single term representing Pennsylvania in the U.S. House of Representatives.

Another officer of the Pennsylvania field artillery would leave his mark in the history of the Church. Robert J. Nevin, erstwhile commander of Pennsylvania Independent Battery I, returned to theology studies that had been interrupted by the war, and was ordained as an Episcopalian priest in 1867; he would go on to establish the first ever Protestant Church in the city of Rome.

**The Hon. William McClelland**     **The Rev. Robert J. Nevin**

Image of William McClelland, former captain of Battery B, 1st Pennsylvania Light Artillery from the P.R.V.C. Historical Society; Image of Robert J. Nevin, former captain of Pennsylvania Independent Battery I, from Trinity Episcopal Church, Bethlehem, PA.

Even before the Civil War ended, a movement began to preserve portions of certain battlefields as places to honor the sacrifices of the soldiers who fought there. In 1864, a group called the Gettysburg Battlefield Memorial Association began safekeeping the site of the largest battle ever fought on American soil. In 1895 the lands under their charge were transferred to the federal government and became the Gettysburg National Military Park.

By that time societies had been organized all over the country to raise funds for erecting monuments to particular military organizations. Each Pennsylvania battery that had fought at Gettysburg eventually had a monument marking one or more of the positions it occupied during the struggle. The dedication of such monuments was a significant occasion for which the surviving veterans would all gather together. The program usually included a speech in which a member of the unit, usually the former commander, if he was still alive, would retell the story of the unit's wartime service.

At the dedication of the monument of Pennsylvania Independent Battery C, Captain James Thompson, who had immigrated to the United States from Ireland in 1856 (the same year he was discharged from the British Royal Regiment of Artillery with the rank of sergeant), raised a battery for the defense of his adopted country in 1861, and only gained formal American citizenship in 1863, greeted his old comrades and recounted the roll they played in preserving their country on the ground of the war's most famous battlefield. Colonel Ricketts prepared a sketch of the services of Batteries F & G, 1$^{st}$ Pennsylvania Light Artillery, which were combined under his command during that battle. Lieutenant James A. Gardner gave the address at the dedication of the monument of Battery B, 1$^{st}$ Pennsylvania Light Artillery. Gardner retold the story of the battery's creation and wartime service, and ended by speaking to his comrades about the future. Although he was addressing his fellow veterans of Battery B, his message could just as easily have been for all of the veterans of the Pennsylvania field artillery service, or indeed every veteran of the Civil War:

> Almost a quarter of a century has rolled around since the war closed, and you are all growing old. Soon the cold hand of the destroyer will lay hold of you; and though your locks are becoming gray with fast declining years, though your steps are

unsteady and your bodily infirmities are fast increasing, all caused by the hardships and privations of a cruel war; yet this we know - the fires of your lofty patriotism will continue to burn brightly to the end. You have fought a good fight[;] you have run the course. May the glory of your mighty deeds, and the cloudy pillar which hovered over all of us upon many a well-fought field, ever keep us in the way of truth and righteousness, and direct us onward and upward to the Promised Land, where we shall enroll ourselves anew in the armies of the Great Ruler who hath given all the victories.[*]

The greatest reunion of Civil War veterans occurred in 1913 and commemorated the fiftieth anniversary of the Battle of Gettysburg. The Commonwealth of Pennsylvania invited every living honorably discharged veteran of the Civil War, whether they fought for the Union or the Confederacy, to attend a massive encampment at the site of the battle. More than 50,000 veterans attended the weeklong event, which included a reenactment of Pickett's Charge in which the former antagonists exchanged handshakes instead of bullets. On the 4$^{th}$ of July they were addressed by President Woodrow Wilson, who expressed the gratitude of the nation: "These venerable men crowding here to this famous field have set us a great example of devotion and utter sacrifice. They were willing to die that the people might live. But their task is done."

Another reunion was held in 1938 to commemorate the seventy-fifth anniversary of the battle, but by that time far fewer veterans were still alive, and only about 18,000 were able to attend.

Today, Gettysburg National Military Park draws large crowds of visitors each year who come to stand on the ground where the fate of the country was decided in 1863. Rows of old cannon and stone monuments still mark the spots where Cooper's Battery B

---

[*] *Pennsylvania at Gettysburg* at vol. 2, 916.

fought on the first and second days of the battle, where Ricketts' combined Battery F & G broke the charge of the Louisiana Tigers on Cemetery Hill, where Thompson's Battery C & F struggled in the shadow of Little Round Top, where Knap's Battery E faced the enemy near Culp's Hill, and where the rising Confederate tide was scattered by the repulse of Pickett's Charge.

●○●

# APPENDIX A:
# OFFICER LISTINGS BY ORGANIZATION

\* Officers with asterisks after their names commanded the organization.

### The Ringgold Light Artillery

**James McKnight\***
James McKnight founded the Ringgold Light Artillery in 1850 and commanded the organization through its entire pre-war period and through its active service in 1861. Before the war he was the co-owner of a Reading hardware store.

**Henry Nagle**
First lieutenant of the Ringgold Light Artillery, Henry Nagle was later promoted to captain and given command of a new company comprising extra men from the Ringgold Light Artillery and the National Light Infantry Company of Pottsville. This new company, sometimes referred to as the "Second Ringgold Infantry," became Company "C" of the 25th Pennsylvania Infantry Regiment (the original Ringgold Light Artillery became Company "A" of the same regiment).

**William Graeff**
Second lieutenant of the Ringgold Light Artillery.

### Regimental Headquarters, 1st Pennsylvania Light Artillery

**Charles T. Campbell\***
Mustered in on May 29, 1861. Campbell was promoted from captain of Battery A to lieutenant colonel when the regiment was formed. When Colonel Richard H. Rush declined the command of the regiment, Lt. Col. Campbell became the commanding officer. Campbell left the regiment on December 9, 1861 to take command of the 57th Pennsylvania Infantry Regiment. In November of 1862 Campbell became a brigadier general and was given command of a military district in Wisconsin.

### Henry T. Danforth*
Mustered in on September 13, 1861. During the organization of the regiment Danforth was promoted from captain of Battery B to major on August 1, 1861, and was again promoted to lieutenant colonel on September 13, 1861. Danforth resigned his commission on December 21, 1861 and enlisted back into Battery B, where he was soon commissioned as a second lieutenant. He was killed at the Battle of Glendale on June 30, 1862. Henry T. Danforth had previously served in Battery C, $3^{rd}$ U.S. Artillery during the Mexican War.

### Robert M. West*
Mustered in on July 26, 1861. Originally the captain of Battery G, West was promoted to major on September 13, 1861 and again to colonel on July 29, 1862. Following the Peninsula Campaign, West spent the next two years on detached service commanding various combined armed forces in the vicinity of Yorktown. On May 29, 1864 Colonel West transferred to the $5^{th}$ Pennsylvania Cavalry Regiment.

### James Brady*
Mustered in on July 8, 1861. The original promoter of the regiment and the first captain of Battery H, James Brady was promoted to major on July 19, 1862 and to lieutenant colonel on November 13, 1863. Brady served as Chief of Artillery for the Department of the Susquehanna during the Gettysburg campaign and assisted in the defense of Harrisburg. In late 1863 Brady briefly commanded the First Volunteer Brigade of the Artillery Reserve of the Army of the Potomac before becoming Chief of Artillery for a section of the Washington defenses. On the transfer of Colonel West, Lieutenant Colonel Brady acceded to the command of the regiment, but continued to actually serve in the Washington defenses with his headquarters at Fort Corcoran. Brady was brevetted to colonel on March 13, 1865 and mustered out on July 19, 1865.

### R. Bruce Ricketts
Mustered in on July 8, 1861. Ricketts was promoted from captain of Battery F to major on December 1, 1864. Major Ricketts served variously as a provisional artillery brigade commander in the Second Corps, an Inspector of Artillery in the Ninth Corps, and as the Chief of Artillery for the Ninth Corps. On March 15, 1865 he was again promoted to colonel, but never mustered in under that rank. He then served as Inspector of Artillery for the Artillery Reserve until discharged

from the service on June 3, 1865. Ricketts' descendants transferred a large part of his estate to the state of Pennsylvania to form the nucleus of a state park that was named in his honor. Ricketts' Glen State Park is located across 13,000 acres of Luzerne, Sullivan and Columbia counties.

**Edward H. Flood**
Mustered in on May 29, 1861. Formerly the captain on Battery D, Flood was promoted to lieutenant colonel on July 19, 1862 and was discharged from the service on September 22, 1863.

**Alfred E. Lewis**
Mustered in on July 6, 1861. Originally the captain on Battery E, Lewis was promoted to lieutenant colonel on August 1, 1861 and discharged on July 29, 1862.

**Ezra W. Matthews**
Mustered in on July 8, 1861. Originally the captain on Battery F, Matthews was forced to leave Battery F in late 1862 on account of illness. He was promoted to major on March 14, 1863 and discharged on July 29, 1863.

**Theodore Miller**
Mustered in on August 1, 1861. Formerly the captain of Battery E, Miller left Battery E on July 4, 1862 to serve as an Assistant Adjutant General. He was promoted to major on February 24, 1865 and assigned as Inspector of Artillery for the Ninth Corps. On March 25, 1865, during the siege of Petersburg, Major Miller was present during the Confederate attack on Fort Stedman, and was captured by a party of the enemy. The Union artillery fire being too intense to permit the Confederates to withdraw to their own lines with their prisoner, Major Miller convinced them to surrender to him instead, and led between 250 and 300 of them back into Union lines as his prisoners. Miller was discharged on June 2, 1865.

**Edward Shippen**
Regimental Surgeon. Mustered in on August 5, 1861 and resigned on September 17, 1862.

**M. F. Price**
Regimental Surgeon. Mustered in on August 2, 1862 to replace Surgeon Edward Shippen and resigned on September 18, 1863.

**James R. Riley**
Assistant Surgeon. Mustered in on August 5, 1861. On August 26, 1862 Riley was promoted to full Surgeon and transferred to the 127th Pennsylvania Infantry.

**B. M. Patterson**
Assistant Surgeon. Mustered in on August 26, 1862 as a replacement for Assistant Surgeon James Riley, who was promoted and transferred. Patterson died on December 16, 1862.

**W. A. P. Eberhart**
Chaplain. Mustered in on September 13, 1861 and discharged for medical reasons on July 21, 1862.

## Battery A, 1st Pennsylvania Light Artillery

**Hezekiah Easton\***
Mustered in on May 29, 1861. Hezekiah Easton was promoted to captain and given command of the battery when Charles T. Campbell (who organized the battery) was chosen as lieutenant colonel of the regiment. Easton was killed at the Battle of Gaines' Mill on June 27, 1862. Prior to the war, Easton had been a successful businessman in the Greencastle-Antrim area of Franklin County, Pennsylvania.

**John G. Simpson\***
Mustered in on August 5, 1861. First Lieutenant (later Captain) John G. Simpson assumed command of the battery after the death of Captain Easton, and continued in command until dismissed from the service on August 21, 1864.

**William Stitt\***
Mustered in on May 29, 1861. One of the batteries original second lieutenants, William Stitt was promoted to first lieutenant on December 26, 1861. He assumed command of the battery following Captain Simpson's dismissal, and was promoted to captain on September 17, 1864. William Stitt remained in command of the battery until the entire unit mustered out on July 25, 1865.

**W. H. Sullenberger**
Mustered in on May 29, 1861. One of the batteries original first lieutenants, W. H. Sullenberger resigned his commission on November 12, 1861.

**H. E. Palsgrove**
Mustered in on May 29, 1861. One of the batteries original first lieutenants, H. E. Palsgrove resigned his commission on December 1, 1861.

**Charles T. Campbell**
Mustered in on May 29, 1861. Charles T. Campbell was promoted to first lieutenant on December 21, 1861 (following the resignations of W. H. Sullenberger and H. E. Palsgrove) and resigned his commission on February 8, 1862.

**Samuel D. Martin**
Samuel D. Martin enlisted on May 29, 1861. On March 6, 1862 he was promoted to first sergeant. He received his commission as a second lieutenant on February 24, 1864. He was promoted to first lieutenant on November 27, 1864, and mustered out with the battery on July 25, 1865.

**William R. Brown**
William R. Brown enlisted on May 29, 1861 as a private and was promoted to first sergeant on December 1, 1864. He received his commission as a first lieutenant on March 1, 1865, and mustered out with the battery on July 25, 1865.

**Jacob L. Deitriek**
Mustered in on May 29, 1861. Second Lieutenant Jacob L. Deitriek was wounded during the Second Battle of Bull Run on August 30, 1862 and was discharged on medical grounds on January 24, 1863.

**Peter Cummings**
Mustered in on May 29, 1861. Second Lieutenant Peter Cummings was dismissed from the service on December 18, 1863.

**John H. Kline**
John H. Kline enlisted on May 29, 1861. Kline was promoted to corporal on December 18, 1862, and to sergeant on December 24, 1863. He received his commission as a second lieutenant on March 1, 1865, and mustered out with the battery on July 25, 1865.

## Battery B, 1st Pennsylvania Light Artillery

**James H. Cooper***
Mustered in on June 28, 1861. Originally the battery's first sergeant during the brief tenure of Henry T. Danforth (promoted to major when the regiment was organized), James H. Cooper was commissioned as a second lieutenant on June 28, 1861, and promoted to captain on August 2, 1861. Cooper left the battery on August 8, 1864 at the expiration of his term of service. In September of 1864 Cooper was promoted to major but never mustered in under that rank.

**William McClelland***
William McClelland enlisted as a private and was mustered in on June 28, 1861. On April 8, 1864 he was commissioned as a second lieutenant, and on September 12, 1864 he was promoted to first lieutenant. Following the expiration of James H. Cooper's term of service, McClelland took command of the battery and was promoted to captain on February 23, 1865. He mustered out with the battery on June 9, 1865. McClelland was elected to Congress in 1870, served for one term in the House of Representatives, and died in 1892.

**Isaac A. Nesbit**
Mustered in on June 28, 1861. First Lieutenant Isaac A. Nesbit was dismissed from the service on March 14, 1864.

**James S. Fullerton**
Mustered in on June 28, 1861. First Lieutenant James S. Fullerton was discharged from the service on December 7, 1862.

**William C. Miller**
William C. Miller enlisted as a private on July 13, 1861. He was commissioned as a second lieutenant on August 1, 1862 and promoted to first lieutenant on April 8, 1864. He mustered out at the expiration of his term on November 22, 1864. Miller was wounded at the Second Battle of Bull Run on August 29, 1862, and again during the Battle of Gettysburg, on July 2, 1863.

189

### Thomas C. Rice
Thomas C. Rice enlisted as a private on October 6, 1861, and was promoted to first sergeant on June 28, 1864. On September 13, 1864 Rice was commissioned as a second lieutenant, and on February 23, 1865 he was promoted to first lieutenant. He mustered out with the battery on June 9, 1865.

### James A. Gardner
James A. Gardner enlisted as a private on July 23, 1861. He was promoted to corporal on April 1, 1864, to sergeant on June 28, 1864, and to first sergeant on September 13, 1864. On March 1, 1865 Gardner was commissioned as a first lieutenant. He mustered out with the battery on June 9, 1865. On September 11, 1889 James A. Gardner delivered the keynote address at the dedication ceremony for the battery's monument on Cemetery Hill in Gettysburg.

### Thomas Cadwalader
Thomas Cadwalader enlisted on June 28, 1861. Formerly the battery's first sergeant, he was commissioned as a second lieutenant on August 2, 1861. Second Lieutenant Cadwalader was killed at the Battle of Glendale on June 30, 1862.

### Henry T. Danforth
The original organizer and commander of the battery, Henry T. Danforth was promoted to major during the organization of the regiment. After a brief period of service as a staff officer (during which he was promoted again to lieutenant colonel), Danforth resigned his commission and enlisted back into Battery B, where he was soon commissioned as a second lieutenant. He was killed at the Battle of Glendale on June 30, 1862. Henry T. Danforth had previously served in Battery C, $3^{rd}$ U.S. Artillery during the Mexican War.

### James P. Alcorn
Having originally enlisted in the battery in 1862, and having since then been promoted first to corporal and then to sergeant, James P. Alcorn was commissioned as a second lieutenant on April 8, 1864. He mustered out at the expiration of his term on November 23, 1864.

### J. M. Pennypacker
Having originally enlisted in the battery in 1862, and having since then been promoted first to corporal and then to sergeant, J. M. Pennypacker

was commissioned as a second lieutenant on March 1, 1865. He mustered out with the battery on June 9, 1865.

**John H. Gealy**
Having originally enlisted in the battery in 1862, Corporal John H. Gealy was commissioned as a second lieutenant on Mar. 1, 1865. He mustered out with the battery on June 9, 1865.

## Battery C, 1st Pennsylvania Light Artillery

**J. G. Simpson***
Mustered in on June 15, 1861. Simpson was succeeded by McCarthy as commander of the battery on August 5, 1861 and was discharged on December 9, 1861.

**Jeremiah McCarthy***
Mustered in on June 15, 1861. McCarthy replaced J. G. Simpson as commander of the battery and was promoted to captain on August 5, 1861. In early 1863 Battery C was disbanded and the men reassigned to Battery D, at which time McCarthy took command of Battery D in place of Captain Michael Hall, who resigned. McCarthy left the service in June of 1863 due to illness.

**Sharp L. Richards**
Mustered in on July 24, 1861. Second Lieutenant Sharp L. Richards was promoted to first lieutenant on July 20, 1862. Lieutenant Richards appears to have transferred to Battery D in early 1863 when Batteries C and D were consolidated. On February 23, 1865 Richards was briefly discharged from the service before returning on March 5, at which time he was commissioned as a captain and given command of a new Battery C, 1st Pennsylvania Light Artillery which was raised to replace the original Battery C. He mustered out with that battery on June 29, 1865.

**M. J. Byrne**
Mustered in on June 15, 1861. Second Lieutenant Byrne was promoted to first lieutenant on August 5, 1861, and resigned his commission on January 1, 1862.

### Solomon Barnes
Mustered in on June 15, 1861. First Lieutenant Barnes was discharged from the service on December 9, 1861.

### M. Reichenbach
Mustered in on December 19, 1861. First Lieutenant Reichenbach was discharged from the service on March 31, 1863 following the consolidation of Battery C with Battery D.

### Richard M. Ball
Mustered in on June 15, 1861. Second Lieutenant Ball appears to have transferred to Battery D in early 1863 when Batteries C and D were consolidated and was promoted to first lieutenant on September 16, 1863. Lieutenant Ball appears was discharged from the service on March 28, 1865.

### Joseph Benson
Having originally enlisted in the battery on June 15, 1861, Joseph Benson was commissioned as a second lieutenant on February 6, 1862. He resigned his commission on March 16, 1863 following the consolidation of Battery C with Battery D.

### Frederick Fiedler
Mustered in on June 15, 1861. Second Lieutenant Fiedler resigned his commission on March 14, 1863 following the consolidation of Battery C with Battery D.

### Robert B. Kennedy
Mustered in on November 23, 1863. Second Lieutenant Kennedy resigned his commission on an unknown later date.

## Battery C, 1st Pennsylvania Light Artillery (Second)

### Sharp L. Richards*
Mustered into the original Battery C on July 24, 1861 and was promoted to first lieutenant on July 20, 1862. Lieutenant Richards appears to have transferred to Battery D in early 1863 when the original Battery C was consolidated with Battery D. On February 23, 1865 Richards was briefly discharged from the service before returning on March 5, at which time he was commissioned as a captain and given command of the new

Battery C, which was raised to replace the original Battery C. Captain Richards mustered out on June 29, 1865.

**Charles C. Wentz**
Having originally enlisted on November 23, 1863, Sergeant Charles C. Wentz was commissioned as a second lieutenant in the new Battery C on March 9, 1865, and promoted to first lieutenant on March 30, 1865. He mustered out with the battery on June 29, 1865.

**Frank Langle**
Having originally enlisted on November 27, 1863, Quartermaster Sergeant Langle transferred to the new Battery C and was commissioned as a second lieutenant on June 5, 1865. He mustered out with the battery on June 29, 1865.

## Battery D, 1<sup>st</sup> Pennsylvania Light Artillery

**Edward H. Flood\***
Mustered in on July 6, 1861. The battery's original commander, Captain Flood was promoted to lieutenant colonel on July 19, 1862 and was discharged from the service on September 22, 1863.

**Michael Hall\***
Mustered in on October 1, 1861. Hall took command of the battery upon the promotion of Edward H. Flood to lieutenant colonel on July 19, 1862 and was himself promoted from first lieutenant to captain on June 29, 1862. Captain Hall resigned his commission on March 21, 1863 after Battery C and Battery D were consolidated and Captain McCarthy, as the senior of the two, retained command.

**Jeremiah McCarthy\***
Mustered into Battery C on June 15, 1861 and was promoted to captain on August 5, 1861. In early 1863 Battery C was disbanded and the men reassigned to Battery D, at which time McCarthy took command of Battery D in place of Captain Hall. McCarthy left the service in June of 1863 due to illness.

**William Munk\***
Mustered in on June 15, 1861. William Munk was commissioned as a second lieutenant on November 28, 1863, and promoted to first

lieutenant on January 21, 1864. McCarthy's successor in command, Munk was promoted to captain on March 9, 1865. He mustered out with the battery on June 30, 1865.

### Andrew Rosney
Enlisted on June 15, 1861. Formerly the battery's first sergeant, Rosney was commissioned as a second lieutenant on August 23, 1862, and promoted to first lieutenant on August 11, 1863. He appears to have been promoted to captain on January 20, 1864, but does not appear to have served in command of the battery. Rosney resigned his commission on September 6, 1864.

### Edward Dougherty
Mustered in on July 6, 1861. Second Lieutenant Dougherty was promoted to first lieutenant on August 5, 1861 and resigned his commission on March 3, 1863.

### F. McLaughlin
Mustered in on July 6, 1861. First Lieutenant McLaughlin died on June 4, 1862.

### George Munce
Enlisted on July 6, 1861. Munce was commissioned as a second lieutenant on July 20, 1862 and promoted to first lieutenant ten days later on July 30, 1862. He resigned his commission on March 21, 1863.

### Thomas Malone
Enlisted on July 6, 1861. Malone was commissioned as a second lieutenant on August 5, 1861. He resigned his commission on September 20, 1861.

### James Boyle
Enlisted on August 27, 1861. Boyle was commissioned as a second lieutenant on August 12, 1863, and mustered out with the battery on June 30, 1865.

### William Caley
Enlisted on July 25, 1861. Caley was commissioned as a second lieutenant on June 21, 1864 and mustered out with the battery on June 30, 1865.

## Battery E, 1st Pennsylvania Light Artillery

**Alfred E. Lewis***
Mustered in on June 20, 1861. The original captain of the battery, Alfred E. Lewis was promoted to major on August 1, 1861. Lewis was discharged from the service on July 29, 1862.

**Jacob M. Barr***
Mustered in on June 20, 1861. Temporarily Alfred E. Lewis' successor in command of the battery, Captain Barr resigned his commission on December 12, 1861.

**Theodore Miller***
Mustered in with Battery H on August 1, 1861. When Captain Barr resigned on December 12, 1861, First Lieutenant Miller was promoted to captain and given command of Battery E the following day. Captain Miller left the battery on July 4, 1862 to serve as an Assistant Adjutant General. Miller was subsequently promoted to major on February 24, 1865 and assigned as Inspector of Artillery for the Ninth Corps. On March 25, 1865, during the siege of Petersburg, Major Miller was present during the Confederate attack on Fort Stedman, and was captured by a party of the enemy. The Union artillery fire being too intense to permit the Confederates to withdraw to their own lines with their prisoner, Major Miller convinced them to surrender to him instead, and led between 250 and 300 of them back into Union lines as his prisoners. Miller was discharged on June 2, 1865.

**Thomas G. Orwig***
Mustered in on June 20, 1861. First Lieutenant Orwig succeeded Theodore Miller in command of the battery when Miller left on July 4, 1862 to serve as an Assistant Adjutant General. Thomas G. Orwig was promoted to captain on August 11, 1862, and resigned his commission on September 21, 1864.

**Henry Y. Wildey***
Mustered in with Battery H on August 1, 1861. Thomas G. Orwig's successor in command of the battery, Wildey was transferred to Battery E and promoted to captain on November 1, 1864, and mustered out with the battery on July 20, 1865.

### Abington W. Minich
Mustered in on June 20, 1861. First Lieutenant Abington W. Minich was dismissed from the service on February 28, 1862.

### John Hardy
Mustered in on June 20, 1861. First Lieutenant John Hardy resigned his commission on November, 1861.

### Frank C. Choate
Mustered in on June 20, 1861. Second Lieutenant Choate transferred to Battery H on July 16, 1862. He was promoted to captain and given command of a battery of U.S. Colored Light Artillery on December 28, 1863.

### Benjamin M. Orwig
Enlisted on June 20, 1861. Benjamin M. Orwig was commissioned as a second lieutenant on November 17, 1863, and promoted to first lieutenant on August 30, 1864. He was discharged from the service on March 16, 1865.

### William C. Wick
Mustered in on June 22, 1861. Second Lieutenant Wick was dismissed from the service on July 18, 1863.

### William H. Kilgore
Enlisted on June 20, 1861. Originally the battery's quartermaster sergeant, Kilgore was commissioned as a second lieutenant on June 1, 1864 and promoted to first lieutenant on February 27, 1865. He mustered out with the battery July 20, 1865.

### John Hassler
Enlisted on June 20, 1861. Hassler was commissioned as a second lieutenant on August 12, 1862, and resigned his commission on September 6, 1862 to join Company "D" of the 158th Pennsylvania Infantry, still as a second lieutenant. He mustered in to that company on November 4, 1862 and mustered out with them on August 12, 1863.

### Gustavus Reeling
Enlisted on June 20, 1861. Reeling was commissioned as a second lieutenant on August 31, 1864 and resigned his commission on June 5, 1865.

### John Perrin
John Perrin originally enlisted as a private on November 4, 1861. He was promoted to corporal on August 10, 1864 and to sergeant on October 4, 1864. Perrin was commissioned as a second lieutenant on February 27, 1865. He was promoted to first lieutenant on March 17, 1865 but never mustered in under that rank. John Perrin mustered out with the battery on July 20, 1865.

## Battery F, 1st Pennsylvania Light Artillery

### Ezra W. Matthews*
Mustered in on July 8, 1861. The original commander of the battery, Captain Matthews was forced to leave the battery due to illness shortly after the Battle of Antietam in late 1862. He was later promoted to major on March 14, 1863 and discharged on July 29, 1863.

### Robert Bruce Ricketts*
Mustered in on July 8, 1861. Ricketts was promoted from second lieutenant to first lieutenant on August 5, 1861. On September 23, 1862, immediately after Captain Matthews left the battery, Ricketts was given command. He was later promoted to captain in early 1863. On December 1, 1864 Ricketts was promoted to major, and on March 15, 1865 he was promoted to colonel, but never mustered in under that rank. Robert Bruce Ricketts was discharged from the service on June 3, 1865. Ricketts' descendants transferred a large part of his estate to the state of Pennsylvania to form the nucleus of a state park that was named in his honor. Ricketts' Glen State Park is located across 13,000 acres of Luzerne, Sullivan and Columbia counties.

### John F. Campbell*
Enlisted on July 8, 1861. John F. Campbell was commissioned to second lieutenant on May 20, 1864 and to first lieutenant on December 6, 1864. He assumed command of the battery following the promotion of R. Bruce Ricketts to major, and was himself promoted to captain on April 17, 1865. He mustered out with the battery on June 9, 1865

### Charles B. Brockway
Mustered in on July 8, 1861. Sergeant Charles B. Brockway was commissioned as a second lieutenant on February 28, 1862. He was taken prisoner during the Second Battle of Bull Run and, following his

exchange in late 1862, was promoted to first lieutenant on March 16, 1863. He was promoted to captain on November 30, 1864 but never mustered in under that rank. On March 13, 1865 he was brevetted to the rank of captain, and on October 22, 1864 he was discharged from the service.

### Elbridge McConkey
Mustered in on July 8, 1861. Second Lieutenant McConkey was promoted to first lieutenant on August 5, 1861 and resigned his commission on February 20, 1

### Henry L Godbald
Mustered in on July 8, 1861. Lieutenant Godbald lost a leg on August $21^{st}$ at Rappahannock Station and died of his wounds a month later on September 22, 1862.

### Henry Wireman
Mustered in on July 8, 1861. Second Lieutenant Henry Wireman was promoted to first lieutenant on December 6, 1864 and mustered out with the battery on June 9, 1865.

### William M. Thurston
Mustered in on July 8, 1861. Second Lieutenant William M. Thurston was promoted to first lieutenant on April 22, 1865 and mustered out with the battery on June 9, 1865.

### T. LeRoy Case
Mustered in on July 8, 1861. Second Lieutenant T. LeRoy Case was discharged from the service on February 4, 1863.

### Francis H. Snider
Mustered in on July 8, 1861. Snider was commissioned as a second lieutenant on January 31, 1864. He was wounded during the Battle of Mine Run (November 27 through December 2, 1863) and was discharged from the service on October 8, 1864.

### George W. Mowrer
Enlisted on July 8, 1861. Mowrer was commissioned as a second lieutenant on April 22, 1865 and mustered out with the battery on June 9, 1865.

**F. P. Brockway**
Enlisted on January 1, 1862. F. P. Brockway was commissioned as a second lieutenant on December 21, 1864 and mustered out with the battery on June 9, 1865.

## Battery G, 1st Pennsylvania Light Artillery

**Robert M. West***
Mustered in on July 26, 1861. The original captain of the battery, West was promoted to major on September 13, 1861 and again to colonel on July 29, 1862. On May 29, 1864 Colonel West transferred to the 5th Pennsylvania Cavalry Regiment.

**Mark Kern***
Mustered in on July 26, 1861. Mark Kern succeeded Robert West in command of the battery when West was promoted to major on September 13, 1861. The following day he was himself promoted to captain. Captain Kern was killed on August 30, 1862 at the Second Battle of Bull Run.

**Frank P. Amsden***
Mustered in with Battery H on July 8, 1861. First Lieutenant Amsden was promoted to captain on November 12, 1862 and transferred to Battery G to replace Captain Kern who had been killed during the Second Battle of Bull Run. Captain Amsden resigned his commission on May 25, 1863 after the battery was consolidated with Captain Ricketts' Battery F.

**Belden Spence***
Mustered in on July 26, 1861. Spence was promoted to first lieutenant on May 11, 1863 and given command of the section of Battery F comprised of the remaining men of Battery G. Spence was promoted to captain on January 20, 1864 shortly before the battery was separated from Battery F and reconstituted, but does not appear to have ever commanded the battery in the field. Captain Spence mustered out on December 4, 1864 at the expiration of his term of service.

**William Jennings***
Mustered in on March 24, 1862. Jennings was promoted to first lieutenant on May 16, 1864 and took command of the battery after it was

separated from Battery F. Lieutenant Jennings was discharged from the service at the end of his term on March 17, 1865.

**Eugene C. Moore***
Enlisted on March 17, 1862. Moore was commissioned as a second lieutenant on February 23, 1865 and took command of the battery when Lieutenant Jennings left the service. Moore was promoted to first lieutenant on April 24, 1865 and to captain on May 15, 1865. Captain Moore mustered out with the battery on June 29, 1865.

**Gustavus Braun**
Mustered in on July 26, 1861. First Lieutenant Braun resigned his commission on October 8, 1861.

**James Kincade**
Mustered in on July 30, 1861. Kincade was promoted to first lieutenant on October 8, 1861 and resigned his commission on January 8, 1862.

**Charles H. Mitchell**
Enlisted on July 26, 1861. Mitchell was commissioned as a second lieutenant on September 9, 1863 and was promoted to first lieutenant on March 5, 1864. First Lieutenant Mitchell mustered out on December 31, 1864 at the expiration of his term of service.

**William C. Hays**
Enlisted on April 14, 1864. William C. Hays was commissioned as a second lieutenant on April 20, 1865 and was promoted to first lieutenant on May 12, 1865. First Lieutenant Hays mustered out with the battery on June 29, 1865.

**George W. Reisinger**
Mustered in on July 30, 1861. Second Lieutenant Reisinger resigned his commission on January 16, 1862.

**Edward Fitzki**
Mustered in on July 11, 1861. Second Lieutenant Fitzki resigned his commission on October 2, 1862.

**George R. Buffum**
Enlisted on September 9, 1861. Buffum was commissioned as a second lieutenant on August 1, 1862 and granted a medical discharge on April 7, 1863 as a result of wounds received in battle.

### M. C. Gillespie
Enlisted on July 1, 1861. Gillespie was commissioned as a second lieutenant on June 12, 1863 and resigned his commission on July 13, 1863.

### De Lafayette Chandler
Enlisted on July 31, 1861. Chandler was commissioned as a second lieutenant on June 14, 1864 and mustered out on March 10, 1865 at the expiration of his term of service.

### Charles H. Clark
Enlisted on July 8, 1861. Clark was commissioned as a second lieutenant on June 14, 1864 and mustered out on January 4, 1865 at the expiration of his term of service.

### William Dixon
Enlisted on February 23, 1864. Dixon was commissioned as a second lieutenant on May 12, 1865 and mustered out with the battery on June 29, 1865.

## Battery H, 1$^{st}$ Pennsylvania Light Artillery

### James Brady*
Mustered in on July 8, 1861. The original promoter of the regiment and the first captain of Battery H, James Brady was promoted to major on July 19, 1862 and to lieutenant colonel on November 13, 1863. On the transfer of Colonel West to the 5$^{th}$ Pennsylvania Cavalry Regiment, Lieutenant Colonel Brady acceded to the command of the 1$^{st}$ Pennsylvania Light Artillery. Brady was brevetted to colonel on March 13, 1865 and mustered out on July 19, 1865.

### Andrew Fagan*
Mustered in on August 1, 1861. Second Lieutenant Fagan was promoted to first lieutenant on March 12, 1862 and again to captain on August 1, 1862 following the promotion of Captain Brady to major. Captain Fagan was discharged from the service on May 1, 1865.

**Lord B. Richards***
Enlisted on August 1, 1861. Richards was commissioned as a second lieutenant on May 25, 1864 and promoted to first lieutenant on September 19, 1864. Richards succeeded Andrew Fagan as commander of the battery and was promoted to captain on June 5, 1865. Captain Richards mustered out with the battery twenty-two days later on June 27, 1865.

**Theodore Miller**
Mustered in on August 1, 1861. First Lieutenant Miller was promoted to captain and transferred to Battery E on January 13, 1862. Captain Miller left Battery E on July 4, 1862 to serve as an Assistant Adjutant General and was subsequently promoted to major on February 24, 1865. Miller was discharged on June 2, 1865.

**Frank P. Amsden**
Mustered in on July 8, 1861. First Lieutenant Amsden was promoted to captain and given command of Battery G on November 12, 1862. Captain Amsden resigned his commission on May 25, 1863 after Battery G was consolidated with Captain Ricketts' Battery F.

**Henry Y. Wildey**
Mustered in on August 1, 1861. First Lieutenant Wildey was promoted to captain and given command of Battery E on November 1, 1864. Captain Wildey mustered out with Battery E on July 20, 1865.

**Frank C. Choate**
Mustered in with Battery E on June 20, 1861. Second Lieutenant Choate was transferred to Battery H on July 16, 1862. On December 28, 1863 he was promoted to captain and given command of a battery of U.S. Colored Light Artillery.

**William J. Park**
Mustered in on August 1, 1861. First Lieutenant Park resigned his commission on January 12, 1862.

**George E. Bentz**
First Lieutenant Bentz was mustered in 1861 and resigned his commission on an unknown date.

### William McLaughlin
Mustered in on August 1, 1861. Second Lieutenant McLaughlin was promoted to first lieutenant on December 29, 1862.

### Joseph Cogan
Enlisted on August 1, 1861. Cogan was commissioned as a second lieutenant on March 18, 1864 and was promoted to first lieutenant on May 25, 1864. Lieutenant Cogan was discharged from the service on July 27, 1864.

### Horace Templeton
Enlisted on August 1, 1861. Templeton was commissioned as a second lieutenant on May 25, 1864 and was promoted to first lieutenant on March 8, 1865. Lieutenant Templeton mustered out with the battery on June 27, 1865.

### Thomas Thornton
Mustered in on March 12, 1862. Second Lieutenant Thornton died at Washington D.C. on March 26, 1862.

### Richard Cooper
Enlisted on August 5, 1861. Cooper was commissioned as a second lieutenant on August 2, 1862 and resigned his commission on October 18, 1862.

### Robert McNight
Mustered in on September 20, 1864. Second Lieutenant McNight mustered out with the battery on June 27, 1865.

### Samuel L. Richards
Mustered in on August 5, 1861. Richards was commissioned as a second lieutenant on March 8, 1865 and mustered out with the battery on June 27, 1865.

## Battery I, 1st Pennsylvania Light Artillery

### Sylvester B. Cameron*
Mustered in on March 2, 1865. Captain Cameron mustered out with the battery on July 1, 1865.

**Lindley J. Taylor**
Mustered in on March 2, 1865. First Lieutenant Taylor mustered out with the battery on July 1, 1865.

**W. D. Schoenlieber**
Mustered in on March 2, 1865. Second Lieutenant Schoenlieber mustered out with the battery on July 1, 1865.

## Pennsylvania Independent Battery A

**Frank Schaffer***
Mustered in on September 19, 1861. Captain Schaffer, the original commander of the battery, resigned his commission on February 28, 1862.

**Stanley Miotkowski***
Mustered in on September 11, 1861. First Lieutenant Miotkowski was promoted to captain on March 1, 1862 to replace Captain Schaffer. Captain Miotkowski mustered out with the battery on June 30, 1865.

**Charles Steck**
Enlisted on August 29, 1861. Formerly the battery's first sergeant, Steck was commissioned as a second lieutenant on October 1, 1861 and promoted to first lieutenant on March 1, 1862. First Lieutenant Steck was discharged from the service on October 21, 1863.

**August Reineke**
Mustered in on August 29, 1861. Sergeant Reineke was promoted to first sergeant on May 11, 1862 and was commissioned as a second lieutenant on August 1, 1862. He was promoted to first lieutenant on June 29, 1863 and mustered out with the battery on June 30, 1865.

**David J. DeHaven**
Enlisted on September 14, 1861. Sergeant DeHaven was commissioned as a second lieutenant on July 27, 1863 and was promoted to first lieutenant on October 22, 1863. He mustered out with the battery on June 30, 1865.

**Phillip Secker**
Enlisted on September 10, 1861. Corporal Secker was promoted to first sergeant on October 1, 1861 and commissioned as a second lieutenant on March 1, 1862. Second Lieutenant Secker died on July 30, 1862.

**Louis F. Reger**
Louis F. Reger originally enlisted as a private on September 19, 1861 and was promoted to corporal on October 1, 1861. Reger was promoted to sergeant on July 27, 1862 and commissioned as a second lieutenant on June 29, 1863. Second Lieutenant Reger mustered out with the battery on June 30, 1865.

**Louis Deitz**
Louis Deitz originally enlisted as a private on September 2, 1861 and was promoted to corporal on May 1, 1862 and again to sergeant on August 8, 1862. Sergeant Deitz was commissioned as a second lieutenant on October 22, 1863 and mustered out with the battery on June 30, 1865.

**Moritz F. Glaffey**
Mustered in on September 20, 1861 and resigned his commission on September 30, 1861.

## Pennsylvania Independent Battery B

**Charles F. Muehler\***
Mustered in on October 11, 1861. Captain Muehler resigned his commission on November 16, 1862.

**Alanson J. Stevens\***
Mustered in on October 11, 1861. The nephew of Congressman Thaddeus Stevens, First Lieutenant Alanson J. Stevens succeeded Muehler in command of the battery and was promoted to captain on January 5, 1863. Captain Stevens was killed during the Battle of Chickamauga on September 21, 1863.

**Samuel M. McDowell\***
Mustered in on October 11, 1861. First Lieutenant McDowell assumed command of the battery after the death of Captain Stevens and was

promoted to captain on January 11, 1864. McDowell was killed at Kennesaw Mountain on June 27, 1864.

### Jacob Zeigler*
Mustered in on October 11, 1861. Second Lieutenant Zeigler was promoted to first lieutenant on January 11, 1864. Following the death of Captain McDowell, Zeigler became commander of the battery and was promoted to captain on August 16, 1864. Captain Zeigler mustered out with the battery on October 12, 1865.

### William F. Lutje
Mustered in on October 11, 1861. Second Lieutenant Lutje was promoted to first lieutenant on January 5, 1863. Lutje was discharged from the service on June 21, 1864 as a result of wounds received in battle.

### Emanuel F. Shatzer
Enlisted on October 11, 1861. Shatzer was commissioned as a second lieutenant on January 5, 1863 and promoted to first lieutenant on August 16, 1864. Shatzer mustered out with the battery on October 12, 1865.

### John H. Hassinger
Enlisted on October 11, 1861. Formerly the battery's first sergeant, Shatzer was commissioned as a second lieutenant on January 11, 1864. He was promoted to first lieutenant on August 16, 1864 and mustered out with the battery on October 12, 1865.

### John Muller
Enlisted on October 11, 1861. Formerly the battery's first sergeant (after Hassinger), Muller was commissioned as a second lieutenant on August 16, 1864 and mustered out with the battery on October 12, 1865.

### Clarence M. Camp
Enlisted on October 11, 1861. Formerly the battery's quartermaster sergeant, Camp was commissioned as a second lieutenant on August 16, 1864 and mustered out with the battery on October 12, 1865.

## Pennsylvania Independent Battery C

**James Thompson***
Mustered in on August 24, 1861. Formerly a sergeant in the British Royal Regiment of Artillery, Thompson immigrated to the United States in 1856. The original captain of Battery C, Thompson commanded Battery C through the entire war and mustered out with the battery on June 30, 1865.

**John P. Barry**
Mustered in on November 6, 1861. First Lieutenant Barry was discharged from the service on October 10, 1862.

**James Stephenson**
Enlisted on November 6, 1861. Formerly one of the battery's sergeants. Stephenson was commissioned as a first lieutenant on January 1, 1862. He was wounded during the Second Battle of Bull Run on August 30, 1862 and again at Gettysburg on July 2, 1863. Stephenson resigned his commission on January 22, 1864. On March 13, 1865 he received a brevet to the rank of captain.

**Robert C. Hazlett**
Hazlett enlisted as a private on September 27, 1861. He was promoted to sergeant on November 6, 1861. On November 4, 1862 he was commissioned as a second lieutenant. Hazlett was wounded on July 2, 1863 during the Battle of Gettysburg and on February 8, 1864 he was promoted to first lieutenant. Hazlett was discharged from the service on February 7, 1865 and received a brevet to the rank of captain on March 13, 1865.

**Thomas Brown**
Enlisted as a private on November 6, 1861. Brown was promoted to corporal on January 1, 1862 and again to sergeant one year later on January 1, 1863. Brown was commissioned as a second lieutenant on June 26, 1864 and was discharged on October 22, 1864.

**Francis Eichelberger**
Eichelberger enlisted on November 6, 1861. He was promoted to first sergeant on July 1, 1863 and was commissioned as a second lieutenant on August 3, 1864. On November 25, 1864 Eichelberger was promoted to first lieutenant. He resigned his commission on June 17, 1865.

**James Mitchell**
Enlisted on October 28, 1861. Mitchell was commissioned as a second lieutenant on September 6, 1864 and was promoted to first lieutenant on February 28, 1865. He mustered out with the battery on June 30, 1865.

**Adam J. Longsdorf**
Second Lieutenant Longsdorf mustered in on January 1, 1862 and resigned his commission on October 10, 1862.

**James L. McKee**
Enlisted on July 6, 1863. McKee was commissioned as a second lieutenant on November 25, 1864 and mustered out with the battery on June 30, 1865.

**William H. Bruce**
Bruce enlisted on August 21, 1862. He was commissioned as a second lieutenant on February 28, 1865 and mustered out with the battery on June 30, 1865.

## Pennsylvania Independent Battery D

**George W. Durell***
Mustered in on September 24, 1861. Captain Durell was discharged at the end of his term on September 23, 1864.

**Samuel H. Rhoads***
Enlisted on September 24, 1861. Originally one of the battery's sergeants, Rhoads was commissioned as a second lieutenant on August 19, 1864. Durell's successor in command, he was promoted to captain on October 3, 1864 and mustered out with the battery on June 13, 1865.

**Lemuel Gries**
Mustered in on September 24, 1861. First Lieutenant Gries resigned his commission on June 19, 1863.

**Howard McIlvaine**
Mustered in on September 24, 1861. First Lieutenant McIlvaine was wounded at White Sulphur Springs on November 15, 1862 and died of his wounds one year later on November 15, 1863.

**Henry Sailor**
Enlisted on September 24, 1861. Originally one of the battery's sergeants, Rhoads was commissioned as a second lieutenant on August 12, 1864. Sailor was promoted to first lieutenant on October 17, 1864 and mustered out with the battery on June 13, 1865.

**Adley B. Lawrence**
Enlisted on September 24, 1861. Private Lawrence was promoted to corporal on April 22, 1863 and again to sergeant on May 1, 1864. On October 8, 1864 he became the battery's first sergeant and on November 24, 1864 he was commissioned as a first lieutenant. Lieutenant Lawrence mustered out with the battery on June 13, 1865.

**George W. Silvis**
Mustered in on September 24, 1861. Second Lieutenant Silvis was promoted to first lieutenant on November 16, 1862 but never mustered in under that rank. He left the service at the end of his term on October 8, 1864.

**Christopher Loeser**
Mustered in on May 2, 1862. Second Lieutenant Loeser resigned his commission on October 12, 1864.

**Charles A. Cuffel**
Enlisted on September 24, 1861. Private Cuffel was promoted to corporal on May 1, 1864 and again to sergeant on September 24, 1864. Cuffel was commissioned as a second lieutenant on November 24, 1864 and mustered out with the battery on June 13, 1865.

**James L. Mast**
Enlisted on September 24, 1861. Private Mast was promoted to corporal on October 1, 1863 and again to sergeant on May 1, 1864. Mast was commissioned as a second lieutenant on November 24, 1864 and mustered out with the battery on June 13, 1865.

## Pennsylvania Independent Battery E

**Joseph M. Knap***
Mustered in on July 20, 1861 as a first lieutenant in Company "L" of the 28th Pennsylvania Infantry. Lieutenant Knap was separated from

Company "L" on November 1, 1861 and given command of the newly organized Independent Battery E. Captain Knap resigned his commission on May 16, 1863 to assume the superintendancy of the Fort Pitt Foundry, but would later return to the field first with "Knap's Independent Militia Battery," and then again with "Knap's Independent Artillery Battalion," *which see.*

**Charles A. Atwell\***
Mustered in on September 21, 1861. First Lieutenant Atwell was wounded at Chancellorville on May 2, 1863. Lieutenant Atwell took command of the battery after the resignation of Captain Knap and was promoted to captain on July 16, 1863. Captain Knap was mortally wounded at the Battle of Wauhatchie Station on October 29, 1863 and died of his wounds on November 1, 1863.

**Edward R. Geary**
Mustered in on September 6, 1861. Second Lieutenant Geary was wounded at the Battle of Cedar Mountain on August 9, 1862, and promoted to first lieutenant on July 16, 1863. On October 20, 1863 a commission for Geary was issued that would have made him the captain of Pennsylvania Independent Battery F, but Geary was killed at the Battle of Wauhatchie Station on October 29, 1863 before the commission could be delivered (it was in his father General John W. Geary's pocket during the battle). Edward Geary was posthumously brevetted to lieutenant colonel on March 13, 1865.

**James D. McGill\***
Mustered in on September 21, 1861. Lieutenant McGill assumed command of the battery after the death of Captain Atwell and was promoted to captain on March 12, 1864. Captain McGill resigned his commission on July 8, 1864, but briefly remained in the field with the battery and was wounded at the Battle of Peach Tree Creek on July 20, 1864.

**James A. Dunlevy\***
Mustered in on October 39, 1861. Dunlevy was promoted to first lieutenant on March 13, 1863 and assumed command of the battery after the resignation of Captain McGill. Dunlevy was promoted to captain on July $9^{th}$, 1864, but never mustered in under that rank. He resigned his commission on August 5, 1864.

### Thomas S. Sloan*
Mustered in on September 21, 1861. Sloan was commissioned as a second lieutenant on July 16, 1863, and was promoted to first lieutenant on March 12, 1864. Sloan assumed command of the battery after the resignation of Lieutenant Dunlevy and was promoted to captain on September 11, 1864. Captain Sloan mustered out with the battery on June 14, 1865.

### Clement Tingley, Jr.
Mustered in on August 23, 1861. First Lieutenant Tingley resigned his commission on May 13, 1862.

### Adam Shaw
Enlisted on July 11, 1861. Shaw was wounded during the Battle of Antietam on September 17, 1862. Shaw was commissioned as a second lieutenant on March 30, 1864 and was promoted to first lieutenant on October 15, 1864. He mustered out with the battery on June 14, 1865.

### William R. Stokes
Enlisted on July 11, 1861. Stokes was commissioned as a second lieutenant on March 31, 1864 and was promoted to first lieutenant on September 16, 1864. He mustered out with the battery on June 14, 1865

### Sylvestor W. McCloskey
Enlisted on July 6, 1861. First Sergeant McCloskey was commissioned as a second lieutenant on October 15, 1864 and mustered out with the battery on June 14, 1865

### Edward Hammann
Enlisted on October 29, 1861. Quartermaster Sergeant Hammann was wounded at Front Royal, Virginia on May 23, 1862. He was commissioned as a second lieutenant on September 16, 1864 and mustered out with the battery on June 14, 1865

## Pennsylvania Independent Battery F

### Robert B. Hampton*
Mustered in on October 17, 1861. Captain Hampton was killed during the Battle of Chancellorsville on May 3, 1863.

### Nathaniel Irish*
Mustered in on January 31, 1862. After the death of Captain Hampton at Chancellorsville, First Lieutenant Irish was promoted to captain on May 24, 1863, but Battery F was temporarily consolidated with Pennsylvania Independent Battery C that same month and Captain Thompson of Battery C retained command of the whole. Irish was wounded during the Battle of Gettysburg on July 2, 1863. When Battery F was separated from Battery C and reconstituted on March 25, 1864 Irish was selected as Battery F's new commander. Captain Irish mustered out with the battery on June 26, 1865.

### Lewis S. Tarr
Mustered in on October 17, 1861. First Lieutenant Tarr was discharged from the service on December 28, 1861.

### James P. Fleming
Mustered in on October 17, 1861. First Lieutenant Fleming resigned his commissioned on June 3, 1863.

### Robert Paul
Enlisted on October 8, 1861. Sergeant Paul was commissioned as a first lieutenant on June 2, 1862 and was discharged from the service at the end of his term on January 3, 1865.

### Joseph B. Todd
Enlisted on October 8, 1861. Sergeant Todd was wounded during the Battle of Gettysburg on July 2, 1863 and was commissioned as a first lieutenant on March 3, 1864. Todd was discharged from the service at the end of his term on February 16, 1865.

### Frederick L. Atwood
Enlisted on October 8, 1861. Sergeant Atwood was commissioned as a second lieutenant on November 9, 1863 and was promoted to first lieutenant on March 8, 1865. Atwood was brevetted to lieutenant colonel on March 13, 1865, and mustered out with the battery on June 26, 1865.

### George Ritchie
Enlisted on October 8, 1861. Private Ritchie was wounded during the Battle of Gettysburg on July 2, 1863 and was sometime thereafter promoted to first sergeant. Ritchie was commissioned as a second lieutenant on February 25, 1865 and was promoted to first lieutenant on

March 9, 1865. Ritchie was brevetted to lieutenant colonel on March 13, 1865, and mustered out with the battery on June 26, 1865.

**Joseph L. Miller**
Mustered in on August 6, 1862. Second Lieutenant Miller was wounded during the Battle of Gettysburg on July 2, 1863 and died of his wounds on August 6, 1863.

**Samuel D. Glass**
Enlisted on October 8, 1861. First Sergeant Glass was commissioned as a second lieutenant on July 26, 1863. Glass was promoted to first lieutenant on January 4, 1865 but never mustered in under that rank. Glass was discharged on February 22, 1865 at the expiration of his term of service.

**Alfred N. Harbours**
Mustered in on January 1, 1862. Second Lieutenant Harbours resigned his commission on July 26, 1863.

**Frank H. Shiras**
Enlisted on October 8, 1861. Sergeant Shiras was commissioned as a second lieutenant on March 9, 1865 and mustered out with the battery on June 26, 1865.

**Frank A. Merrick**
Enlisted on October 8, 1861. Sergeant Merrick was commissioned as a second lieutenant on March 10, 1865 and mustered out with the battery on June 26, 1865.

## Pennsylvania Independent Battery G

**John Jay Young\***
Mustered in on August 22, 1862. Captain Young mustered out with the battery on June 18, 1865.

**Alfred Kerr, Sr.**
Mustered in on August 22, 1862. First Lieutenant Kerr mustered out with the battery on June 18, 1865.

**George W. Ahl, Jr.**
Mustered in on August 22, 1862. First Lieutenant Ahl was promoted to captain and given command of the $1^{st}$ Delaware Heavy Artillery Company, "Ahl's Heavy Artillery Company," on July 27, 1863. Ahl's company was raised from among Confederate prisoners at Fort Delaware who were released in exchange for enlisting in the Union army. Captain Ahl mustered out with his heavy artillery company on July 25, 1865.

**J. G. McConnell, Jr.**
Mustered in on August 22, 1862. Second Lieutenant McConnel was promoted to first lieutenant on July 27, 1863 and mustered out with the battery on June 18, 1865.

**Joseph C. Young**
Mustered in on September 2, 1862. Second Lieutenant Young was discharged on March 15, 1863.

**William Hall, Sr.**
Enlisted on August 22, 1862. First Sergeant Hall was commissioned as a second lieutenant on May 4, 1863 and mustered out with the battery on June 18, 1865.

**Henry Warner, Jr.**
Enlisted on August 22, 1862. Sergeant Warner was promoted to quartermaster sergeant on December 9, 1862, to first sergeant on August 30, 1863, and immediately commissioned as a second lieutenant on September 1, 1863. In January of 1864 Second Lieutenant was made post adjutant of Fort Delaware. He mustered out with the battery on June 18, 1865.

## Pennsylvania Independent Battery H

**John I. Nevin\***
Mustered in on July 11, 1861. Formerly a second lieutenant in the $28^{th}$ Pennsylvania Infantry (in which service he was captured and spend six months in southern prisons), John I. Nevin was promoted to captain and given command of Battery H on October 25, 1862. Nevin left the battery on February 14, 1863 to serve with the $93^{rd}$ Pennsylvania Infantry, in which organization he attained the rank of lieutenant colonel. Nevin was in temporary command of the $93^{rd}$ Pennsylvania Infantry during the

Battle of Gettysburg, and was later wounded during the Battle of the Wilderness. Only 28 years old at the end of the war, he traveled west and spent several years in Montana and Utah before returning to Pennsylvania as the editor of a Pittsburgh newspaper. He died on January 5, 1884.

**William Borrowe***
Formerly an officer of the $2^{nd}$ Regiment of United States Artillery, William Borrowe was promoted to captain when John I. Nevin resigned on February 14, 1863, and commanded the battery until he was dismissed from the service on March 8, 1865.

**Edwin H. Nevin, Jr.***
Mustered in on September 30, 1862. First Lieutenant Edwin H. Nevin, Jr. was given command of the battery after the dismissal of William Borrowe, and was promoted to captain on April 3, 1865. He mustered out with the battery on June 18, 1865.

**Theodore M. Finlay**
Formerly a private in Pennsylvania Independent Battery F, Theodore M. Finlay was transferred to this battery and commissioned as a first lieutenant on October 21, 1862. He mustered out with the battery on June 18, 1865.

**William H. Askine, Jr.**
Formerly the battery's first sergeant, Askine was commissioned as a second lieutenant on July 14, 1864. He was promoted to first lieutenant on April 3, 1865, and mustered out with the battery on June 18, 1865.

**John C. Klett, Jr.**
Mustered in on October 21, 1862. Second Lieutenant John C. Klett, Jr. resigned his commission on February 14, 1863.

**John N. Brown**
Mustered in on October 21, 1862. Second Lieutenant John N. Brown resigned his commission on February 28, 1863.

**A. J. B. Baumstarck**
Mustered in on October 10, 1862. Formerly the battery's first sergeant, Baumstarck was commissioned as a second lieutenant on August 5, 1863. He was discharged on May 29, 1864.

**Morris W. Gibbs**
Mustered in on September 4, 1862. Formerly the first sergeant of Independent Company C, Pennsylvania Volunteer Infantry. Gibbs was transferred to this battery and commissioned as a second lieutenant on July 22, 1864. He mustered out with the battery on June 18, 1865.

**William F. Hoag**
Mustered in on September 30, 1862. Formerly the battery's first sergeant, Hoag was commissioned as a second lieutenant on April 17, 1865. He mustered out with the battery on June 18, 1865.

## Pennsylvania Independent Battery I

**Robert Jenkins Nevin\***
Formerly a first lieutenant in the 122$^{nd}$ Pennsylvania Infantry, Robert Jenkins Nevin raised an emergency militia battery bearing his name in June of 1863. At the end of the 6-months' term of the militia battery, enough men were willing to reenlist for 3 years' terms to create this battery. Nevin mustered as captain of this battery on January 26, 1864. He was later brevetted to major and was given command of a brigade in the Washington defenses. Nevin mustered out with the battery on June 23, 1865. A theology student both before and after the war, Nevin received a D.D. from the Union Theological Seminary in 1874 and an L.L.D from Hobart College in 1887. In 1867 he was ordained as an Episcopalian priest and went on to establish the first ever Protestant Church within the city of Rome, Italy. Nevin died on September 20$^{th}$, 1906.

**Martin Bachman**
Mustered in Nevin's Independent Militia Battery on July 6, 1863, and in this battery on January 27, 1864, following the conversion of Nevin's Independent Militia Battery into this battery. First Lieutenant Bachman mustered out with the battery on June 23, 1865.

**Louis M. Johnston**
Mustered in on January 26, 1864. Second Lieutenant Johnston was promoted to first lieutenant on March 11, 1864 and mustered out with the battery on June 23, 1865.

**Eliphalet O. Lyte**
Mustered in Nevin's Independent Militia Battery on June 30, 1863 and remained with the battery through its conversion into this battery in January of 1864. Sergeant Lyte was commissioned as a second lieutenant on March 11, 1864 and mustered out with the battery on June 23, 1865.

**John Weltmore**
Mustered in on January 26, 1864. First Sergeant Weltmore was promoted to second lieutenant on March 11, 1864 and mustered out with the battery on June 23, 1865.

## The Keystone Battery

**Matthew Hastings***
Captain Hastings was the original commander of the company in 1861 when it was raised as part of the Philadelphia Home Guard. He continued in command through the company's transition to a full volunteer field battery for its first term of one year between August of 1862 and August of 1863, and resumed command in 1864 when the battery was re-instituted for 100-days' service between July and October of that year.

**John Shipley Newlin**
Corporal Newlin mustered in on August 7, 1862, and mustered out with the battery one year later on August 20, 1863. Newlin was later commissioned as a second lieutenant on July 12, 1864 when the battery was re-instituted for 100-days' service, and mustered out again on October 25, 1864.

**(Other officers of this battery are unknown)**

## Battery H, 3$^{rd}$ Pennsylvania Heavy Artillery

**William D. Rank***
Mustered in on January 19, 1863. Captain Rank mustered out with the company on July 25, 1865.

**William. M. Runkel**
Mustered in on October 23, 1862. First Lieutenant Runkel mustered out with the company on July 25, 1865.

**Thomas B. Nelson**
Mustered in on January 19, 1863. First Lieutenant Nelson mustered out with the company on July 25, 1865.

**John A. Light**
Enlisted on September 16, 1862. Sergeant Light was commissioned as a second lieutenant on March 2, 1863 and resigned his commission on May 10, 1865.

**Frederick A. Knocekey**
Enlisted on October 2, 1862. First sergeant Knocekey was commissioned as a second lieutenant on May 3, 1864, and mustered out with the company on July 25, 1865.

**Byron Pope**
Enlisted on September 15, 1862. Believed to have been commissioned as a second lieutenant on June 13, 1865 from First Sergeant, and brevetted to first lieutenant on June 13, 1865. Pope mustered out with the company on July 25, 1865.

## Ermentrout's Independent Militia Battery

**W. C. Ermentrout***
Captain Ermentrout's militia battery mustered in on July 3, 1863 and mustered out 23 days later on July 26, 1863.

**(Other officers of this battery are unknown)**

## Frishmuth's Independent Militia Battery

**Benoni Frishmuth***
Captain Frishmuth's militia battery mustered in on June 26, 1863 and mustered out on August 1, 1863.

**(Other officers of this battery are unknown)**

### Guss' Independent Militia Battery
### "The Chester County Artillery"

**George R. Guss***
Captain Guss' militia battery mustered in on July 1, 1863 and mustered out on August 24, 1863.

**(Other officers of this battery are unknown)**

### The Keystone Independent Militia Battery
### "The Second Keystone Battery"

**Edward Fitzki***
Captain Fitzki's militia battery mustered in on July 6, 1863 and mustered out on August 24, 1863.

**(Other officers of this battery are unknown)**

### Knap's Independent Militia Battery

**Joseph M. Knap***
Formerly commander of Pennsylvania Independent Battery E, Captain Joseph Knap returned to the field during the 1863 emergency as the commander of a militia battery.

**(Other officers of this battery are unknown)**

### Knap's Independent Artillery Battalion

**Joseph M. Knap***
Formerly commander of Pennsylvania Independent Battery E and "Knap's Independent Militia Battery," Joseph Knap returned to the field

in the spring of 1864 as the commander of this battalion, with the rank of major.

**(Other officers of this organization are unknown)**


### Landis' Independent Militia Battery

**Henry D. Landis***
Captain Landis' militia battery was formed in 1861, under Landis' command, as part of the Philadelphia defenses, but did not muster until the emergency caused by the Confederate invasion of Pennsylvania. The battery was formally mustered on June 27, 1863 and mustered out one month later on July 27, 1863.

**(Other officers of this battery are unknown)**


### Miller's Independent Militia Battery

**E. Spenser Miller***
Captain Miller's militia battery mustered during June of 1863 and mustered out on July 25, 1863.

**(Other officers of this battery are unknown)**


### Nevin's Independent Militia Battery

**Robert J. Nevin***
Formerly a first lieutenant in the $122^{nd}$ Pennsylvania Infantry, Robert Jenkins Nevin raised this battery in June of 1863. At the end of the battery's 6-months' term, enough men were willing to reenlist for 3 years' terms to create Pennsylvania Independent Battery I. Nevin remustered as captain of Battery I on January 26, 1864, and mustered out with Battery I on June 23, 1865. A theology student both before and after the war, Nevin received a D.D. from the Union Theological Seminary in 1874 and an L.L.D from Hobart College in 1887. In 1867 he was ordained as an Episcopalian priest and went on to establish the

first ever Protestant Church within the city of Rome, Italy. Nevin died on September 20th, 1906.

**Martin Bachman**
Mustered in on July 6, 1863. First Lieutenant Bachman remained with the battery following its conversion from a militia battery into Pennsylvania Independent Battery I, and mustered with that battery on January 27, 1864.

**Coleman Twining**
Mustered in on June 30, 1863. Twining was promoted from second lieutenant to first lieutenant on August 26, 1863, and mustered out with the battery on January 7, 1864.

**Walter S. Ditto**
Mustered in on October 6, 1863. Second Lieutenant Ditto mustered out with the battery on January 7, 1864.

**William. R. Gerhart**
Enlisted on July 2, 1863. Formerly the battery's first sergeant, Gerhart was commissioned as a second lieutenant on August 26, 1863, and mustered out with the battery on January 7, 1864.

## Tyler's Independent Militia Battery

**Horatio K. Tyler***
Captain Tyler's militia battery mustered in on July 16, 1863 and mustered out on January 28, 1864.

**(Other officers of this battery are unknown)**

## Woodward's Independent Militia Battery

**W. H. Woodward***
Captain Woodwards's militia battery mustered in on July 9, 1863 and mustered out on November 4, 1863.

**(Other officers of this battery are unknown)**

# APPENDIX B:
# BATTERY ASSIGNMENTS

### The Ringgold Light Artillery

Pre-war militia organization. Organized 1850. Mustered in on April 18, 1861. Attached to the 25th Pennsylvania Infantry Regiment as Company "A" during the summer of 1861. Discharged during the summer of 1861 after 3-months' service.

### Battery A, 1st Pennsylvania Light Artillery

#### 1861

Organized during the spring in Franklin County under the command of Charles T. Campbell.
**August:**
Mustered with the regiment at Philadelphia on the 5th, at which time Campbell was promoted to lieutenant colonel (and later colonel), leaving the command of the battery to Captain Hezekiah Easton. Transferred to Washington and attached to McCall's Pennsylvania Reserve Division, Army of the Potomac.

#### 1862

**March:**
Attached to the 2nd Division, First Corps, Army of the Potomac.
**April:**
Attached to McCall's Division, Dept. of the Rappahannock.
**June:**
Attached to the 3rd Division, Fifth Corps, Army of the Potomac. Captain Easton was killed on the 27th and Lieutenant John G. Simpson succeeded him in command.
**August:**
Attached to the 3rd Division, Third Corps, Army of Virginia.

**September:**
Attached to the 3$^{rd}$ Division, First Corps, Army of the Potomac.

### 1863

**February:**
Attached to the 3$^{rd}$ Division, Ninth Corps, Army of the Potomac.
**April:**
Attached to the 2$^{nd}$ Division, Seventh Corps, Dept. of Virginia.
**July:**
Attached to the forces at Norfolk and Portsmouth, Dept. of Virginia and North Carolina.

### 1864

**January:**
Attached to Heckman's Division, Eighteenth Corps, Dept. of Virginia and North Carolina.
**April:**
Attached to Portsmouth defenses, Dept. of Virginia and North Carolina.
**May:**
Attached to the Eastern Virginia District, Dept. of Virginia and North Carolina.
**July:**
Attached to the Artillery Brigade of the Tenth Corps.
**August:**
Lieutenant Simpson left the service on the 21$^{st}$ and Lieutenant William Stitt succeeded him in command.
**September:**
Lieutenant Stitt was promoted to captain on the 17$^{th}$.
**October:**
Attached to the Artillery Brigade of the Eighteenth Corps.
**December**
Attached to the Artillery Brigade of the Twenty-fourth Corps (Dept. of Virginia).

### 1865

**July:**
Mustered out on the 25th.

## Battery B, 1st Pennsylvania Light Artillery

### 1861

**April:**
Organized at Mount Jackson in Laurence County on the 26th under the command of Henry T. Danforth.

**August:**
Mustered with the regiment in Philadelphia on the 5th, at which time Danforth was selected as one of the majors of the regiment and command of Battery B was given to Captain (formerly First Sergeant) James H. Cooper. Transferred to Washington and attached to McCall's Pennsylvania Reserve Division, Army of the Potomac.

### 1862

**March:**
Attached to the 2nd Division, First Corps, Army of the Potomac.

**April:**
Attached to McCall's Division, Dept. of the Rappahannock.

**June:**
Attached to the 3rd Division, Fifth Corps, Army of the Potomac.

**August:**
Attached to the 3rd Division, Third Corps, Army of Virginia.

**September:**
Attached to the 3rd Division, First Corps, Army of the Potomac.

### 1863

**May:**
Attached to the Artillery Brigade of the First Corps.

### 1864

**March:**
Attached to the Artillery Brigade of the Fifth Corps.

**August:**
Captain Cooper left the service on the 8th and Lieutenant William McClelland succeeded him in command.

## 1865

**February:**
Lieutenant McClelland was promoted to captain on the 23rd.
**March:**
Attached to the Artillery Reserve of the Army of the Potomac.
**June:**
Mustered out on the 9th.

## Battery C, 1st Pennsylvania Light Artillery

### 1861

**April:**
Organized in Philadelphia in response to James Brady's call for volunteers issued on the 13th. Initially commanded by Captain J. G. Simpson.
**August:**
Mustered with the regiment in Philadelphia on the 5th, around which time Captain Simpson was succeeded by Captain Jeremiah McCarthy. Transferred to Washington.
**October:**
Attached to W. F. Smith's Division, Army of the Potomac.

### 1862

**March:**
Attached to the 1st Division, Fourth Corps, Army of the Potomac.
**September:**
Attached to the 3rd Division, Sixth Corps, Army of the Potomac.

### 1863

Consolidated with Battery C, 1st Pennsylvania Light Artillery during the spring. The consolidated battery kept the name

'Battery D' but Captain Hall agreed to resign from the service and command was given to Captain McCarthy of Battery C.

## Battery C, 1st Pennsylvania (Second)

### 1864

**December:**
Organized under the command of Captain Sharp L. Richards as a replacement for the original Battery C.

### 1865

**June:**
Mustered out on the 30th.

## Battery D, 1st Pennsylvania Light Artillery

### 1861

**April:**
Organized in Philadelphia in response to James Brady's call for volunteers issued on the 13th. Initially commanded by Captain Edward H. Flood.

**August:**
Mustered with the regiment in Philadelphia on the 5th. Transferred to Washington.

**October:**
Attached to Buell's Division, Army of the Potomac.

### 1862

**March:**
Attached to the 1st Division, Fourth Corps, Army of the Potomac.

**September:**
Attached to the 3rd Division, Sixth Army Corps, Army of the Potomac.

## 1863

Consolidated with Battery C, 1st Pennsylvania Light Artillery during the spring. The consolidated battery kept the name 'Battery D' but Captain Hall agreed to resign from the service and command was given to Captain McCarthy of Battery C.

**May:**
Attached to the Artillery Brigade of the Sixth Corps.

**June:**
Assigned to Camp Barry, Defenses of Washington, D.C. Captain McCarthy left the service due to illness and was lieutenant William Munk succeeded him in command.

**July:**
Captain Flood was promoted to lieutenant colonel on the 19th and Captain Michael Hall succeeded him in command.

**August:**
Unattached Artillery of the Dept. of West Virginia.

**December:**
Attached to the 1st Brigade of the 1st Division, Dept. of West Virginia.

## 1864

**January:**
Attached to Wheaton's Brigade, Dept. of West Virginia.

**April:**
Attached to the Artillery Brigade of the Dept. of West Virginia.[*]

## 1865

**January:**
Attached to the 1st Separate Brigade of the Dept. West Virginia.

**May:**
Attached to the 2nd Infantry Division, Dept. of West Virginia.

---

[*] Between August and December, 1864 the forces assigned to the Department of West Virginia were referred to as the "Army of West of Virginia." Commanded by General George Crook, the Army of West Virginia was in reality a nominal corps of General Philip Sheridan's Army of the Shenandoah.

**June:**
Mustered out on the 30th.

## Battery E, 1st Pennsylvania Light Artillery

### 1861

Organized under the leadership of Captain Alfred E. Lewis of men from Blair and Philadelphia counties during the spring.
**August:**
Mustered with the regiment in Philadelphia on the 5th, at which time Captain Lewis was promoted to major and Captain Jacob M. Barr succeeded him in command. Transferred to Washington.
**October:**
Attached to W. F. Smith's Division, Army of the Potomac.
**November:**
Attached to Buell's Division, Army of the Potomac.
**December:**
Captain Barr resigned on the 12th and Captain Theodore Miller succeeded him in command.

### 1862

**March:**
Attached to the 1st Division, Fourth Corps, Army of the Potomac.
**June:**
Attached to the Reserve Artillery, Fourth Corps.
**July:**
Captain Miller left the battery on the 4th to serve as an Assistant Adjutant General and Lieutenant Thomas G. Orwig succeeded him in command.
**August:**
Lieutenant Orwig was promoted to captain on the 11th.

### 1863

**June:**
Attached to the 2nd Brigade, 1st Division, Fourth Corps.
**July:**

Attached to the forces at Norfolk and Portsmouth, Dept. of Virginia and North Carolina.

## 1864

**June:**
Unattached Artillery of the Dept. of Virginia and North Carolina.
**July:**
Attached to the Artillery Brigade of the Eighteenth Corps.
**August:**
Attached to the Artillery Brigade of the Tenth Corps.
**September:**
Captain Orwig resigned his commission on the 21st and Lieutenant Henry Y. Wildey succeeded him in command.
**November:**
Lieutenant Wildey was promoted to captain on the 1st.
**December:**
Attached to the Artillery Brigade of the Twenty-fifth Corps (Dept. of Virginia).

## 1865

**July:**
Mustered out on the 20th.

## Battery F, 1st Pennsylvania Light Artillery

### 1861

Organized under the leadership of Captain Ezra W. Matthews of men from Philadelphia County during the spring.
**August:**
Mustered with the regiment at Philadelphia on the 5th. Transferred to Washington and attached to Bank's Division, Army of the Potomac.
**October:**
Attached to the 1st Division, Fifth Corps.

## 1862

**March:**
Attached to the 1st Division, Dept. of the Shenandoah.
**May:**
Attached to the 2nd Division, Dept. of the Rappahannock.
**June:**
Attached to the 2nd Division, Third Corps, Army of Virginia.
**September:**
Attached to the 2nd Division, First Corps, Army of the Potomac. Captain Matthews was forced to leave the battery due to illness and Lieutenant R. Bruce Ricketts succeeded him in command.

## 1863

**January:**
Attached to the 3rd Division, First Corps.
**May:**
Attached to the 3rd Volunteer Brigade, Artillery Reserve of the Army of the Potomac. Battery G, 1st Pennsylvania Light Artillery was consolidated with this battery on the 12th with Captain Ricketts retaining command.
**July:**
Attached to the Artillery Brigade of the Second Corps, Army of the Potomac.

## 1864

**April:**
Battery G was separated from this battery and reconstituted on the 3rd.
**September:**
Attached to the Artillery Reserve of the Army of the Potomac.
**December:**
Captain Ricketts was promoted to major in the 1st and Lieutenant John F. Campbell succeeded him in command.

## 1865:

**April:**
Lieutenant Campbell was promoted to captain on the 17th.

**July:**
Mustered out on the 9th.

## Battery G, 1st Pennsylvania Light Artillery

### 1861

**April:**
Organized in Philadelphia in response to James Brady's call for volunteers issued on the 13th. Initially commanded by Captain Robert M. West.

**August:**
Mustered with the regiment at Philadelphia on the 5th, at which time West was promoted to major (and later colonel), leaving the command of the battery to Captain Mark Kern. Transferred to Washington and attached to McCall's Pennsylvania Reserve Division, Army of the Potomac.

### 1862

**March:**
Attached to the 2nd Division, First Corps, Army of the Potomac.

**April:**
Attached to McCall's Division, Dept. of the Rappahannock.

**June:**
Attached to the the 3rd Division, Fifth Corps, Army of the Potomac.

**August:**
Attached to the 3rd Division, Third Corps, Army of Virginia. Captain Kern was killed on the 30th.

**September:**
Attached to the 3rd Division, First Corps, Army of the Potomac.

**November:**
Lieutenant Frank P. Amsden of Battery H, 1st Pennsylvania Light Artillery was promoted to captain and transferred to Battery G as a replacement for Captain Kern.

## 1863

**May:**
Attached to the 3rd Volunteer Brigade, Artillery Reserve, Army of the Potomac. Consolidated with Battery F, 1st Pennsylvania Light Artillery on the 12th. Captain Amsden resigned his commission on the 25th following the consolidation and Captain R. Bruce Ricketts of Battery F retained command of the whole.

**July:**
Attached to the Artillery Brigade of the Second Corps, Army of the Potomac.

## 1864

**April:**
Attached to the Twenty-second Corps and assigned to Camp Barry. Separated from Battery F on the 3rd and reconstituted under the command of Lieutenant William Jennings.

**May:**
Attached to the 1st Brigade, DeRussy's Division, Twenty-second Corps.

**July:**
Attached to the Reserve Division, Dept. of West Virginia.

## 1865

**January:**
Attached to the 1st Infantry Division, West Virginia.

**March:**
Lieutenant Jennings left the service at the end of his term on the 17th and Lieutenant Eugene C. Moore succeeded him in command.

**April:**
Attached to the 3rd Brigade, Hardins' Division, Twenty-second Corps.

**May:**
Lieutenant Moore was promoted to captain on the 15th.

**June:**
Mustered out on the 29th.

## Battery H, 1st Pennsylvania Light Artillery

### 1861

**April:**
Organized in Philadelphia in response to James Brady's call for volunteers issued on the 13$^{th}$. Initially commanded by Captain James Brady.

**August:**
Mustered with the regiment at Philadelphia on the 5$^{th}$ and transferred to Washington.

**October:**
Attached to Buell's Division, Army of the Potomac.

### 1862

**March:**
Attached to the 1$^{st}$ Division, Fourth Corps, Army of the Potomac

**July:**
Attached to the Reserve Artillery of the Fourth Corps. Captain Brady was promoted to major on the 19$^{th}$ and Lieutenant Andrew Fagan succeeded him in command.

**August:**
Lieutenant Fagan was promoted to captain on the 1$^{st}$.

### 1863

**June:**
Attached to the Twenty-second Corps and assigned to Camp Barry.

### 1864

**May:**
Attached to the 1$^{st}$ Brigade, DeRussy's Division, Twenty-second Corps.

### 1865

**May:**
Captain Fagan left the service on the 1$^{st}$ and Lieutenant Lord B. Richards succeeded him in command.

**June:**
Lieutenant Richards was promoted to captain on the 5$^{th}$ and the battery mustered out on the 27$^{th}$.

## Battery I, 1st Pennsylvania Light Artillery

### 1865

**March:**
Organized on the 2$^{nd}$ under the command of Captain Sylvester B. Cameron and attached to DeRussy's Division, Twenty-second Corps. Entire term of service spent in the Washington defenses.

**July:**
Mustered out on the 1$^{st}$.

## Pennsylvania Independent Battery A

### 1861

**September:**
Organized at Philadelphia on the 19$^{th}$ under the initial command of Captain Frank Schaffer. Assigned to Fort Delaware, where they spend their entire term of service.

### 1862

**February:**
Captain Schaffer resigned in the 28$^{th}$ and Lieutenant Stanley Miotkowski succeeded him in command.

**March:**
Lieutenant Miotkowski was promoted to captain on the 1$^{st}$.

### 1865

**June:**
Mustered out on the 30$^{th}$.

## Pennsylvania Independent Battery B

### 1861

Organized during the summer as a company of the 77th Pennsylvania Infantry Regiment; originally commanded by Peter B. Housum. Later reinforced by a combination with an independent company from Erie County under Charles F. Muehler.

**August:**
Transferred to Camp Nevin, Kentucky and assigned to Negley's Brigade, Army of the Ohio.

**November:**
Mustered in with the 77th Pennsylvania Regiment; under the command of Captain Charles Muehler.

**December:**
Attached to 2nd Division of the Army of the Ohio.

### 1862

**June:**
Attached to 5th Division, Army of the Ohio.

**September:**
Attached to 5th Division, Second Corps, Army of the Ohio.

**November:**
Captain Muehler resigned and Alanson J. Stevens succeeded him. Attached to 3rd Division, Fourteenth Corps, Army of the Cumberland.

### 1863

**January:**
Attached to 3rd Division, Twenty-first Corps, Army of the Cumberland. Lieutenant Stevens was promoted to captain on the 5th.

**September:**
Captain Stevens was killed at the Battle of Chickamauga on the 21st and was succeeded in command by Lieutenant Samuel M. McDowell.
**October:**
Attached to 3rd Division, Fourth Corps, Army of the Cumberland.

## 1864

**January:**
Lieutenant McDowell was promoted to captain on the 11th.
**April:**
Attached to 1st Division, Fourth Corps.
**June:**
Captain McDowell was killed at Kennesaw Mountain on the 27th and was succeeded by Lieutenant Jacob Ziegler.
**August:**
Lieutenant Jacob Ziegler was promoted to captain on the 16th.
**July:**
Attached to the Fourth Corps Artillery Brigade.

## 1865

**August:**
Attached to the Department of Texas.
**October:**
Mustered out on the 12th.

# Pennsylvania Independent Battery C

## 1861

**September:**
Organized at Pittsburgh under the command of Captain James Thompson.
**November:**
Mustered in on the 6th and moved to Washington

## 1862

**May:**
Attached to Ord's Division, Dept. of the Rappahannock.
**June:**
Attached to the 2$^{nd}$ Division, Third Corps, Army of Virginia.
**September:**
Attached to the 2$^{nd}$ Division, First Corps, Army of the Potomac

## 1863

**June:**
Attached to the 1$^{st}$ Volunteer Brigade, Artillery Reserve, Army of the Potomac.
**November:**
Attached to the Artillery Brigade of the Second Corps, Army of the Potomac.

## 1864

**March:**
Attached to the Twenty-second Corps and assigned to Camp Barry.

## 1865

**June:**
Mustered out on the 30$^{th}$.


# Pennsylvania Independent Battery D

## 1861

**September:**
Organized at Doylestown on the 24$^{th}$ under the command of George W. Durell.
**November:**
Transferred to Washington and attached to McDowell's Division, Army of the Potomac.

## 1862

**March:**
Assigned to the 1st Division, First Corps, Army of the Potomac.
**April:**
Attached to King's Division, Dept. of the Rappahannock.
**June:**
Attached to the 1st Division, Third Corps, Army of Virginia.
**August:**
Attached to the 2nd Division, Ninth Corps, Army of the Potomac.

## 1863

**April:**
Attached to the Army of the Ohio
**June:**
Attached to the Army of the Tennessee
**August:**
Covington, Ky., Dept. of the Ohio

## 1864

**March:**
Attached to the 4th Division, Ninth Corps, Army of the Potomac.

## 1865

**June:**
Mustered out in the 13th.


## Pennsylvania Independent Battery E

### 1861

Organized during the early summer by Charles A. Atwell and James D. McGill and originally intended for service with the 63rd Pennsylvania Infantry Regiment.
**July:**

Attached to the oversized 28th Pennsylvania Infantry Regiment and reinforced by transfers from other companies of that regiment.
**September:**
Mustered into service at Camp DeKorponay under the command of Captain Joseph M. Knap. Attached to W. F. Smith's Division, Army of the Potomac.
**November:**
Attached to Banks' Division, Army of the Potomac.

### 1862

**March:**
Attached to Geary's Brigade (formerly the 28th Pennsylvania Infantry Regiment), Fifth Corps
**April:**
Transferred with Geary's Brigade to the Dept. of the Shenandoah.
**May:**
Transferred with Geary's Brigade to the Dept. of the Rappahannock.
**June:**
Attached to the artillery of the Second Corps, Army of Virginia.
**September:**
Attached to the 2nd Division, Twelfth Corps, Army of the Potomac.

### 1863

**May:**
Attached to the Artillery Brigade of the Twelfth Corps

**December:**
Attached to the 2nd Division, Twelfth Corps, Army of the Cumberland.

### 1864

**April:**
Attached to the 2nd Division, Twentieth Corps.
**July:**
Attached to the Artillery Brigade of the Twentieth Corps.

## 1865

**June:**
Mustered out at Pittsburgh on the 14$^{th}$.

## Pennsylvania Independent Battery F

## 1861

**October:**
Recruited and organized at Pittsburgh.
**December:**
Mustered in on the 7$^{th}$ under the command of Captain Robert B. Hampton and assigned to General Bank's command on the Upper Potomac.

## 1862

**March:**
Attached to the 1$^{st}$ Division, Fifth Corps, Dept. of the Shenandoah.
**June:**
Attached to the artillery of the Second Corps, Army of Virginia.
**September:**
Attached to the 2$^{nd}$ Division, Twelfth Corps, Army of the Potomac.

## 1863

**May:**
Attached to the 4$^{th}$ Volunteer Brigade, Artillery Reserve, Army of the Potomac.
**October:**
Attached to the Artillery Brigade of the Second Corps, Army of the Potomac.

## 1864

**March:**
Attached to the Twenty-second Corps and assigned to Camp Barry.

**May:**
Attached to the 2nd Brigade, DeRussy's Division, Twenty-second Corps.
**July:**
Attached to the Reserve Division, Dept. of West Virginia.

### 1865

**January:**
Attached to the 1st Separate Brigade, 3rd Division, West Virginia.
**March:**
Attached to the Artillery Reserve of the Army of the Shenandoah.
**April:**
Attached to the 3rd Brigade, Hardins' Division, Twenty-second Corps, Dept. of Washington.
**June:**
Mustered out on the 26th at Washington, D.C.

## Pennsylvania Independent Battery G

### 1862

**August:**
Organized at Harrisburg on the 22nd under the command of Captain John J. Young and assigned to Fort Delaware, where they spent their entire term of service.

### 1865

**June:**
Mustered out on the 15th.

## Pennsylvania Independent Battery H

### 1862

**October:**
Organized at Pittsburgh on the 21st under the command of Captain John Nevin and temporarily assigned to the 1st Division, Fifth Corps.

**December:**
Assigned to Camp Barry in the Washington defenses.

## 1863
**March:**
Attached to the Twenty-second Corps and assigned to the Alexandria garrison.

## 1865
**January:**
Reassigned the Camp Barry (still attached to the Twenty-second Corps).

**June:**
Mustered out on the 23$^{rd}$ in Philadelphia.

## Pennsylvania Independent Battery I

## 1864
**January:**
Formerly Nevin's Independent Militia Battery. This battery was converted into a fully-fledged volunteer field battery and mustered in at Harrisburg on the 7$^{th}$ under the command of Captain Robert J. Nevin. From Harrisburg they were transferred to Washington, attached to the Twenty-second Corps, and assigned to Camp Barry.

**May:**
Attached to the 2$^{nd}$ Brigade, DeRussy's Division, Twenty-second Corps.

**July:**
Attached to the 3$^{rd}$ Brigade, DeRussy's Division, Twenty-second Corps.

**December:**
Attached to the 1$^{st}$ Brigade, DeRussy's Division, Twenty-second Corps.

## 1865
**June:**
Mustered out on the 23$^{rd}$.

## Selected Bibliography

Bates, Samuel P. *History of the Pennsylvania Volunteers, 1861-1865*. Harrisburg: B. Singerly, State Printer, 1869.

Billings, John D. *Hardtack & Coffee: The Unwritten Story of Army Life*. Boston: George M. Smith & Co., 1887.

Buell, Augustus. *The Cannoneer: Recollections of Service in the Army of the Potomac by a Detached Volunteer in the Regular Army*. Washington: The National Tribune, 1890.

Clark, William. *History of Hampton Battery F Independent Pennsylvania Light Artillery*. Akron and Pittsburgh: Werner Company, 1909.

Downey, Fairfax. *The Guns at Gettysburg*. New York: David McKay Company, 1958.

Dyer, Frederick H. *A Compendium of the War of the Rebellion*. Cedar Rapids, IA: Torch Press, 1908.

Foote, Shelby. *The Civil War: A Narrative*. (3 vols.) New York: Random House, 1958, 1963, 1974.

Fox, Authur B. *Pittsburgh During the American Civil War, 1860-1865*. Butler, PA: Mechling Bookbindery, 2004.

French, William H., William F. Barry, & Henry J. Hunt. *Instruction for Field Artillery*. Philadelphia: J.B. Lippincott & Co., 1861.

Hazlett, James C., Edwin Olmstead, & M. Hume Parks. *Field Artillery Weapons of the Civil War*. Associated University Presses, 1988, (rev. ed.).

Katcher, Philip, & Tony Bryan. *American Civil War Artillery 1861-1865*. University Park, IL: Osprey Publishing, 2001.

Kautz, August V. *Customs of Service for Non-commissioned Officers and Soldiers*. Philadelphia: J.B. Lippincott & Co., 1864.

Leslie, Frank. *Famous Leaders and Battle Scenes of the Civil War*. New York: Mrs. Frank Leslie, 1896.

Miller, Francis Trevelyan and Robert Sampson Lanier. *Photographic History of the Civil War: In Ten Volumes*. New York: Review of Reviews Company, 1911.

Naisawald, L. VanLoan. *Grape and Canister: The Story of the Field Artillery of the Army of the Potomac, 1861-1865*. Oxford University Press: 1960.

Nicholson, Bvt. Lt. Col. John P., ed. *Pennsylvania at Gettysburg: Ceremonies at the Dedication of the Monuments Erected by the Commonwealth of Pennsylvania to Major-General George G. Meade, Major General Winfield S. Hancock, Major General John F. Reynolds and to Mark the Positions of the Pennsylvania Commands Engaged in the Battle*. Harrisburg: Wm. Stanley Ray, State Printer, 1914.

*Ordnance Manual for the Use of the Officers of the United States Army, 1861*. Philadelphia: J. B. Lippincott & Co., 1862.

Poore, Benjamin Perley. *The Political Register and Congressional Directory: A Statistical Record of the Federal Officials, Legislative, Executive, and Judicial, of the United States of America, 1776-1878.* Boston: Houghton, Osgood and Co., 1878.

Rodenbough, Theophilis Francis, & William L. Haskin. *The Army of the United States Historical Sketches of Staff and Line with Portraits of Generals-in-Chief.* (New York: Maynard, Merrill, & Co., 1896).

Scharf, Thomas J. *History of Delaware, 1609-1888.* Philadelphia: L. J. Richards & Co., 1888.

Scharf, Thomas J., & Thompson Westcott. *History of Philadelphia, 1609-1884.* Philadelphia: L. H. Everts & Co., 1884.

Scott, Bvt. Lieut. Col. Robert N., ed. *The War of the Rebellion: A Compilation of the Official Records of the Union and Confederate Armies.* Washington: Government Printing Office, 1880.

Sears, Stephen W. *Gettysburg.* Boston: Houghton Mifflin, 2003.

Thomas, Dean. *Cannons: An Introduction to Civil War Artillery.* Gettysburg: Thomas Publications, 1985.

# Image Bibliography

1. **Going into Action by William Henry Shelton (1840 – 1932)**
   From the Library of Congress, Prints & Photographs Division, [LC-USZ62-7360] ............................. xi

2. **The Ringgold Light Artillery at drill**
   Image from the National Archives .................. 2

3. **National Flag of the Ringgold Light Artillery Company**
   Image from Brian Hunt and the
   Pennsylvania Capitol Preservation Committee .......... 4

4. **The U.S. Capitol in 1860**
   Image from the National Archives. .................. 4

5. **Governor Andrew Curtin of Pennsylvania**
   Image from the Penna. Historical and Museum Commission. ................................................ 6

6. **National Flag of the 1st Pennsylvania Artillery Regiment**
   Image from Brian Hunt and the
   Pennsylvania Capitol Preservation Committee .......... 9

7. **Lt. Col. Charles T. Campbell**
   Image from the P.R.V.C. Historical Society
   www.pareserves.com ........................... 10

8. **Battery A, 1st Pennsylvania Light Artillery at the Battle of Dranesville**
   Engraving from Frank Leslie's Illustrated Newspaper (January 11, 1862). .............................. 21

9. **14 Pdr. James Rifle**
   Photograph by the Author, taken at Gettysburg National Military Park. ................................. 23

10. **10 Pdr. Parrott Rifle**
    Photograph by the Author, taken at Gettysburg National Military Park. ................................. 23

11. **3-in. Ordnance Rifle**
    Photograph by the Author, taken at Gettysburg National
    Military Park. . . . . . . . . . . . . . . . . . . . . . . . . . . . . . . . . . . 24

12. **The Battle of Shiloh: Pittsburg Landing
    on the evening of April 6th**
    Engraving from Frank Leslie's Illustrated Newspaper
    (May 17, 1862). . . . . . . . . . . . . . . . . . . . . . . . . . . . . . . . 26

13. **Battery C, 1st Pennsylvania Light Artillery at Fair Oaks**
    Image from the P.R.V.C. Historical Society
    www.pareserves.com . . . . . . . . . . . . . . . . . . . . . . . . . . . 29

14. **Unknown Union Battery at the Battle of Fair Oaks**
    Image from the Library of Congress, Prints & Photographs Division,
    [LC-B811- 2510]. . . . . . . . . . . . . . . . . . . . . . . . . . . . . . . 29

15. **Confederate attack at Beaver Dam Creek,
    from a contemporary sketch**
    From the National Park Service (Richmond National
    Battlefield Park). . . . . . . . . . . . . . . . . . . . . . . . . . . . . . . 31

16. **Captain Hezekiah Easton,
    Battery A, 1st Pennsylvania Light Artillery**
    Image from the Allison-Antrim Museum,
    Greencastle, PA. . . . . . . . . . . . . . . . . . . . . . . . . . . . . . . .32

17. **The Napoleon**
    Photograph by the Author, taken at Gettysburg National
    Military Park. . . . . . . . . . . . . . . . . . . . . . . . . . . . . . . . . . 35

18. **Knapp's Battery E at Cedar Mountain,
    Sketch by Edwin Forbes (1839 – 1895)**
    Image from the Library of Congress, Prints & Photographs Division,
    [LC-USZC4-4197]. . . . . . . . . . . . . . . . . . . . . . . . . . . . . 42

19. **Lieutenant Henry L. Godbald,
    Battery F, 1st Pennsylvania Light Artillery**
    Image from the P.R.V.C. Historical Society
    www.pareserves.com . . . . . . . . . . . . . . . . . . . . . . . . . . . 42

20. **The Rappahannock Bridge**
    Image from the Library of Congress, Prints & Photographs Division,
    [LC-B815- 517]. . . . . . . . . . . . . . . . . . . . . . . . . . . . . . . . 43

21. **Lieutenant Charles Brockway,**
    **Battery F, 1st Pennsylvania Light Artillery**
    Image from the P.R.V.C. Historical Society
    www.pareserves.com . . . . . . . . . . . . . . . . . . . . . . . . . . . . 50

22. **The Keystone Battery at Drill**
    Image from the National Archives. . . . . . . . . . . . . . . . . . . 53

23. **Fort Delaware on Pea Patch Island in the Delaware River**
    From a painting by Seth Eastman (1808 – 1875). . . . . . . . 53

24. **Abandoned Limber and Confederate Dead**
    **in front of the Dunker Church**
    Image from the National Park Service. . . . . . . . . . . . . . . . .57

25. **Knap's Pennsylvania Independent Battery E at Antietam**
    Image from the National Archives. . . . . . . . . . . . . . . . . . . 59

26. **Burnside's Bridge (September 1862)**
    Image from the Library of Congress, Prints & Photographs Division,
    [LC-B817- 7930]. . . . . . . . . . . . . . . . . . . . . . . . . . . . . . . .62

27. **Private Harvey Bryant, McCarthy's Battery C,**
    **1st Pennsylvania Light Artillery**
    Image from the P.R.V.C. Historical Society
    www.pareserves.com. . . . . . . . . . . . . . . . . . . . . . . . . . . . 65

28. **Pontoon Bridges at Fredericksburg**
    **(Stafford Heights in the Background)**
    Image from the National Archives. . . . . . . . . . . . . . . . . . . 67

29. **A Hard Pull; sketch by Edwin Forbes (1839 – 1895)**
    Image from the Library of Congress, Prints & Photographs Division,
    [LC-USZ62-7169]. . . . . . . . . . . . . . . . . . . . . . . . . . . . . . .73

30. **Captain R. Bruce Ricketts;**
    **Battery F, 1st Pennsylvania Light Artillery**
    Image from the P.R.V.C. Historical Society
    www.pareserves.com . . . . . . . . . . . . . . . . . . . . . . . . . . . . . 78

31. **Captain Joseph M. Knap,**
    **Pennsylvania Independent Battery E**
    Image from the U.S.A.H.E.C. (Carlisle, Penna.). . . . . . . . 81

32. **General Henry J. Hunt**
    Image from the Library of Congress, Prints & Photographs Division,
    [LC-B813- 1912 A]. . . . . . . . . . . . . . . . . . . . . . . . . . . . . . . 84

33. **Captain Frank P. Amsden**
    **Battery G, 1st Pennsylvania Light Artillery**
    Image from the P.R.V.C. Historical Society
    www.pareserves.com . . . . . . . . . . . . . . . . . . . . . . . . . . . . . 85

34. **General Reynolds**
    Image from the National Archives. . . . . . . . . . . . . . . . . . 90

35. **Gettysburg Cemetery Gatehouse (July, 1863)**
    Image from the Library of Congress, Prints & Photographs Division,
    [LC-B811- 2388]. . . . . . . . . . . . . . . . . . . . . . . . . . . . . . . . 93

36. **Sketch of Cemetery Hill (July 3rd)**
    **by Alfred R. Waud (1828 – 1891)**
    Image from the Library of Congress, Prints & Photographs Division,
    [LC-USZ62-160]. . . . . . . . . . . . . . . . . . . . . . . . . . . . . . . . 96

37. **Little Round Top as seen from below**
    Image from the Library of Congress, Prints & Photographs Division,
    [LC-B817- 7318]. . . . . . . . . . . . . . . . . . . . . . . . . . . . . . . . 99

38. **Pickett's Charge from *The Battle of Gettysburg*. Painting by Paul Dominic Philippoteaux (1846-1923)**
    Image from the National Park Service. . . . . . . . . . . . . . . 103

39. **Pursuit of Lee's Army. Near Emmitsburg, Maryland on July 7th. Painting by Edwin Forbes (1839 – 1895)**
    Image from the Library of Congress, Prints & Photographs Division,
    [LC-USZC4-1003] . . . . . . . . . . . . . . . . . . . . . . . . . . . . . . 106

40. **Men of the Keystone Battery**
    Image from the National Archives................... 108

41. **The Battle of Chickamauga
    from a Contemporary Lithograph**
    Image from the Library of Congress, Prints & Photographs Division,
    [LC-USZ62-1598].............................. 111

42. **Captain Charles Atwell,
    Pennsylvania Independent Battery E**
    Image from the U.S.A.H.E.C. (Carlisle, Penna.)......... 121

43. **Lieutenant Edward R. Geary,
    Pennsylvania Independent Battery E**
    Image from History of Hampton Battery F Independent Penna.
    Light Artillery (Clark) at 132...................... 121

44. **General John W. Geary**
    Image from the Library of Congress, Prints & Photographs Division,
    [LC-B813- 2033 A].............................. 121

45. **Battle of Missionary Ridge;
    sketch by Alfred R. Waud (1828-1891)**
    Image from the Library of Congress, Prints & Photographs Division,
    [LC-USZC4-5681]...............................124

46. **The Steamboat Chickamauga**
    Image from the Hamilton County Tennessee Genealogical Society,
    www.hctgs.org .................................. 131

47. **Artillery crossing the Rappahannock
    at Germanna Ford (Spring 1864)**
    Image from the Library of Congress, Prints & Photographs Division,
    [LC-B815- 701].................................132

48. **Lieutenant Francis H. Snider, Battery F,
    1st Pennsylvania Light Artillery**
    Image of Lieutenant Snider from the P.R.V.C. Historical Society
    www.pareserves.com ........................... 134

49. **Pontoon Bridge over Jericho Mills (May 24th 1864)**
    Image from the Library of Congress, Prints & Photographs Division, [LC-B811- 746]. . . . . . . . . . . . . . . . . . . . . . . . . . . . . . . . . 136

50. **Battle of Kennesaw Mountain by
    Bror Thure de Thulstrup (1848 – 1930),
    From a Lithograph by L. Prang & Co., 1887**
    Image from the Library of Congress, Prints & Photographs Division, [LC-USZC4-1521]. . . . . . . . . . . . . . . . . . . . . . . . . . . . . . 142

51. **Colonel Robert M. West,
    1st Pennsylvania Light Artillery**
    Image from the U.S.A.H.E.C. (Carlisle, Penna.). . . . . . . . 147

52. **Officers of the Keystone Battery**
    Image from the National Archives. . . . . . . . . . . . . . . . . . . 151

53. **Battery B, 1st Pennsylvania Light Artillery at Petersburg**
    Image from the National Archives. . . . . . . . . . . . . . . . . . . 152

54. **Destruction of the Ram *Savannah*.**
    Image from *Harper's Weekly* (February 4, 1865) . . . . . . . 159

55. **Captured Confederate Siege Artillery at Richmond,
    Spring 1865**
    Image from the Library of Congress, Prints & Photographs Division, [LC-B811- 3158] . . . . . . . . . . . . . . . . . . . . . . . . . . . . . . 169

56. **Colonel R. Bruce Ricketts**
    Image from the Sullivan County Historical Society. . . . . . .177

57. **The Honorable William McClelland**
    Image from the P.R.V.C. Historical Society
    www.pareserves.com . . . . . . . . . . . . . . . . . . . . . . . . . . . . 178

58. **The Rev. Robert J. Nevin**
    Image from the Trinity Episcopal Church, Bethlehem, PA,
    www.trinitybeth.org . . . . . . . . . . . . . . . . . . . . . . . . . . . . . 178

# Index

101st Ohio Infantry Regiment... 163
102nd New York Infantry Regiment ............ 125
111th Pennsylvania Infantry Regiment............ 120
112th Pennsylvania Regiment....*See* 2nd Pennsylvania Heavy Artillery Regiment
14th Indiana Infantry Regiment. 133
14th Pennsylvania Reserves.. *See* 1st Pennsylvania Light Artillery
152nd Pennsylvania Regiment ...*See* 3rd Pennsylvania Heavy Artillery Regiment, *See* 3rd Pennsylvania Heavy Artillery Regiment
15th New York Independent Battery ............ 136
16th Virginia Cavalry Regiment.. 88
1st Delaware Cavalry Regiment 105
1st Maryland Brigade............ 12
1st Maryland Infantry Regiment . 37
1st Pennsylvania Light Artillery. 19, 22, 27, 32, 34, 65, 96, 107, 115, 147, 153, 165, 183
204th Pennsylvania Regiment... *See* 5th Pennsylvania Heavy Artillery Regiment
212th Pennsylvania Regiment... *See* 6th Pennsylvania Heavy Artillery Regiment
25th Pennsylvania Infantry Regiment............ 3, 183
27th Pennsylvania Infantry Regiment............ 6
28th Pennsylvania Infantry Regiment............ 13, 208, 213
2nd Maine Battery............ 55
2nd New York Battery............ 5
2nd New York Independent Battery ............ 46
2nd Pennsylvania Heavy Artillery Regiment............ 9
2nd Rhode Island Battery............ 5
2nd U.S. Artillery Regiment........ 74
32nd Pennsylvania Infantry Regiment............ 30
3-in. Ordnance Rifles.... 24, 35, 159
3rd Pennsylvania Heavy Artillery Regiment............ 9, 104, 105
3rd Wisconsin Battery............ 71
42nd Pennsylvania Infantry Regiment............ 30
43rd Pennsylvania Regiment .... *See* 1st Pennsylvania Light Artillery
48th Pennsylvania Infantry Regiment............ 149
4th U.S. Artillery Regiment...... 105
57th Pennsylvania Infantry Regiment............ 10
5th Indiana Battery............ 145
5th Maine Battery............ 96
5th Massachusetts Battery......... 135
5th Pennsylvania Cavalry Regiment ............ 148
5th Pennsylvania Heavy Artillery Regiment............ 9
63rd Pennsylvania Infantry Regiment............ 13
6th Massachusetts Militia Regiment ............ 2
6th Pennsylvania Cavalry Regiment ............ 7
6th Pennsylvania Heavy Artillery Regiment............ 9
77th Pennsylvania Infantry Regiment............ 11, 12
82nd Ohio Infantry Regiment.... 158
8th Ohio Infantry Regiment...... 133
Abercrombie, Gen. John J.......... 38
Acquia Creek, Maryland...... 35, 76
Adairsville, Georgia ............ 140

Adjutant General of Pennsylvania ...... 82
Ahl, Capt. George W. ....... 117, 213
Ahl's Heavy Artillery Company ...... 117
Alabama ............ 117, 119, 157, 160
Alcorn, Lt. James P. ................. 189
Alexander, Col. E. Porter ......... 100
Alexandria, Virginia ........... 38, 118
Allegheny County, Pennsylvania ...... 52, 104
Ames Company of Massachusetts ...... 23, 34, 35
Ames, Capt. Nelson .................. 97
Amissville, Virginia .................. 63
Amsden, Capt. Frank P. . 67, 68, 85, 198, 201, 230, 231
Amsden's Battery G *See* Battery G, 1st Pennsylvania Light Artillery
Antietam Creek ............... 56, 57, 61
Appomattox Courthouse .......... 169
Appomattox River ................... 167
Armstrong County, Pennsylvania ...... 104
Army of Northern Virginia .. 29, 41, 54, 56, 62, 89, 106, 108, 109, 113, 125, 154, 166, 171
Army of Tennessee.. 109, 138, 157, 159, 164
Army of the Cumberland 65, 70, 72, 112, 115, 117-120, 122, 123, 124, 143
Army of the James ................... 164
Army of the Ohio ........... 25, 65, 70
Army of the Potomac 26, 28-29, 32-33, 47, 54-56, 63, 65-66, 72, 74, 77-81, 83-90, 104, 106, 108, 113-115, 118, 127, 129, 131, 134, 137-138, 143, 148, 154-155, 221-225, 227-230
Army of the Shenandoah ......... 155
Army of the Tennessee .... 118, 123, 139
Army of Virginia. 45, 48, 51, 54-55
Army of West Virginia ..... 155, 226
Artificers ................................... 17
Artillery brigade system ...... 84, 143

Artillery Reserve ...... 84-86, 94, 96, 101, 105, 114-115, 136, 148, 166, 224, 229
Askine, Lt. William H. ............ 214
Atlanta, Georgia ...... 125, 138, 143, 144-145, 157-159
Atwell, Capt. Charles A. . 13, 37-38, 77, 81, 86, 93, 117, 119, 121-122, 139, 174, 209
Atwell's Battery E .................... *See* Pennsylvania Independent Battery E
Bachman, Lt. Martin ......... 215, 220
Baker, Col. Edward D. ................ 6
Ball, Lt. Richard M. ................ 191
Baltimore and Ohio Railroad ... 105
Baltimore, Maryland 2, 83, 105, 118
Bank's Ford ...................... 72, 80
Banks, Gen. Nathan P. ... 13, 36, 37, 41, 48
Barnes, Lt. Solomon ............... 191
Barr, Capt. Jacob M. ................ 194
Barr's Battery E ..*See* Battery E, 1st Pennsylvania Light Artillery
Barry, Col. William F. ... 10, 66, 108
Battert C, 1st Pennsylvania Light Artillery ............................... 29
Battery (field) ........................ 10
Battery A, 1st Pennsylvania Light Artillery ..... 7, 20, 21, 30, 31, 32, 34, 47, 54, 57, 62, 66, 69, 113, 168, 172, 186, 221
Battery B, 1st Pennsylvania Light Artillery.7, 11, 21-23, 30-35, 45, 47-48, 54, 57-58, 62, 67-69, 75, 78, 81, 86, 89, 90-92, 94, 101, 102, 104, 113, 126, 128, 131, 134-137, 152, 168, 172, 177, 179, 180, 188, 223
Battery B, 4th U.S. Artillery ..... 136
Battery C, 1st Illinois Light Artillery ............................... 71
Battery C, 1st Pennsylvania Light Artillery 7, 19, 27-28, 33, 56, 61, 66, 72, 114, 165, 172, 190, 224
Battery C, 1st Pennsylvania Light Artillery ($2^{nd}$) ....... 165, 172, 191

255

Battery C, 3rd U.S. Artillery ..... 7, 184, 189
Battery C, 5th U.S. Artillery ....... 45
Battery D, 1st Pennsylvania Light Artillery.7, 11, 27-28, 33-34, 56, 61, 66, 72, 79-81, 114, 155-157, 165, 172, 192, 225
Battery E & L, 1st New York Light Artillery............................. 135
Battery E, 1st Pennsylvania Light Artillery.8, 19, 27-28, 32-34, 64, 114, 164-168, 172, 194, 227
Battery F, 1st Pennsylvania Light Artillery.8, 21-23, 38, 42-44, 47, 49-51, 55, 58-59, 62-63, 66, 69, 73, 75, 77-78, 81, 85-86, 94- 96, 100, 104, 114, 116, 126, 128, 132-134, 136-137, 148, 165, 172, 179, 181, 196, 198, 201, 228, 230-240
Battery G, 1st New York Light Artillery............................... 97
Battery G, 1st Pennsylvania Light Artillery 7, 30, 32-33, 47-48, 67-68, 85-86, 94-95, 100, 104, 114, 116, 126, 128, 154, 165, 171, 173, 179, 181, 198
Battery H, 1st Ohio Light Artillery ............................................ 76, 85
Battery H, 1st Pennsylvania Light Artillery.7, 11, 27-28, 32-34, 64, 115, 129, 148, 165, 173, 200
Battery I, 1st New York Light Artillery......................... 92, 95
Battery I, 1st Pennsylvania Light Artillery............... 165, 173, 202
Battery K, 4th U.S. Artillery ....... 77
Battery L, 1st New York Light Artillery................................ 92
Battery M, 1st New York Light Artillery................................ 60
Battery M, 4th U.S. Artillery..... 164
Battle Above the Clouds........... 122
Baumstarck, Lt. A. J. B............. 214
Beatty, Col. Samuel................... 70
Beauregard, Gen. P.G.T........ 25, 65
Beaver Dam Creek ............... 30-31

Benner's Hill............................. 94
Benson, Lt. Joseph................... 191
Bentz, Lt. George E................. 201
Berks County, Pennsylvania...... 12
Berryville, Virginia ................. 155
Best, Capt. Clermont L. ............. 60
Beverly House......................... 134
Big Round Top......................... 93
Billings, John ............................. 3
Black Water, Virginia.............. 153
Blair County, Pennsylvania.......... 8
Blue Ridge ................... 39, 83, 153
Blue Springs, Tennessee.......... 139
Bolton, Lt. James..................... 170
Booth, John Wilkes ................. 170
Borrowe, Capt. William......74, 214
Borrowe's Battery H................. See Pennsylvania Independent Battery H
Boyle, Lt. James...................... 193
Brady, Lt. Col. James ..6, 7, 28, 32-34, 64, 115, 129, 148, 168, 184, 200, 224-225, 230, 232
Brady's Battery H See Battery H, 1st Pennsylvania Light Artillery
Bragg, Gen. Braxton 7, 65, 70, 118, 122, 123, 124, 125, 138
Brander, Capt. T. A. .................. 92
Braun, Lt. Gustavus................. 199
Breck, Lt. George.................... 135
Bridgeport, Alabama 117, 119, 130
Bridges, Capt. Lyman.............. 144
Bristoe Station.....47, 114, 116, 125
British Royal Regiment of Artillery ............................................ 179
Brockway, Capt. Charles B. ..21, 44, 49, 63, 73, 95, 133, 196
Brockway, Lt. F. P................... 198
Brown, Lt. John N. .................. 214
Brown, Lt. William R. ............. 187
Brown's Ferry, Tennessee........ 119
Brown's Gap........................... 155
Bryant, Pvt. Harvey .................. 65
Buckhead, Georgia.................. 143
Bucks County, Pennsylvania...... 12
Bucktails............................ 30, 57

Buell, Gen. Don Carlos.. 25, 64, 65, 70, 227
Buffum, Lt. George R. ............... 199
Buford, Gen. John ............... 89, 91
Buglers ...................................... 17
Bull Run, First Battle of ............... 5
Bull Run, Second Battle of... 46–51
Burnside, Gen. Ambrose 61, 62, 65, 66, 69, 72, 74, 129, 132, 149
Butler, Gen. Benjamin ............. 164
Butterfield, Gen. Daniel ...... 35, 141
Byrne, Lt. M. J. ........................ 190
Cadwalader, Lt. Thomas .......... 189
Caissons ..................................... 16
Caley, Lt. William .................... 193
California Regiment ..................... 6
Cameron, Capt. Sylvester B. ... 165, 202
Cameron's Battery I *See* Battery HI, 1st Pennsylvania Light Artillery
Camp Barry. 10, 107, 114-115, 129, 226
Camp Camden ......................... 104
Camp DeKorponay ..................... 13
Camp Hill ............ *See* Oyster Point
Camp Lamon ............................. 12
Camp Nevin ............................... 12
Campbell, Col. Charles T ...... 7, 10, 183, 186, 187, 221
Campbell, Lt. Charles T ........... 187
Campbell, Lt. John F. ....... 166, 196
Campbell's Battery F *See* Battery F, 1st Pennsylvania Light Artillery
Canister ..................................... 16
Cannoneers (duties of) ............... 15
Captain (duties of) ..................... 14
Carlisle, Pennsylvania .... 83, 87, 88, 99
Carlisle, Pvt. Casper R. ......... 98, 99
Carroll, Gen. Samuel S. ...... 96, 133
Case shot ................................... 16
Case, Lt. T. Leroy ... 49, 50, 63, 197
Cassville, Georgia ................... 140
Cedar Creek ............................ 155
Cedar Mountain, Battle of ........ 209
Cemetery Hill .... 92-94, 96, 99-101, 181, 189

Cemetery Ridge 93, 94, 96- 99, 101, 102, 105
Centreville, Virginia ....... 20, 49, 51
Chancellorsville . 75-77, 79, 80, 81, 132
Chandler, Lt. De Lafayette ....... 200
Chantilly, Virginia ..................... 51
Charles City Crossroads ............. 33
Charleston, South Carolina .......... 1
Charlestown, Virginia ................ 64
Charlottesville Virginia Artillery Battery .................................. 88
Chattahoochee River ......... 142-145
Chattanooga, Tennessee.. 109, 111-112, 115-120, 122, 138, 144
Chester County Artillery ... 107, 218
Chickahominy River .. 27-28, 30-33
*Chickamauga (steamboat)* 130, 131
Chickamauga creek ................. 109
Chickamauga, Battle of ............ 174
Chief of the caisson (duties of) ... 15
Chief of the line of caissons (duties of) ........................................ 14
Chief of the piece (duties of) ...... 15
Choate, Lt. Frank C. ......... 195, 201
Clark, Lt. Charles H. ................ 200
Cleburne, Gen. Patrick ...... 123, 125
Cobb's Mills, Georgia ............. 145
Cobham, Col. George A., Jr. ..... 120
Cogan, Lt. Joseph .................... 202
Cold Harbor, Virginia 137-138, 148
Columbia, Tennessee ............... 160
Company H, 3rd Pennsylvania Heavy Artillery .... 104-105, 118, 216
Conrad House .................... 45, 47
Cooper, Capt. James .. 8, 11, 55, 58-59, 68, 101, 135-137, 152, 153, 188, 223
Cooper, Capt. James H. ........... 188
Cooper, Lt. Richard ................. 202
Corey, Pvt. John ...................... 169
Corinth, Mississippi ............ 25, 64
Couch, Gen. Darius .. 27-28, 56, 61, 87
Covington, Kentucky ............... 117
Crab Orchard, Kentucky ............ 74

Cracker line............................ 120
Crampton's Gap...................... 56
Crawfish Spring, Tennessee..... 109
Crawford County, Pennsylvania 104
Crook, Gen. George.. 155, 157, 226
Cross Keys, Virginia ................. 36
Culp's Hill ...... 93-94, 99, 100, 181
Cumberland River ................... 162
Cummings, Lt. Peter................ 187
Curtin, Gov. Andrew................ 5-6
Dallas, Georgia....................... 140
Dam No. 5 ........................... 21-22
Danforth, Lt. Col. Henry T.... 7, 11, 33, 184, 189
Danforth, Lt. Col? Henry T..... 152, 184, 188, 223
Dauphin County, Pennsylvania 104
Davis, Jefferson........................ 29
Decatur, Alabama.................... 130
Deep Bottom, Virginia............. 153
DeHaven, Lt. David J. ............. 203
Deitriek, Lt. Jacob L. ............... 187
Deitz, Lt. Louis ....................... 204
Delaware. 11, 52-53, 104, 113, 115, 117-118, 173-174
Devil's Den.............................. 97
Ditto, Lt. Walter S. ................... 220
Dixon, Lt. William .................. 200
Doubleday, Gen. Abner ............ 90
Dougherty, Lt. Edward ............ 193
Dranesville, Battle of................. 19
Drewry's Bluff......................... 27
Dug's Gap.............................. 139
Dunker Church................... 57, 60
Dunlevy, Lt. James... 142, 144, 209
Dunlevy, Lt. James?......... 209-210
Dunlevy's Battery E .................*See* Pennsylvania Independent Battery E
DuPont, Capt. Henry A..... 155-156
Durell, Capt. George W. .....12, 150, 153, 207
Early, Gen. Jubal............... 154-156
Easton, Capt. Hezekiah....7, 20, 32, 47, 172, 186, 221, 230
Easton's Battery A... *See* Battery A, 1st Pennsylvania Light Artillery

Easton's Battery B... *See* Battery B, 1st Pennsylvania Light Artillery
Eberhart, Chaplain W. A. P...... 186
Eighteenth Corps...... 138, 222, 228
Einstein, Col. Max......................6
Eleventh Corps. 74, 76, 80, 91, 130, 144
Elliot's Salient........................ 149
Ely's Ford ........................126, 132
Emmitsburg Road..................... 97
Emmitsburg, Maryland............ 106
Erie County, Pennsylvania......... 12
Ermentrout, Capt. W. C. .......... 107
Ermentrout's Independent Militia Battery .........................107, 217
Eshelman's Battery.................. 102
Ewell, Gen. Richard .. 83, 87-89, 91
Fagan, Capt. Andrew... 34, 200-201
Fagan's Battery H... *See* Battery H, 1st Pennsylvania Light Artillery
Fair Oaks, Battle of ........ 28-29, 32
Fairfield Road ..................... 89-90
Falmouth, Virginia .............. 38-39
Ferrero, Gen. Edward ....... 149-150
Fiedler, Lt. Frederick............... 191
Field artillery............................8
Field Howitzers.............. 25, 34-35
Fifth Corps..... 30, 74, 93, 128, 131, 135-136, 221, 223-224, 228
Finlay, Lt. Theodore M............ 214
First Corps .... 54-55, 57, 59, 66-69, 74-77, 86, 89-93, 113, 126, 128, 221-223, 229
First Corps (Army of Virginia).. 45, 48
First sergeant (duties of) ............ 14
Fisher's Hill ........................... 155
Fitzki, Capt. Edward. 107, 199, 218
Fitzki's Battery..........*See* Keystone Independent Militia Battery F
Flat Rock Shoals ..................... 158
Flood, Lt. Col. Edward H...... 7, 34, 115, 192, 225, 230, 232
Flood's Battery D ...*See* Battery D, 1st Pennsylvania Light Artillery
Foot artillery ............................8
Ford's Theater........................ 169

Fort Corcoran .......................... 148
Fort Couch ............................... 87
Fort Darling ............................ 153
Fort Delaware ....... 52-53, 104, 115, 117-118, 173-174
Fort Meikel ............................ 167
Fort Pitt Foundry ... 24, 81, 87, 151, 209
Fort Stedman ..... 166, 167, 185, 194
Fort Sumter ............................ 1, 2
Fort Washington ....................... 87
Fort Whipple .......................... 129
Fortress Monroe ................. 26, 113
Fourth Corps .... 27, 34, 56, 64, 114, 138, 140, 143-145, 157, 160, 163, 224-225, 227
Franklin County, Pennsylvania .... 7
Franklin Pike .......................... 163
Franklin, Tennessee ... 161-162, 164
Frederick, Maryland ................ 154
Fredericksburg .. 64,-67, 69, 72, 75, 76, 79-80, 134
Fredericksburg, Virginia. 72, 74, 83
Fremont, Gen. John C. ................ 38
French, Gen. William H. ...... 10, 108
Frishmuth, Capt. Benoni ............ 86
Frishmuth's Independent Militia Battery .................. 86, 107, 217
Front Royal, Virginia ...... 37, 38, 39
Fullerton, Lt. James S. .............. 188
Gaines' Mill, Battle of ............... 31, 137, 172
Gardner, Lt. James A. ........ 179, 189
Gealy, Lt. John H. .................... 190
Geary, Gen. John W. ...81, 119-120, 122, 130, 138-139, 143-144, 158
Geary, Lt. Col. Edward R. 13, 119-120, 122, 139
Geary, Lt. Edward R. .. 94, 121, 174, 209
Georgia ............................ 157-159
Gerhart, Lt. William R. ............. 220
Germanna Ford ......... 126, 131-132
Germantown, Virginia ............... 51
Getty, Gen. George W. ............. 132
Gettysburg Battlefield Memorial Association ......................... 178
Gettysburg Cemetery Gatehouse 93
Gettysburg National Military Park ................................. 178, 180
Gettysburg, Pennsylvania 87-94, 96, 104-105, 107-108, 115, 178-180, 188-189, 214
Gibbs, Lt. Morris W. ................ 215
Gillespie, Lt. M. C. ................... 200
Glaffey, Lt. Moritz F. ............... 204
Glendale, Battle of ...... 33, 184, 189
Gloucester, Virginia .................. 64
Godbald, Lt. Henry L. ..... 42, 43, 50, 63, 172, 197
Gordon's Mills, Tennessee ....... 110
Graeff, Lt. William .................. 183
Grand Review of 1865 ............. 171
Granny White Pike .................. 163
Grant, Gen. Ulysses S.. 25, 74, 116, 118, 122-123, 128, 131, 135-138, 148-149, 153-154, 158, 164, 166, 169, 171
Great Falls, Maryland ................ 19
Greene, Gen. George S. ............. 60
Griffen Gun .............................. 24
Griffen, James .......................... 24
Griffiths, Pvt. Jabez .......... 169-170
Groveton, Battle of ............. 45-47
Groveton, Virginia ................ 45-47
Gunner (duties of) ..................... 15
Guntersville, Alabama ............. 130
Guss, Capt. George R. ............. 107
Hagerstown Pike ................. 57, 60
Hall, Capt. Michael ...... 34, 73, 192
Hall's Battery D ..*See* Battery D, 1st Pennsylvania Light Artillery
Halleck, Gen. Henry W.. 25-26, 64-65
Hampton, Capt. Robert B. ..... 13, 22, 77, 81, 174, 210
Hampton's Battery F ................ *See* Pennsylvania Independent Battery F
Hancock, Gen. Winfield Scott ... 21, 101, 132-133
Hancock, Maryland ............. 21-22
Hanover Junction, Pennsylvania ................................. 105

Hanover Road .......................... 105
Hardaway's Alabama Battery .. 116
Hardee, Gen. William .............. 140
Hardy, Lt. John ........................ 195
Harper's Ferry ...... 54, 64, 108, 114, 127, 154-155, 157, 165
Harpeth River .......................... 161
Harrisburg, Pennsylvania ..... 2, 3, 7, 52, 83, 86-87, 89, 108, 115, 127, 137, 148, 172
Harrison's Landing, Virginia ... 33, 36, 41
Hart, Capt. Patrick ................... 136
Hassler, Lt. John ...................... 195
Hasting's Battery ....... *See* Keystone Battery
Hastings, Capt. Matthew ... 52, 107-108, 151, 216
Hays, Gen. Harry ....................... 95
Hays, Lt. William C ................. 199
Herr's Ridge ............................... 91
Hill, Gen. A.P ... 48, 61, 89, 91, 114, 126
Hillsborough Pike .................... 163
Hoag, Lt. William F ................. 215
Hood, Gen. John Bell ...... 141, 143, 145, 157, 159, 160-162, 164
Hooker, Gen. Joseph 47, 55, 57, 72, 74-76, 79, 82-83, 119-120, 122, 124, 126, 130-131, 138
Houghtaling, Capt. Charles ........ 71
Housum, Capt. Peter B. ............. 12
Howard, Gen. Oliver .......... 76, 123
Hummel Heights ....................... 88
Hunt, Gen. Henry J .. 10, 66, 84- 86, 90, 101-102, 108, 143
Hunting Run ......................... 76-77
Huntington, Capt. James ............ 85
Huntington's Battery ... *See* Battery H, 1st Ohio Light Artillery
Hurt, Capt. William B .............. 116
Hutchinson's Island, Georgia ... 158
Illinois ..................................... 170
Instruction for Field Artillery ..... 10
Irish, Capt. Nathaniel ............... 128
Irish's Battery F .. *See* Pennsylvania Independent Battery F

Ives, Pvt. Henry B. ..................... 63
Jackson, Capt. William L. .......... 88
Jackson, Gen. Thomas ................ 21
Jackson, Gen. Thomas "Stonewall" 36-38, 41, 44-49, 51, 75, 79-80, 83
Jackson, Mississippi ................ 116
Jacob's Ford ............................ 126
James Rifles ................. 23, 25, 110
James River .... 27, 33, 35, 113, 138, 148
Jenkins, Gen. Albert G .......... 87-88
Jennings, Lt. William ............... 128, 129, 154, 165, 198
Jennings' Battery G *See* Battery G, 1st Pennsylvania Light Artillery
Jericho Mills, Virginia ............. 136
Jerusalem Plank Road .............. 168
Johnson, President Andrew ...... 171
Johnson's Island, Ohio ............. 129
Johnston, Gen. Albert Sydney .... 25
Johnston, Gen. Joseph E. ...28, 116, 138-143, 171
Jonesborough, Georgia ............ 145
Keene, Laura ................... 169-170
Kelly's Ford ................ 44, 47, 113
Kenly, Col. John R. .............. 37-38
Kennedy, Lt. Robert B ............. 191
Kennesaw Mountain .. 141-142, 174
Kentucky 12, 65, 73, 116-117, 129, 153
Kern, Capt. Mark 7, 32, 49, 67, 173, 198
Kern's Battery G .*See* Battery G, 1st Pennsylvania Light Artillery
Keystone Battery ... 52-53, 108-109, 151, 216
Keystone Independent Militia Battery ........................ 107, 218
Kilgore, Lt. William H. ............ 195
Kimball, Gen. Nathan ....... 161, 163
Kincade, Lt. James ................... 199
King, Lt. Rufus .......................... 88
Kirby, Col. Isaac M. ................ 163
Klett, Lt. John C. ..................... 214
Kline, Lt. John H. .................... 187
Knap, Maj. Joseph ..................... 77

Knap, Maj. Joseph M. .... 13, 24, 60, 81, 86, 117, 151, 218
Knap's Battery E. *See* Pennsylvania Independent Battery E
Knap's Independent Light Artillery Battalion............................ 151
Knap's Independent Militia Battery ...................................... 87, 107
Kolb's Farm........................... 141
Lake Erie ................................ 129
Lamon, Gen. Ward H................. 12
Landis, Capt. Henry D. ....... 87, 219
Landis' Independent Militia Battery ..................... 87-88, 107
Lane, Col. James C.................. 125
Langle, Lt. Frank..................... 192
Laurel Hill ............................. 134
Lawrence County, Pennsylvania .. 7
Leale, Dr. Charles.................... 170
Lebanon County, Pennsylvania 104
Lee, Gen. Robert E. ...29-30, 34- 36, 38, 41, 46, 54, 56, 62, 79, 83, 89, 99-100, 103, 106, 113, 126, 131, 149, 154, 164, 166, 168-169, 171
Letcher Artillery....................... 92
Lewis, Lt. Col. Alfred E... 7-8, 185, 194, 227
Lewis' Battery E. *See* Battery E, 1st Pennsylvania Light Artillery
Lieutenant (duties of)................. 14
Light artillery............................. 8
Limbers.................................... 16
Lincoln, President Abraham.... 1, 5, 36, 54, 169, 170
Lithonia, Georgia .................... 158
Little Harpeth River................. 164
Little River Turnpike................. 51
Little Round Top.... 93, 96-98, 100, 181
Longstreet, Gen. James...41, 44-49, 89, 96-97, 100-101
Lookout Mountain.... 119, 122, 124
Lookout Valley ....................... 119
Louisiana Tiger Brigade .....95, 181
Lovejoy's Station, Georgia ...... 145
Lutheran Theological Seminary . 91

Luzerne County, Pennsylvania.... 7, 104
Malone, Lt. Thomas ................ 193
Malvern Hill............................. 35
Malvern Hill, Battle of............... 33
Manassas Gap ......................... 109
Manassas Junction........3, 38, 44-45
Mansfield, Gen. Joseph K. ......... 60
Marietta road........................... 140
Marietta, Georgia ............. 140, 142
Marsh Creek....................... 89-90
Martin, Lt. Samuel D............... 187
Maryes Heights .............. 75, 79, 81
Maryland 12-13, 19, 21, 25, 37, 54, 63, 83, 89, 105-106, 154
Maryland Heights..... 154, 157, 165
Matthews, Capt. Ezra W. . 8, 59, 63, 73, 196, 228
Matthews' Battery F. *See* Battery F, 1st Pennsylvania Light Artillery
Maximilian I .......................... 173
McCarthy, Capt. Jeramiah .73, 114, 192
McCarthy, Capt. Jeremiah .......... 7, 190, 192, 224
McCarthy's Battery C...*See* Battery C, 1st Pennsylvania Light Artillery
McCarthy's Battery D...*See* Battery D, 1st Pennsylvania Light Artillery
McClellan, Gen. George B... 26-28, 30, 36, 38, 41, 54, 56-57, 64, 65, 138
McClelland, Capt. William ..... 152, 168, 177-178, 188
McClelland's Battery B .........*See* Battery B, 1st Pennsylvania Light Artillery
McConkey, Lt. Elbridge .......... 197
McDowell, Capt. Samuel M.... 141, 174, 204
McDowell, Capt.? Samuel M.. 110, 111, 123
McDowell, Gen. Irvin.....28, 38, 47

McDowell's Battery B ............... *See* Pennsylvania Independent Battery B
McGill, Capt. James D. 13, 60, 122, 142, 143, 209
McGill's Battery E .................... *See* Pennsylvania Independent Battery E
McGilvery, Lt. Col. Freeman .... 96, 101
McIlvaine, Lt. Howard 63, 174, 207
McKnight, Capt. James M. .. 1, 183
McLaughlin, Lt. William .. 193, 202
McLaws, Gen. Lafayette ............ 97
McNight, Lt. Robert ................. 202
McPherson, Gen. James ........... 139
McPherson's Wood .............. 90-91
Meade, Gen. George. 45, 67-68, 83-84, 89, 103, 106-107, 109, 114, 126, 131, 149
Mechanicsburg, Pennsylvania ... 87-88
Mechanicsville, Virginia ..... 30, 137
Mexican War. 1, 7, 22, 25, 184, 189
Mexico .................................... 173
Middletown, Virginia .... 36-37, 155
Miller, Capt. E. Spenser ............. 86
Miller, Lt. Joseph L. ................. 174
Miller, Lt. William C. 92, 136, 137, 188
Miller, Maj. Theodore.... 8, 34, 167, 185, 194, 201, 227
Miller's Battery E ... *See* Battery E, 1st Pennsylvania Light Artillery
Miller's cornfield .................. 57-58
Miller's Independent Militia Battery ................. 87, 107, 219
Miller's cornfield ....................... 57
Mine Run ......................... 126, 197
Mineral Spring Run ................... 77
Minich, Lt. Abington W ........... 195
Miotkowski, Capt. Stanley 115, 203
Miotkowski's Battery A ............. *See* Pennsylvania Independent Battery A
Missionary Ridge ............. 122-124

Mississippi ..... 25, 64, 74, 113, 116, 129, 153
Mitchell, Lt. Charles H. ........... 199
Mitchell's Ford ........................ 116
Monocacy River ...................... 105
Moore, Lt. Eugene C. ........ 165, 199
Moore's Battery G ... *See* Battery G, 1st Pennsylvania Light Artillery
Morton's Ford ......................... 127
Mount Jackson, Pennsylvania ...... 7
Mount Sterling, Kentucky .......... 74
Mowrer, Lt. George W. ............ 197
Mud March ............................... 72
Muehler, Capt. Charles F. .... 12, 70, 204
Muehler's Battery B ................. *See* Pennsylvania Independent Battery B
Muhlenburg, Lt. Edward ............ 86
Munce, Lt. George ................... 193
Munk, Capt. William 114, 155-157, 192-193
Munk's Battery D *See* Battery D, 1st Pennsylvania Light Artillery
Murfreesboro ............. 70, 109, 117
Myer's house ........................... 134
Nagle, Capt. Henry ............. 3, 183
Napoleons ............. 34-35, 129, 133
Nashville and Chattanooga Railroad ............................. 119
Nashville, Tennessee . 71, 119, 160, 162-163
National Light Infantry Company of Pottsville, Pennsylvania ...... 3
Neal Dow Station, Georgia ...... 142
Nesbit, Lt. Isaac A. .................. 188
Nevin, Capt. Edward H ............ 174
Nevin, Capt. Edwin H .............. 214
Nevin, Capt. John I. ..... 63, 74, 213-214
Nevin, Capt. Robert J. 86, 127, 175, 178, 215
Nevin's Battery H .................... *See* Pennsylvania Independent Battery H
Nevin's Battery I *See* Pennsylvania Independent Battery I

Nevin's Independent Militia Battery ... 86, 107, 127, 215-216, 219
New Hope Church, Georgia .... 140-141
New Jersey .......................... 6, 104
New Market, Virginia ................. 45
New York ................. 5-6, 23, 46, 60
Newlin, Lt. John S. ................... 216
Ninth Corps.. 51, 55, 61, 63, 66, 73, 116, 129, 132, 137, 166-168, 185, 194, 222
Norfolk, Virginia 27, 113, 149, 222, 228
North Anna River ..................... 135
North Carolina ........................ 171
Noyes' Creek ........................... 140
Oak Hill ..................................... 91
Ohio ................. 25, 47, 64, 129, 153
Old Church, Virginia ............... 137
Oostanula River ................. 139, 140
Opequon. *See* Winchester, Virginia
Orange & Alexandria Railroad. 114
Orange Plank Road .................. 133
Ord, Gen. E.O.C. ....................... 20
Orderly sergeant. *See* First Sergeant
Ordnance Rifles 23, 25, 55, 67, 105, 116, 127, 133, 158
Orwig, Capt. Thomas ... 34, 64, 165, 194, 195
Orwig's Battery E *See* Battery E, 1st Pennsylvania Light Artillery
Ox Ford .................................. 137
Ox Hill ...................................... 51
Oyster Point (Camp Hill), Pennsylvania ................... 87-88
Palsgrove, Lt. H. E. ................. 187
Pamunkey River ....................... 137
Paris, Kentucky ......................... 74
Park, Lt. William J. ................. 201
Parrott Rifles. 22-25, 35, 42-43, 50, 129, 156
Parrott, Robert Parker ................ 23
Patterson, Asst. Surgeon B. M.. 186
Patterson, Gen. Robert .................. 6
Pea Patch Island *See* Fort Delaware
Peach orchard ....................... 97-98

Peach Tree Creek ..... 142-143, 145, 209
Pegram's Battalion ..................... 91
Pelham, Maj. John ..................... 68
Pennsylvania Independent Battery A ............. 11, 52, 115, 117, 173
Pennsylvania Independent Battery B 11-12, 25, 64, 70-71, 109-111, 115, 123, 138-145, 157, 160-163, 173, 204
Pennsylvania Independent Battery C ... 12, 38, 41-44, 47, 49-51, 55, 58-59, 62, 69, 75, 79, 81, 85-86, 96-98, 101-102, 104, 116, 119, 126-128, 169, 174, 179, 181, 206
Pennsylvania Independent Battery D.. 12-13, 38, 44, 47, 49, 51, 55, 61-63, 66, 73, 116-117, 129, 132, 137, 148-150, 153, 167-168, 174, 207
Pennsylvania Independent Battery E ... 13, 19, 24-25, 37, 41-42, 48, 56, 59-60, 62, 64, 76-79, 81, 86, 93-94, 104, 117, 119-122, 125, 129-130, 138-145, 151, 157-159, 171, 174, 181, 208-209
Pennsylvania Independent Battery F ... 13, 22, 36-37, 45-46, 48, 56, 60, 62, 64, 76-78, 81, 85-86, 96-98, 101-102, 104, 116, 119, 127-128, 154, 170-171, 174, 181, 209-210, 214
Pennsylvania Independent Battery G ............ 52, 117-118, 174, 212
Pennsylvania Independent Battery H ............ 63, 74, 118, 174, 213
Pennsylvania Independent Battery I ................. 127, 175, 178, 215
Pennsylvania Reserve Volunteer Corps ....................................... 5
Pennypacker, Lt. J. M. ............. 189
Perkins, Lt. Samuel C. ............... 88
Perrin, Lt. John ......................... 196
Perryville, Battle of ................... 65
Petersburg, Virginia. 138, 148, 152, 153, 164, 166-168, 185, 194

Petersen, William .................. 170
Philadelphia, Pennsylvania 6-8, 11, 24, 52, 83, 87-88, 104, 107-108, 127, 148, 172-175, 216, 219, 221, 223-225, 227-228, 230, 232
Phillips, Capt. Charles A. ......... 135
Pickett, Gen. George................ 102
Pickett's Charge ........ 103, 180-181
Pilot Knob............................. 140
Pine Mountain....................... 140
Pittsburg Landing, Tennessee 25-26
Pittsburgh, Pennsylvania.12-13, 24, 63, 81, 87, 151, 174, 214
Pleasants, Lt. Col. Henry ......... 149
Po River................................ 134
Poffenberger's Ridge............ 57-58
Point of Rocks, Maryland .. 19, 154, 165
Pope, Gen. John . 26, 35, 41-42, 45-48, 51, 54, 64, 217
Potomac River.... 13, 19, 21, 35, 54, 56, 62, 109, 113, 129, 154
Potter County, Pennsylvania ........ 7
Power's Ferry, Georgia............ 142
Power's Hill......................... 93-94
Powhatan Point ...................... 148
Price, Regt. Surgeon M. F. ....... 185
Proctor's Creek ...................... 145
Quartermaster sergeant (duties of) ........................................ 14
Raleigh, North Carolina........... 171
Rank, Capt. William D. .... 104, 216
Rank's Battery H..*See* Company H, 3rd Pennsylvania Heavy Artillery
Ransom, Capt. Dunbar............... 45
Rapidan River . 41, 75-77, 126-127, 131-132, 137-138
Rappahannock Bridge..... 38, 42-44
Rappahannock River.38, 42-44, 49-50, 63-65, 69, 72, 74-81, 106, 109, 113-114, 132, 172, 197, 221, 223, 229
Red Oak, Georgia.................... 145
Reeling, Lt. Gustavus .............. 195
Reger, Lt. Louis F................... 204
Reichenbach, Lt. M. .............. 191

Reineke, Lt. August................ 203
Reisinger, Lt. George W. ......... 199
Reno, Gen. Jesse ...................... 51
Resaca, Georgia ............... 139-140
Reynolds, Capt. John A. ............ 92
Reynolds, Capt. William............. 5
Reynolds, Gen. John 68, 83, 89, 91, 152
Reynolds, Maj. John A. ........... 120
Rhoads, Capt. Samuel H. . 153, 167, 207
Rhodes, Lt. Samuel H. ......... 55, 61
Rice, Lt. Thomas C...........168, 189
Rice's Station, Virginia............ 169
Richards, Capt. Lord B. ........... 201
Richards, Capt. Sharp L... 165, 190, 191
Richards, Lt. Samuel L ............ 202
Richards' Battery C . *See* Battery C, 1st Pennsylvania Light Artillery
Richards' Battery H.*See* Battery H, 1st Pennsylvania Light Artillery
Richmond, Virginia ..26-29, 31, 34, 138, 143, 166, 168-169
Ricketts, Col. R. Bruce .. 22, 49, 63, 73, 77-78, 85, 94-95, 100, 165, 167, 177, 179, 196, 198, 201, 231
Ricketts, Gen. James B. ..44-45, 51, 59
Ricketts' Battery F....*See* Battery F, 1st Pennsylvania Light Artillery
Ricketts' Glen State Park . 177, 185, 196
Riggin, Guidon-bearer James H. 95
Riley, Regt. Surgeon James R. . 186
Ringgold Gap, Battle of .......... 125
Ringgold Light Artillery ... 183, 221
Ringgold, Georgia ................... 125
Rio Grande............................. 173
Roberts, Col. Joseph................ 105
Robertson's Crossroads, Virginia ........................................ 126
Robinson, Col. James S. ........... 158
Rocky Face Ridge ................... 139
Rodes, Gen. Robert ................... 91
Roemer, Capt. Jacob................. 46

Rosecrans, Gen William S. ..65, 70, 109, 115, 119
Rosney Battery D... *See* Battery D, 1st Pennsylvania Light Artillery
Rosney, Capt. Andrew............. 193
Rossville, Georgia................... 125
Rough-and-Ready, Georgia...... 145
Rush, Col. Richard H.................. 7
Sailor, Lt. Henry............... 167, 208
Salem Church, Virginia............. 80
Sample, Pvt. William........ 169, 170
Sandusky, Ohio....................... 129
Savannah (Ironclad).......... 158-159
Savannah, Georgia..... 157-158, 171
Schaffer, Capt. Frank... 11, 52, 115, 203
Schaffer's Battery A ................. *See* Pennsylvania Independent Battery A
Schoenlieber, Lt. W. D. ........... 203
Schofield, Gen. John......... 160-162
Schurz, Gen. Carl...................... 45
Schuylkill County, Pennsylvania
 .......................................... 149
Secker, Lt. Phillip.................... 204
Second Bull Run ...... *See* Bull Run, Second Battle of
Second Corps. 74, 93, 98, 101, 105, 114, 126, 128, 132-136, 166, 229
Second Corps (Army of Virginia)
 ...................................... 45, 48
Second Keystone Battery.......... *See* Keystone Independent Militia Battery
Second Manassas ..... *See* Bull Run, Second Battle of
Second Maryland Battery.......... *See* Pennsylvania Independent Battery C
Second Ringgold Infantry .... 3, 183
Sedgwick, Gen. John . 74-75, 79-80
Seeley, Lt. Francis W................. 77
Segebarth, Col. Hermann.. 104-105
Seminary Ridge.... 90-92, 101, 102, 103
Seven Pines.......................28, 153

Seymour, Gen. Truman.............. 33
Sharpsburg, Maryland..... 56-57, 61
Shell ......................................... 15
Shenandoah River ................... 154
Shenandoah Valley.. 36, 38, 41, 83, 109, 153-156, 165, 226, 229
Sheridan, Gen. Phillip...... 154-155, 173, 226
Sherman, Gen. William T. 117-118, 122-123, 125, 138-140, 141, 143, 145, 157-159, 164, 171
Shiloh, Battle of ....................... 25
Shippen, Regt. Surgeon Edward 185
Sickel, Col. Horatio G. .............. 30
Sickles, Gen. Daniel ..........97, 108
Sigel, Gen. Franz...................... 48
Silvis, Lt. George ............. 150, 208
Simpson, Capt. John G. 7, 153, 190
Simpson, Lt. John G. .......7, 34, 186
Simpson's Battery A *See* Battery A, 1st Pennsylvania Light Artillery
Sixth Corps .. 56, 61, 66, 75, 79, 93, 132, 224, 226
Sloan, Capt. Thomas S..... 144, 151, 158, 210
Sloan's Battery E.*See* Pennsylvania Independent Battery E
Slocum, Gen. Henry ................. 76
Slough, Gen. John P. ............... 118
Smith, Gen. W. F..................... 19
Snake Creek Gap..................... 139
Snider, Lt. Francis H.. 133-134, 197
Soles, Pvt. Samuel ............ 169-170
Solid shot.................................. 15
South Carolina ....................... 158
South River............................ 158
Special Order 191..................... 54
Spence, Lt. Belden..... 85, 129, 165, 198
Spence's Battery G .. *See* Battery G, 1st Pennsylvania Light Artillery
Sporting Hill, Pennsylvania ....... 88
Spotsylvania.................... 134-135
Spring Hill .............................. 160
Stafford Heights.................. 66-67
Stanley, Gen. David S....... 138, 145
Steamboat *Chickamauga* .. 130-131

Steck, Lt. Charles .................... 203
Stevens, Capt. Alanson J.... 70, 109, 110, 173, 204
Stevens, Congressman Thaddeus 70
Stevens' Battery B ..................... *See* Pennsylvania Independent Battery B
Stewart, Lt. James ................... 136
Stitt, Lt. William .............. 153, 186
Stitt's Battery A .. *See* Battery A, 1st Pennsylvania Light Artillery
Stoneman, Gen. George ............. 74
Stones River ............................. 70
Stratford, Sgt. Richard ............... 95
Stuart, Gen. J.E.B. ..................... 20
Sudley Spring Road ............. 49-50
Sullenberger, Lt. W. H. ............ 187
Sullivan, Pvt. John ..................... 59
Susquehanna River ......... 83, 87, 88
Susquehanna, Dept. of ..... 115, 148, 152
Swallow, Capt. George R ........... 70
Taylor, Lt. Lindley J. ................ 203
Templeton, Lt. Horace .............. 202
Tennessee . 25, 65, 70, 72, 117-118, 122, 138-139, 160
Tennessee River ....... 119, 130, 160
Texas ...................................... 173
Third Corps ... 47, 49, 74-75, 77, 93, 97, 101, 108-126, 221, 223, 229
Third Corps (Army of Virginia) 45, 47, 51
Thomas, Gen. George H. . 115, 119, 122-123, 140, 157, 159-160, 162, 164
Thompson, Capt. James . 12, 41, 43-44, 49, 58-59, 68, 85, 97-98, 102, 116, 179, 206
Thompson's Battery C .............. *See* Pennsylvania Independent Battery C
Thornton, Lt. Thomas .............. 202
Thoroughfare Gap ............... 47, 49
Thurston, Lt. William M. .......... 197
Tidball, Capt. John C. .............. 168
Totopotomoy Creek .................. 137
Triana, Alabama ...................... 130

Tunnel Hill .............................. 139
Turner's Gap ............................. 55
Twelfth Corps ... 56, 60, 64, 74, 76-77, 86, 93-94, 100, 117, 119-120, 130, 143
Twentieth Corps ...... 130, 138, 141, 143, 157
Twenty-fifth Corps ........... 168, 228
Twenty-first Corps .................. 110
Twenty-third Corps ................. 161
Twining, Lt. Coleman .............. 220
Tyler, Capt. Horatio K. ...... 107, 220
Tyler's Militia Battery ...... 107, 220
Tyndale, Col. Hector ................. 60
United States Colored Troops .. 149
United States Ford ............... 75, 78
Urbana, Virginia ................. 64, 114
Utoy Creek .............................. 145
Valley Turnpike ....................... 155
Van Cleve, Gen. Horatio P.. 70, 109
Van Dyke, Lt. John ................... 71
Vicksburg, Mississippi .... 116, 117, 153
Victoria, Texas ........................ 173
Vine Creek .............................. 140
Vining's Station, Georgia ........ 142
Virginia .... 19, 25-30, 35-36, 38, 41, 47-48, 51, 54-55, 62-64, 67, 92, 102, 106, 109, 113-114, 116, 118, 127, 129, 138, 144, 148, 153, 155, 164, 166, 168, 169, 221-223, 226, 228-229
Virginia Peninsula .... 26-27, 30, 35-36, 38, 41, 45, 64, 113-115, 127, 148, 153
*Virginia, C.S.S. (ironclad)* ......... 27
Wagner, Gen. George ....... 160-161
Wainwright, Col. Charles ..... 86, 89, 92, 94
Wapping Heights ..................... 109
Warren, Gen. Gouverneur K. ... 116, 131, 134
Warrenton Junction ................... 38
Warrenton, Virginia ............ 38, 45
Warwick River ......................... 27
Washington, D.C.. 1-3, 5, 8, 10, 13, 19, 21, 36, 52, 63, 67, 74, 83,

90, 107-108, 114-115, 117-118, 127-129, 148, 151, 153-154, 165, 168-169, 171, 174, 202, 215, 221, 223-228, 230, 232
Washington Arsenal ..................... 3
Washington Artillery of New Orleans............................... 102
Washington Heights ...*See* Hummel Heights
Wauhatchie Station.. 119, 120, 139, 174, 209
Wauhatchie Valley .................. 139
Weitzel, Gen. Godfrey............ 168
Weltmore, Lt. John.................. 216
Wentz, Lt. Charles C. ............... 192
West Point Foundry................... 23
West Virginia.....................114, 165
West, Col. Robert M.. 7, 19, 28, 34, 115, 147, 184, 198
Westminster, Pennsylvania ...... 105
White Bridge, Pennsylvania....... 90
White Sulphur Springs, Virginia .... 63, 174
Whitworth Rifles...................... 116
Wick, Lt. William C. ................ 195
Wiedrich, Capt. Michael....... 92, 95
Wilcox's Alabama Brigade ...... 102
Wilcox's Landing.................... 148
Wilderness .... 75, 80, 126, 131, 134
Wildey, Capt. Henry Y. ... 165, 194, 201
Wildey's Battery E .. *See* Battery E, 1st Pennsylvania Light Artillery
Williams, Gen. Alpheus S.......... 60
Williamsburg, Virginia ..27-28, 148
Williamsport, Maryland.... 106, 109
Willoughby run ........................ 90
Wilson, President Woodrow .... 180
Winchester, Virginia 36-38, 64, 155
Wireman, Lt. Henry................. 197
Woodward, Capt. W. H..... 107, 220
Woodward's Militia Battery..... 107
York County, Pennsylvania ......... 7
Yorktown, Siege of.................... 27
Yorktown, Virginia ..... 27, 64, 114, 115, 148, 153
Young, Capt. John J.................. 52
Young's Battery G....................*See* Pennsylvania Independent Battery G
Zeigler, Capt. Jacob..........141, 205
Zeigler's Battery B ..................*See* Pennsylvania Independent Battery B

www.ingramcontent.com/pod-product-compliance
Lightning Source LLC
Chambersburg PA
CBHW071425150426
43191CB00008B/1045